MAZES

Essays by

HUGH KENNER

NORTH POINT PRESS · SAN FRANCISCO

1989

The author and the publisher wish to thank the
magazines in which these essays originally appeared.

LIBRARY OF CONGRESS
CATALOGING-IN-PUBLICATION DATA
Kenner, Hugh.
Mazes: essays/by Hugh Kenner.
p.   cm.
ISBN 0-86547-341-2
I. Title.
AC8.K45   1989
081—dc19   88-61173

FOR RICHARD G. STERN

Contents

Preface

One morning back in 1969 I ended a long, long book called *The Pound Era* by typing "Thought is a labyrinth," a sentence I lifted from a speculation of Guy Davenport's on how the death of William Carlos Williams might have been linked with the fate of the sick elm he'd said he'd not outlive. If life abounds more in coincidence than in causation, we can't always be sure of telling them apart, and coincidence is an economy that unclutters mental life. Dante dated his vision 1300, Chaucer died in 1400, *Henry V* was 1600, Dryden died 1700, *Lyrical Ballads* was reissued in 1800. Noting an absent 1500, you can recall Pound's remark about a blankness after the death of Chaucer: "And for 180 years almost nothing." And 1900? A thin year. Wilde died, and Ruskin; *The Cardinal's Snuff-Box* got published. . . . That's one way to start drawing a map.

Of his latterly famous son John Stanislaus Joyce said, "If that boy was put down in the Sahara he'd set to making a map." A map to a blankness is just conceivable. Mazes, though, demand maps. Hence my title.

Late in 1985, when Time-Life was still struggling to keep its *Discover* viable, the editors wondered if I'd write them a piece about mazes. Mazes? Well, I'd known Michael Ayrton, our time's premier maze specialist. He'd been commissioned in 1967 to design a maze in the Catskills and create sculptures for placing at its two centers. That commission had come because the patron had chanced on a book of his, a fictional autobiography of Daedalus. What put Ayrton onto Daedalus I don't remember, though what put me onto Ayrton was our shared respect for Wyndham Lewis. Having listened to Ayrton's

discourses, I thought I had enough material to accept the *Discover* assignment (and experience the fantastic scope of Time-Life fact-
checking; their phone calls pursued me even unto a hotel in Toronto,
where I learned that, according to the London Bureau, the guards at
Hampton Court no longer bellow through megaphones as I'd heard
them do in 1964; we recast a sentence).

But my point is the intersection of two causations. Ezra Pound to
Lewis to Ayrton, that was one; and the other was *Discover* to me, facilitated by a former student who happened to be working for them.
But for Ayrton, I'd have had to say I didn't know enough; but for the
student, I'd have had no occasion to say anything. My sense of life is
that it's filled with intersections like that.

As Aristotle himself said, in his parable of the man at the spring.
The spring (vector 1) was in a wooded place; you can fill in the geology. Brigands (vector 2) hid there because it was wooded. And the
man (vector 3) went there because he was thirsty. And the brigands
killed him; and his death (says Aristotle) was "uncaused" because no
clean line of necessity produced it. He was (for explicable reasons) in
the wrong place at the wrong time. But that's the map of most of human fortune, except that for "wrong" we can frequently say "right."

So, little in this collection originated with me; an editor had
thought of me, wanting something I happened to be able to deliver,
by pulling thoughts together and weaving available threads. (If a few
motifs occur more than once, that is understandable. Page by page
over twenty years, I'd no thought of making a *book*.) No claim of orac-
ular unity is made either. Occasions differed, and times, and reader-
ships. The ones collected here are some I still find rereadable. A future collection, more "literary" in emphasis, will be called *Historical
Fictions*.

FEBRUARY 1988

MAZES

Light, Our
One Absolute

Bob Montiegel of National Public Radio phoned on March 6, 1979. He wanted something to air on March 14, the hundredth anniversary of Albert Einstein's birth. And he specified exactly eight minutes of airtime. The funny old uncle nobody understands was a cliché I instinctively rejected; a fit homage to Einstein might try to make one of his ideas intelligible. I chose the Time Dilation. Superbly produced by Montiegel, the vignette won that year's Ohio State Award for educational broadcasting. And many letters I got came from people who'd heard it on the car radio amidst a morning traffic jam.

This morning Earth and its passengers will have completed a hundred trips round the sun since a child named Albert Einstein first blinked at the light in a small town in Germany. Light remained the first fact of his cosmos, as it had been for his remote Jewish forebears. Before the sun was, says the Book of Genesis, there was light. Before God made the sun and moon and stars he created light, the messenger of the universe.

It was 1676 before men were sure that light takes time to get from one part of the universe to another. By the time Albert Einstein was in school, his teachers could tell him pretty nearly how much time it took: a second to travel 186,000 miles: just over a second to reach us from the moon, eight minutes from the sun. And at sixteen, Einstein had found a question to worry about. What if *I* could travel at the speed of light? What would I see? Would a mirror in my hand stay just out of reach of the light streaming toward it from my face, and show me nothing? The answer, when he knew it after ten years, undermined the common-sense world, which knows only common-sense answers. But Einstein believed that a well-defined question can be answered, even though the answer may turn the universe inside out with a Theory of Relativity.

We are used to many things common sense would reject if it confronted them. I am talking in Washington, D.C., with my eye on a clock. You are listening, I don't know where. We both know that we are both on Spaceship Earth, being carried round the sun at nineteen miles a second. Still I don't know where on earth you are, and I don't know what time it is where you are. Your clock ticks along with mine, but I don't know what "now" is your now, because I don't know how long my voice is taking to reach you. The radio waves that carry it dawdle along toward you at the speed of light, which takes a full sixtieth of a second to reach the West Coast, and we are used to a world in which a sixtieth of a second is no insignificant time: long enough to smash up a car, overexpose a snapshot, or tangle a computer's feet.

It gets much stranger, strange enough for Einstein's attention, if we board different spaceships. I'll stay in Washington, you leave Earth: tuck your radio under your arm and blast off toward the stars. As you watch Earth dwindle to a speck you can still hear me, and thanks to technology I can hear you, so we can try an experiment. I have a beeper (*SOUND*) and you have a beeper (*different sound*), and we can sound them together on the count of three. Three, two, one, BEEP. All clear? Count along with me, and BEEP.

Now here's what you hear in your spaceship:

Three, two, one, *BEEP*

beep

But here's what I hear in Washington:

Three, two, one, *BEEP*   *beep*

You say you were right on time: our beeps were simultaneous. And I say yours was late. Clearly, that's because the signals took time to travel. And Einstein says that in a universe where things are milling around, whether two events are simultaneous or not depends on where you are.

Now if you'll let me listen to your clock, I'll say it's running slow. That's not difficult to explain: you are speeding away from me, and every tick has farther to travel than the last one did. But your heartbeat, when I listen, is slowed down, too. From here in Washington I'd say you were living more slowly, even *aging* more slowly. Your time is slower than my time. And if we'd asked Albert Einstein which time was "right," he would have said both were right. There is no universal time.

The faster you speed your spaceship, the more your time slows down. There must be a limit, when your time would stop altogether, and you have probably guessed what it is: the speed of light, which is *therefore* a speed you can never reach. So we can finally answer the question Einstein asked himself at the age of sixteen: what would you see if you were travelling at the speed of light? He asked it when the fastest things that moved were trains, but his answer holds in the age of the Saturn rocket. You cannot reach the speed of light. The most powerful engine could not boost you to that speed, because the universe is so constructed that only light can ever reach it. And light, our one absolute, travels at no other: never hustles, never tires.

The child who was born a hundred years ago took years to gather his wits. At nine he did not even speak with fluency. Normal people, he reflected later, never think about space and time because as children they found such mysteries insoluble. "But my intellectual development was retarded, so I began to wonder about space and time only when I had grown up. Naturally I could go deeper into the problem than a child with normal abilities."

So there is something to be said for delay. Speaking of delay, the light you may see through your window now left the sun just about the moment this program started. In two hundred years it will have reached stars we can point to. Two hundred years are unlikely to bring a second Einstein.

Fractals

For several years Art & Antiques *has printed my "Inside Story" each month on its back page. This one appeared in May 1986.*

The line light draws from Sirius to your eye, 51 million million miles long, is something school mathematics can describe. It's Euclid's "shortest distance between two points." But the line of the ridge of the Jungfrau, an eaten, wavering knife-edge against Swiss skies? The contour of the tumbling cloud above it? The pattern elm boughs etch outside your window? Euclid winces. For the mountain is not a cone, nor the cloud a sphere, nor the elm a tracery of classic curves.

So they are "irregular." Cubism and Brancusi saw failed approximations to Euclid and abstracted irregularity away. But rare eyes, like Leonardo's and Hokusai's, saw self-similarity: shapes repeated on ever smaller scales. So they cherished what the Greeks rejected, unutterable formlessness, the flux Aphrodite renounced as her S-curves crystallized out of it.

Hokusai's *Great Wave* shatters into foamy wavelets that have each the shape of the wave; you can almost see each wavelet doing likewise. Except to the eye of Benoit Mandelbrot, that was the kind of Japanese fancifulness that forced little bonsai trees to mimic big ones.

And Leonardo's *Deluge* was a scribble, unless, like Mandelbrot, you were willing to credit "the superposition of eddies of many diverse sizes."

Mandelbrot, sixty-two, has based a mathematical career on trust in such vision as Hokusai's and Leonardo's. When we see "disorder," we are seeing nature's habit of repeating forms in infinite regress. The moons of Uranus aren't spherical but pitted and pocked. On their surfaces doubtless lie pebbles shaped like them. Mandelbrot's "fractal" functions describe that as effortlessly as Euclid's can describe perfect spheres no eyes have seen.

The twig, he reminds us, has the shape of a limb; the limb, of a tree. (And the tree? Of the human circulatory system. Nature rhymes as resourcefully as Pope.) "Scaling" is his adjective for objects, natural or man-made, in which subsystems of detail echo larger systems ad infinitum. Other objects, like multistory glass boxes, are "scale-bound"; their effect depends on their being the size they are, and the closer you come the less there is to see.

Picasso tended to be a scale-bound artist; his sidewalk construction in Chicago looks strained and empty from having been enlarged to monster size from the size at which it worked. Its bigness now advertises how much isn't in it. Van Gogh, on the other hand, made "scaling" pictures; come close and find detail, clear down to the brush stroke, whose dynamics are like the whole. Shakespeare's metaphors work in miniature like his plays. Ezra Pound's *Cantos*, our time's pre-eminent "scaling" work, is made of Cantos made of episodes made of details made of word constellations, the unique identity patent in the closest close-up.

Mandelbrot's "proofs" have been scamped, a fact that can make the mathematical establishment look down its triangular nose. War made his education so irregular he still isn't sure of the order of the alphabet, an uncertainty shared, oddly, with Picasso. What has made his "Fractal Geometry" irrefutable is the pictures it can generate, pure mathematical fictions that are manifestly moons and mountains. For that we can thank a uniquely American synergy.

In 1958 he left French académie for IBM; a few years later they made him an "IBM Fellow" with a staff including at least two gifted programmers, Richard Voss and Alan Norton, who could make machines hum to his fractal functions. The visions that leap up on color screens cannot fail to carry conviction; if Mandelbrot's math can *create* a plausible mountain, then his claim that it *describes* mountains grows credible. His lectures fall on irregularly willing ears; the art is what persuades. Thanks to IBM, you can turn through his pages comprehending not an x nor y and perceive a universe reclaimed for mind.

The Dead-Letter Office

Commissioned, when I was still in California, for a special museum issue (July-August 1971) of Art in America. *The next year George Braziller reprinted the whole issue as a hardcover called* Museums in Crisis. *But my argument is, more or less, that they* are *the crisis.*

The State of California, through the Buildings and Grounds Committee of its Multiversity, has supplied me with an office in which to meditate, on the explicit understanding that I affix nothing to the walls. It is a totally puritan interior, a plaster cube. I may inflict no holes, insert no fasteners. The penalties would include, presumably, Visitations and Bills for Damages. A man with a pass key comes in every night to empty the wastebasket, and presumably it is he who checks the walls. The State's postulate is clear: my usefulness to the brightest 10 percent of its adolescents will not be enhanced by rectangular arrangements of form and color.

Which is odd, since the campus does maintain a museum. Or not so odd, since the museum (1) is over by the Art Department, and (2) is a Visual Aid, i.e., an accessory to knowledge otherwise formulated. Understanding, you see, is verbal, discursive (how else could they set examinations?).

Or so they think, but the young don't think so. Let the skeleton of a new hive of plaster cubicles commence to be assembled, to the greater glory of discursive understanding, with round it for safety's sake a plyboard fence, and overnight young Giottos modify the assault of that fence with multicolor graffiti: splashes, circles, Blakean injunctions, intricate polychrome-Tenniel cartooned allegories, the illegible ABCs of psychedelia, clouds and birds of iconic aspiration, fragments of Shelleyan hymns to ecology, the works. You walk past it for months till the building gets up and the fence at last comes down: a transient living *musée sans murs* composed wholly of murals. That's what makes the young feel creative, a piece of environment, a silly piece (plywood slabs); it wants transforming.

So there you have it, the familiar paradigm: no art where you use your mind; dead art where the sign says ART; *tachisme* (and a little better) where nothing is supposed to be and nothing will be for long. I rehearse these details because their environment is officially and institutionally educational. Museums have traditionally been educational, so if the museum-atom is splitting, it's on campus that we may find a vector diagram.

Museums have traditionally been educational. What else? In being that they have virtually defined Art. Art is what you can find in a museum. It becomes Art when it is brought there (think of Duchamp's bicycle wheel). Outside, where it was made, it was an altarpiece or a bauble for the Medici summer cottage. Once inside the museum it's divorced from context, from any context save a hushed didactic strenuousness. It becomes good for one. For whom? For anyone. Tourists. Schoolchildren. Religiose barbarians. Writers of guides. Itinerant professors. Folk in quest of a cool place at lunch hour (but no paper bags beyond the front steps!). Dingily, quietly, the artifacts of an inconceivable past soothe or admonish the comers; a visit to the catacombs is not more salutary, nor (in certain moods) would a trip to the morgue be more macabre. Jeremy Bentham thought it a pity to shovel underground the corpses of great men, and then hire sculptors to make imperfect likenesses. Better, he thought, to set up, suitably stuffed, the very bodies. He was not being sardonic; he was saving work and serving truth. That is not a memorial to the Duke of Wellington; no, that *was* the Duke of Wellington. The one "Auto-Ikon" Bentham achieved was his own. At the University of London they display him, seated in a cabinet, during registration week. But supposing we had Botticelli under glass, in a roll-out drawer in an air-conditioned room; supposing, for 500 lire, the *custodi* rolled him out, to let a roomful of visitors gaze at his features and his shroud: *a fifteenth-century Italian Painter*, with his palette on his breast and the brush in his brown right hand. Supposing also, in another room, one could see the *Primavera*, one of the things he was once paid to do: to which room would the 500-lire pieces flow?

But that is a question about unstructured curiosity, to which art museums have never pretended to appeal. They enshrine a structure of cognitions called Art History, and Botticelli's corpse, unless Warhol can be persuaded to sign it, isn't Art History, whereas the *Primavera* is. Some discriminations seem less intelligible. Mummy cases, laboriously and delicately painted with an iconography of the soul's journey, seem not to be Art History; painted Renaissance *cassoni* seem to be. A clavichord, delicately crafted, isn't Art History, nor a ruff; something dribbled by Jackson Pollock is. Art History would seem to be a party line of which the art museum is the teaching machine. It documents, we may say at a venture, the long and intricate story of how painters and sculptors, century after century, have learned from their predecessors and then innovated.

The man with immediate need for that kind of instruction is the apprentice artist. Undeterred by the hush of bourgeois didacticism, he dashes up the museum steps with brio, and looks with a sharpened sense of how to look. But these expensive temples are not maintained for the use of young painters. No, they are temples to Culture: part of the nineteenth-century assumption that a wholly new enterprise, the acculturation of the middle classes, was thinkable; furthermore, that it was best conducted in a sort of orderly attic where things (1) difficult to do, (2) no longer done, and (3) utterly useless were arranged in some graspable sequence (and No Smoking!). Culture, so considered, is communion with the contents of a huge Dead-Letter Office, missives whose addressees have moved on: no longer to be read, as the Medici read the *Primavera*, but filed and acknowledged.

The museum, so considered, has a literary equivalent, the annotated edition, being the repository of poems no longer responded to as formerly, and so turned into teaching machines. At what may be called a dateline in twentieth-century cultural history, in 1922, T. S. Eliot published *The Waste Land* with notes and numbered lines, so creating an instant museum piece. "The Burial of the Dead," the first section was headed, and sure enough, relics of the mighty dead may be discerned embedded in its mellifluity: Chaucer's April, the Bible's desert and its "Son of Man," Shakespeare's pearled eyes, Dante's weary circling throng, a thrill of Webster's, more; and as for you, ". . . you know only / A heap of broken images. . . ." The lines carry numbers, like the lines of official poetry, long dead, and the allusions are itemized, and the "poetry," too, verges on museum poetry: authorized sonorities, validated *frisson*. At the heart of the poem is the myth of the Quester, who enters a ruined temple and notes a miscellany of artifacts. In the myth Eliot took from Jessie Weston's *From Ritual to Romance*, the Quester asks what these forgotten things in fact are, a deed as subversive of quiet as the kind of question Eliot had been asking in the pages of *The Egoist*: "Who, for instance, has a first-hand opinion of Shakespeare?" To ask that is to pluck Shakespeare out of literary history, where his bland stare answers the glazed stares of the docile. When the Quester in the Chapel Perilous asks such questions, then the heavens open, but despite much rumble of thunder Eliot leaves it ambiguous whether or not, in his poem, the question gets properly asked. "Shall I at least set my lands in order?" asks a voice like a desperate curator's on the last page; he proceeds to order exhibits in literary history, from the *Pervigilium Veneris* to *El Desdichado*.

Like its exact contemporary *Ulysses*, *The Waste Land* seems artfully confected to signify the end of culture. If we look at Eliot's prose of the years just before, we discover many testimonials to his sense that Culture has become synonymous with a Museum Civilization, the dead didactic array. The central metaphor in "Tradition and the Individual Talent" is the acquisition of today's work by a museum, as though it could have no other destination. Eliot used the word "monuments" in an elusively ironical paragraph, which notes that "the existing monuments form an ideal order among themselves." And this order is vulnerable, being "modified by the introduction of the new (the really new) work of art among them."

"The existing order is complete before the new work arrives; for order to persist after the subvention of novelty, the *whole* existing order must be, if every so slightly, altered; and so the relations, proportions, values of each work of art toward the whole are readjusted; and this is conformity between the old and the new." Behind the impenetrable tone of that final clause we may discern a sardonic recognition of the way the old at first simply *makes room*, but later finds it is tacitly being revalued. Thus Manet's *Le Déjeuner sur l'Herbe* alters our sense of the Giorgione in the Louvre from which its salient motifs are paraphrased. We might not otherwise have reflected that naked women stood about Giorgione's studio, to help him paraphrase the "classic" conventions of the allegorical Nude. That *Le Déjeuner*, a scandal for the Second Empire, eventually found its way into the very Louvre where Manet saw the Giorgione, is a sequel almost unbelievably neat. It wasn't carried there damp from the studio; still wilder novelties had to moderate its aggressiveness somewhat, so it could slip in as a bit of Art History.

In a different way from the way previous painters had been conscious of their arrayed predecessors, Manet was conscious that in his time one painted in the shadow of the Louvre. He could not have pretended otherwise. And seizing the initiative, he painted a picture that protests against that fact. Scrub, he implies, the tone of time from the colors; replace Venetian dandies in the costume of their day by Parisian dandies in the costume of our day; remove that look of "classical" abstractedness from the nude lady's face—let her self-possessed eyes confront the bourgeois viewer, as though to ask what else he expects if he strays into bohemia—then pretend, if you can, that "cultural" values are enhanced by Sunday afternoon communion with such an artifact. And the Louvre claimed him after all, for History can subdue anything. It has subdued *The Waste Land* also, and Eliot's poem finds its place today amid the poems with notes and numbered lines in those heaps of broken images, the classroom anthologies it once subverted so vigorously.

Manet and Eliot occupy the two ends of an era we agree has ended, the era called Modernist, which is usually said to have protested with all its vigor against the past. That is not accurate; it protested not against the past, against tradition, but against the didactic uses of the past, and the tradition of the handbook. Insofar as *Le Déjeuner sur l'Herbe* is a satirical painting, it is not Giorgione it satirizes but the Louvre; and *The Waste Land* likewise satirizes Palgrave's *Golden Treasury*. The next step, for painters, since museums always triumphed by buying what they painted after a little wait, was to subvert museums from within, and the history of the various post-Modernisms might be written as a war of the United Artists against the place of cool vaults they had come to think deadly.

Thus, about 1917 a curator, roused by the clangor of his doorbell, might shake the cobwebs from his shoulders and swing wide the portals to discover on his marble steps a Duchamp ready-made, the inverted urinal, say, cheekily claiming the right to be admitted. "But you are not sculpture," he splutters, "for you were made in a factory." "Then that Rodin behind you is not sculpture either," responds the urinal, "for it was made in a foundry." "But the Rodin was cunningly and wonderfully designed," rejoins the curator, to whom the urinal: "And do you think my own delicate curves were achieved by accident? They would have enchanted Pythagoras. Observe, moreover, my polished gloss, my pure off-white. A designer stipulated these, craftsmen achieved them; that was not done in a day." "You were made for a low and unmentionable purpose." "Your talk of low and high does not confuse me, and if we are to talk of purposes, the Rodin was made exclusively for the never-mentioned purpose of being sold to someone such as you. And as to the purpose you hint I was made to serve, I no longer mean to serve it, and cheerfully proclaim as much by the fact that I stand before you turned upside down; a procedure, I may add, from which half your collection of sculpture would conceivably profit." "But the Rodin bears the signature of A. Rodin, a sculptor," cries the curator, risking his ace. "As for me," says the urinal, "I bear the signature of R. Mutt." "Who is R. Mutt?" shrieks the curator. "Who is A. Rodin?" rejoins the urinal sweetly. "Do not say, 'an eminent sculptor,' since your only evidence for that is the agreement of your colleagues and yourself that other things he has signed, no more persuasive than the thing your museum so prides itself on, are pieces of eminent sculpture. And right here, on your doorstep, I propose to sit, until the day comes when you shall have accorded my signer, R. Mutt, as much claim to the title of sculptural eminence as the fabricator of that utterly barbarous likeness of Balzac in which a blasted stump modeled in taffy enshrines the sensibility of a coal heaver."

The urinal's point has long since been tacitly conceded, a process a private collector, Walter Arensberg, catalyzed by buying it at once. Soon it had conformed still more closely to the paradigms of classic sculpture by getting lost, even as every piece by Phidias. And even as we guess at Greek sculpture from Roman copies, so at the Sidney Janis Gallery, in 1953, one might assess at one remove the sculptural impulse of Mons. Mutt/Duchamp, glimpsed through a replica.

Meanwhile Picasso, leaving behind him a trail of discarded periods, had been performing yet another kind of museum mimicry. It soon became clear that his Blue Period works, for instance, could be acquired without fear as though they were by a dead artist. No previous painter had done the art-taxonomist's work for him with such thorough effrontery. Soon museums commenced buying easel paintings conceived only decades before as assaults on the museum idea. It could surprise no one that the *Nude Descending a Staircase*, hooted at in 1913 as an explosion in a shingle factory by folk whose perception of heroic paintings did not extend to calling any of them an explosion in a bordello, was received eventually into the Philadelphia Museum of Art.

Impatient with the test of time, Museums of Modern Art arose, hoping to catch creativity on the wing—to capture work done if possible this very morning—whereupon—checkmate!—Jean Tinguely reasoned, and persuaded the New York Museum of Modern Art to credit, that the entire life cycle of a work of art, from the preparation of the palette, say, to the eventual dropping of decayed paint off the canvas, should be condensed from centuries into a few days, and made to occur in its rightful place, a museum. He fabricated in the museum garden a huge rickety "sculpture" the office of which was to destroy itself, right on the spot, with the firemen in attendance (would there be dynamite? the museum queried), the debris to be carted off by garbagemen. The spectacle was accomplished on St. Patrick's Day, 1960. *The Nation* thought it scented social protest and decried a decline in style (garden parties, not barricades), but the Director of Museum Collections accurately perceived a homage to Art History. "Oh, great brotherhood of Jules Verne, Paul Klee, Sandy Calder, Leonardo da Vinci, Rube Goldberg, Marcel Duchamp, Piranesi, Man Ray, Picabia, Filippo Morghen," he wrote, "are you with it?"

The crowning move of the United Artists was the fabrication, wholesale, of artifacts that can have no conceivable destiny except the museum. The *Nude Descending a Staircase* did time in a private collection, the Elgin Marbles decorated a temple, Holbeins once assuaged the vanity of kings; but imagine a way station, en route to the museum, for a piece consisting of a bar interior with stools on which sit life-sized plaster figures! Such works are instant museum pieces; there is simply no other place to put them (a living room? whose?). And an Action Painting bigger than anyone's wall except an institution's, what else can be done with that? They compete in scale with the huge Henry Moores that brood in public courtyards, but being ridiculously perishable they can't be set up outdoors. Such works, moreover, have too equivocal a relation with life to be tolerated for long in the ambiance of any but the most specialized of existences, such an existence as the one the gallery-goer assumes when he checks his parcels just beyond the turnstile. Only the gallery-goer's transience saves him; such things keep no steady company but with their own precarious kind, a Pollock, a Segal, a Giacometti, a Rauschenberg hobnobbing with one another in a world they spin out of one another's proximity: an art world, which is a museum world, an artifice of eternity where there is no marrying nor giving in marriage but only the quizzical intercommunion of artifacts as outrageously unassimilable as dinosaurs. (Could anyone breed a dinosaur, he would give it *at once* to a zoo.)

Considered as a technique for destroying museums, the goings-on in the art world of the sixties had the frenzied effectiveness of a Laurel and Hardy pie-throwing marathon. The program was radical, perhaps uncombatable: as fast as new museums could be constructed, to jam them full of huge objects that no one else can house, that would be ruined in the rain, and that no Selection Committee, conscious of its obligations to History, would think of allowing to perish. Rauschenberg's *Goat*, for heaven's sakes, the stuffed one with the tire around its middle, pensive in its junkyard of painted clutter: what else can be done with *that*? The Moderna Museet, Stockholm, saw its obligation. And more, and more. It resembled an effort at jamming the postal service by addressing tons of mail to the Dead-Letter Office.

Then suddenly the strategy shifted. Instead of art that could only go into museums, art began to be turned out that museums couldn't get at. Earthworks, for instance, defy efforts to dig them up and move them, though a museum may one day be erected over the site of one, and a kinetic sculpture of dyes dropped into a stream will resist all efforts to fit it under a roof in however grandiose a maxi-Jacuzzi. Having goaded the museum mind to a frenzy of blind acquisitiveness, the artist's new ploy is to taunt it with the non-acquirable. Very soon curators, teased beyond bearing, will commence going mad. Their office is to institutionalize Art History, and Art History, so far as they can display it, will seem to have stopped short in the late 1960s, having stepped into a new dimension, out of reach. As for the Ideal Order which Eliot confronted, the order modulated when at long intervals it nodded assent to "the really new," but an order still calm, still constituted of "monuments," still capable of housebreaking a *fauve*, that order stopped decades ago. The history of twentieth-century art may someday appear to have been simply a death struggle with the museum. In that struggle, art being unkillable, the museum was foredoomed. Now, the temples of art history having themselves been relegated to history (we may speak of the Museum Age, and contemplate a Museum of Museums), we may expect art to find more interesting things to do.

Perhaps much that is in museums will be silently returned to where it came from, the Elgin Marbles for instance back to the Acropolis. Athens is now as accessible as London. A transparent dome would protect them from further erosion; surely some disciple of Fuller's will oblige. And the Rubenses, might they not go back to Flanders, and the Munich and London Botticellis to Florence, and the Mantegnas to the Ducal Palace in Mantua? And finally, gathered into a last Museum, those works that never had any other destination. In some Temple of the End of Art History, a terminal moraine, there the Goat, girdled by its tire, will commune thoughtfully forever with the plaster denizens of the bar, who in turn, their backs forever turned to the giant plastic hamburgers, will avoid staring at, or will stare with unseeing plaster eyes at, the thirty-two-foot Hard Edge, its dogmatism offset by the frozen insouciance of a huge dribble from which a Giacometti stick-man strides motionless forever away. And the University may let me put a nail in my wall when I find a picture I like. The fences, though—the kids will go on painting fences, and contractors will pull them down regardless, the paintings having lasted as long as they needed to. Much that's in Art Museums has lasted much longer than that.

The Untidy Desk
and the Larger
Order of Things

From Discover, *early in 1986, when it was still a Time-Life enterprise.
The publication of G. K. Zipf's* Human Behavior and the Principle
of Least Effort *coincided almost exactly with the author's premature
death, thus freeing everyone from the duty of arguing. Benoit Mandelbrot, no less, recently advised me that Zipf's assertions won't hold mathematical water, not least because essentials like "effort" are never defined. So despite a numerical facade, his "Law" stays on the plane of
analogy. But if he did no more than isolate some odd data about language,
those do seem irrefutable.*

There are clean-desk people—you know them, you may even be
one—whose working space always looks scrubbed for surgery. They
make a virtue of handling no paper twice—"Do something with it
right now. Don't dither. 'In doubt? Throw it out.'" Any time the clean-
desker takes down a book, it's no sooner snapped shut than back with
it to the shelf. Each paper summoned from the files is rebounded instantly to the files again. The steady stream from In-Basket gets de-

flected just two ways: to Out-Basket, to trash. Promptly at five, the clean-desker smugly departs from a place where the only hint that anything ever happened all day is an overflowing wastebasket.*

Off duty, clean-deskers measure their vermouth with an eyedropper, walk their dogs by the clock, succor their spouses by the calendar. Such people exist, and some of them ask fees for training decentered souls to be just like them.

But there are also souls like mine, content amid what clean-deskdom calls unholy clutter. Cleaning up the room I'm sitting in at this moment, to the extent of meeting clean-desk standards, would take a week. The few times I have tried it, useful things have invariably disappeared forever: things I routinely laid hands on without fail, back when they were integrated with the mess I fondly manipulate. I am, to put it mildly, an untidy-desker.

But untidy-deskers of the world may take heart. It is we who have mathematical validation. Forget what you may have thought about the swept and tidy world of number. Concentrate on the fine randomness of Einstein's hair. We connoisseurs of scrutable chaos have been guided all along by an inscrutable proposition called the 80-20 rule: a special case, what is more, of Zipf's Law.

Please observe that mess tends to accumulate for good reasons. Taking down Eric Partridge's invaluable *Origins* to check, as I often do, the pedigree of a word, I reflect that before long I'll surely be checking another. So instead of returning *Origins* to the shelf I leave it (for now) on my desk. And this letter from Alabama about the conference: though it's just now been answered, I shall be needing its dates when I call the travel agent. It may as well stay (for now) on my desk on top of Partridge. As for this sheaf of notes for the piece that's due next week, let's leave it here (for now) to remind me to get started. Also it will be handy when I do start. When I've finished, it may as well stay there a while longer, because editors will have queries. . . . Thus "for now" stretches out and out, and stuff accumulates.

There is a principle behind all this, and, despite what prudery may be thinking, it is not sloth. It is this: *what you're needing now you're quite*

*Correction: on noting a wastebasket's tendency to overflow, the dedicated clean-desker gets a bigger one.

likely to need again. Human experience says so. Conversely, *what you needn't lay hands on right now is something you will quite possibly never need*. Human experience again.

Books: every librarian keeps thousands that no one ever seems to ask for; knows, too, that the longer any book goes unwanted the greater are its chances of staying that way. Widgets: the kinds that aren't selling will likely never sell; less rule-bound than librarians, vendors hold clearances. Or language: we've all learned just how much of it we can safely let doze in thesauruses for occasional summoning. But some words—a few hundred, a few thousand—cannot be done without, and they come to mind instantly. We make over 50 percent of our normal talk by recycling only about one hundred words.

Because we've let our word stock dwindle? No. Parsimony is structured into language itself. Shakespeare's glorious vocabulary extended to 29,066 words that we know of, yet just 40 of them make up fully 40 percent of the plays.* If words had to be taken down and put away like books, Shakespeare would have kept those 40 all piled on his desk, and a pox on "clutter."

Time and again such intuitions surface, overwhelming schemes of "order" to become a totem of subsidiary order. Many a secretary has noticed that the file the boss just asked for is the same one he asked for yesterday; if she's shrewd she may stick it (for now) not back in its alphabetical place but in an "active" pile where it will be handy next time. Experience suggests that there *will* be a next time. To avoid any look of disorder the active pile stays in the filing cabinet, but up at the front of the drawer.

Long ago, someone noticed that the files resting out of place at the front—the ones in heavy use—amounted to about one-fifth of the drawer's contents. Further study produced a rule of thumb: *80 percent of the action involved 20 percent of the files*. And the 80-20 rule was born. Though no one seems to know who formulated it, lovers of the untidy desk will want it engraved on a platinum bar for enshrinement at the Bureau of Standards.

*The 40-40 rule and my own discovery. *Of any extensive text sample, just 40 words will make up 40 percent*.

I'll rephrase it: the greater part of any activity draws on but a small fraction of resources. That small fraction may as well stay handy. Though the numbers will vary, 80-20 gives us a feel. Anything of that order—80-20, 75-27, 81-11—says "a lot done with a little."

So if 20 percent of the contents of the room is piled on your desk instead of being stowed in the out-of-sight places where clean-deskers try to tell you it "belongs," then 80 percent of your needs can be satisfied by what's instantly within reach from where you sit. At the cost of a little rummaging, of course. To be sure, not just any 20 percent will do: no, the 20 percent that real activity accumulates, as when the mighty Mississippi builds its delta.

It's a tantalizing proportion, 80-20. In Volume 3, *Sorting and Searching*, of his classic work-in-progress *The Art of Computer Programming*, Donald E. Knuth of Stanford mentions the 80-20 rule as "commonly observed in commercial applications." Knuth cites a 1963 issue of *IBM Systems Journal*, where we find a man named Heising assuring us that the same principle applies in turn to just the active 20 percent.

Thus if we keep 1,000 files of which 200 bear the workaday brunt, then 20 percent of the 200—that's 40 files, or 4 percent—get 80 percent of 80 percent—that's 64 percent—of the use. 80-20; 64-4; by venturing one more stage we find that fully half the busywork entails only about eight of all those 1,000 files: 51 percent versus 0.8 percent. A moderate untidy-desker might prefer to be called a 51-0.8 person. Of a thousand folders, a mere eight scattered on your desk needn't seem unruly.

The reason the *IBM Systems Journal* took notice in 1963 is that back at the dawn of computerdom, when punched cards were clumsy and memory cost a Shah's ransom, searching through thousands of cards for the Widget account was a task to abridge even when steel fingers did it. And the 80-20 rule said, if you've searched for the Widget card once, it's apt to be wanted again; move it up front where the next search will hit on it speedily. Skeptics might have called that fudging, but IBM, adjusting its wide blue tie, pronounced it Computer Science. As it was. The essence of Computer Science is putting numbers on what really goes on.

And this is all very well, but you might like a controlled experiment, not to say a proof. The former, as it happens, I can provide. Not long ago, stuck midway in a wholly different project, I did what I often do while getting unstuck: I tinkered at a computer program meant to do something soothingly irrelevant. Soon it was fetching me some modest statistics on the habits of the novelist Henry James.

James kept a clean desk; in fact at various places in his house in England's Rye, Henry James kept *eight* clean desks. But en route from desk to desk in his ceaseless flight from clutter, he could never leave behind his considerable vocabulary. That he carried with him, and he seems to have used it exactly as I use my mass of papers. The words that he kept, so to speak, within easy reach—say 20 percent of them—were the ones he put to use some 80 percent of the time. They're the same ones we all keep within easy reach. When James did want something fancy he could always hesitate and grope.

In an instance I happen to have handy—2,339 words, most of chapter X of his 1903 novel *The Ambassadors*—there are just 665 different words all told. With no more than those, James somehow managed atmosphere and narrative and dialogue and several instances of psychic crisis, and how he did that is instructive.

The 665 words seem a meager resource. Spread evenly over the pages like soft margarine, they'd turn up with dull uniformity, each one just three or four times, leaving you conscious of a certain poverty. But James used "the" 86 times and "you" 72 times and "to" 62 times and "he" 56 times—you see the pattern. Thus fully 75 percent of the chapter's carpentry is done with a mere 176 of the different words that went into it—only 27 percent of its vocabulary. That left 489 available for special effects. When he mentions a fire "burnt down to the silver ashes of light wood," four of the nine words in that lyrical phrase are making their unique appearance.

Now look back at the paired percentages: 75-27. Not 80-20, but you see the shape.

Or here is T. S. Eliot's *Hollow Men*, a much slenderer artifact, just 417 words total. Eliot managed to include 187 different ones, a surprising proportion when you think how his poem keeps recycling its bleaknesses. And (again) fully 71 percent of the whole is accounted for by just 65 different words—35 percent of the total vocabulary. Ah,

71-35! Remember 80-20? The remainder—122 words—make one-time appearances, as when three of them lend tang to a single line: "The supplication of a dead man's hand."

Thirty-seven years ago, in what he called "An Introduction to Human Ecology," well before "ecology" was a buzzword, George Kingsley Zipf of Harvard (1902–50) spelled out in explicit detail what it was that yielded such uniform numbers. It was human intelligence, constantly estimating the path of minimal bother: exactly what I am doing when I don't put things back where they are said to "belong."

Zipf gave his book a frank title, *Human Behavior and the Principle of Least Effort*, and if he drew much of its data from our behavior in speaking or writing, it was because in that domain statistics were handy. Scholars of language had been extending themselves from compiling word lists to counting the words they'd compiled, and Zipf was the man to see a use for such data. What it illuminated wasn't "linguistics" but the way people manage resources like time and effort.

He got much mileage from a project Miles L. Hanley had completed at the University of Wisconsin in pre-computer 1937, with just $148 of university money and twenty-two students sorting 250 pounds of cards. That was a mimeographed *Word Index to James Joyce's Ulysses*, in the statistical appendices to which G. K. Zipf's eye was caught by a surprising symmetry. Appearances of the tenth most frequent word: 2,653. Of the hundredth: 265. Of the thousandth: 26! That seems too neat to be true. But it is true. Something was balancing.

It resembles one of Zipf's neatest demonstrations, based on the 1930 population of the fifty largest U.S. cities. The largest was New York. The second largest had ½ the population of New York. Number three, ⅓ the population of New York. And on down to number fifty, with, yes, ¹⁄₅₀ of New York's population. A series like 1, ½, ⅓, ¼ . . . is called "harmonic." Zipf's Law says that *any* allocation of resources (people in cities, words in books, tools in a toolbox) will settle down to a harmonic arrangement.

Such tidy balancing had nothing special to do with the verbal fastidiousness of James Joyce. *Ulysses* had simply provided G. K. Zipf with a sample the right size for displaying language in long-term equilibrium. He'd already spotted equilibrium in 44,000 words scribbled against deadlines for Buffalo Sunday papers, and when the Joycean data came to hand he was not surprised to find the same pattern exactly. Zipf in pursuit of his law was a hard man to surprise.

The vocabulary of *Ulysses* happens to be about the size of Shakespeare's—29,899 words. If we think of a circus with that many personnel, we find ringmaster Joyce, like Shakespeare and the Buffalo reporters, depending heavily not on his stars but on his workforce, 135 of whom (the, of, and, a, to, in) account for fully half the bustle in a 260,430-word book. At the other extreme over half the total vocabulary—16,432 words—got to make just one appearance: exotics like "ventripotence" and "yak."

What goes on, according to Zipf, is this. Words that say much, like "entropy" and "ecliptic," help us be brief. That is exactly why technical terms evolve: the few who know what they mean save a lot of time. But short common words that spell things out are easier on the rest of us, though it takes a lot of such words to specify what "entropy" can sew up in three syllables. So a balance is always being negotiated, fifty-dollar words traded against whole handfuls of penny ones. And the working of the language mirrors those tradeoffs. The frenzied action goes on in the bargain basement; hence Shakespeare's—and everyone's—40 or so words to do 40 percent of everything.

If you think I have left my desktop far behind, perhaps to distract your gaze from it, reflect on Zipf's implication that humans use language exactly as they use whatever else gets in its own way out of sheer variousness: papers, books, kitchen tools. The one-time words resemble those kitchen gadgets you must rummage for because you want them so seldom. They are exquisitely fashioned for just one job. The common words, though, are multipurpose, like a paring knife. There's likely an 80-20 rule for the kitchen if only we had data.

What a nutmeg grater does is grate nutmegs, and that's all. What a paring knife does is so many things you'd never finish listing them. Likewise, the hard words give dictionary writers no trouble at all. The big *Oxford* disposes of "colubriform" (snake-shaped) in just five lines.

But on "set," the supreme Swiss Army knife of the English word kit, handy in any thinkable context—get set to set the table with the dinner set, set the alarm so we can set out early, and set things up so we'll not be upset by a prowler but can set our teeth and set a dog on him—the *Oxford* entry was thirty years in the pondering, forty days in the writing, and ran to two-thirds the length of Milton's *Paradise Lost*.

"Set," then, is such a tool as we always keep handy, on the countertop as it were near the paring knife, whereas "colubriform" belongs in the sort of drawer where nutmeg graters and piecrust dimplers languish. If you ever plan to use "colubriform" in public you'd best devote fifteen minutes to making sure it really means what you want it to.

On Zipf's showing, use always tends to draw what is used in close. He scatters odd instances. "The number of people who get on and off an elevator at a given floor is inversely related to the distance of the floor from the bottom." That may reflect heavy traffic generating the cash for lower-floor rents. Nearness, conversely, prompts action. In a 1932 check of Philadelphia marriage licenses, Dr. J. H. S. Bossard found a surprising gravitation toward the girl next door. The shorter the distance, the likelier the pairing. In the range of up to twenty blocks, a 70-30 rule seemed to be operating: some 70 percent of the unions sparked within 30 percent of the distance. And the ghost of 80-20 winks again.

I don't find G. K. Zipf mentioning the 80-20 rule or anything like it. Given his keen ear for anything relevant, that likely means that 80-20 wasn't yet heard of in 1949. But the data he adduces do keep suggesting it. In 80-20 we seem to have a ballpark formulation of Zipf's Law of Least Effort, the law by which he sought to explain absolutely everything.

To make it seem plausible to non-mathematical readers, Zipf invented an analogy I find congenial. He asked us to imagine an artisan (me) with numerous tools (books, papers) on a bench (my desk), this artisan being charged (as am I) to do set jobs with a minimum of total effort. He then showed with ease how the ratios that support Zipf's Law would arise, as the tools got put where they'd be wanted.

My need to minimize my total effort originates with me. I want to save time, thinking I have other uses for it. So the books and papers I expect to have most use for I simply don't put where I'd have to get up and fetch them. And when I judge that I'll be using something again because I am using it now, both Zipf's Law and the 80-20 rule say that probabilities are very much on my side.

If some things, though, do eventually get put away, that is because the efficiencies of clutter can be offset by the effort of fumbling through it. Remember, it is *total* effort that we're trying to minimize; and the human mind, cunning in judging how much of a mess will really abet efficiency, makes estimates you'd need calculus to describe. That is not implausible. An outfielder solves trajectory problems every time he puts his glove where the ball will be.

Zipf's Law and its quick approximation, 80-20, confront a human predicament (much to do, finite time) that's inextricable from the way we cope with it (keep handy whatever we expect to use). The law reflects our expectation of what will be most used, and experience tends to make the expectation reliable. So Zipf and 80-20 end up sketching what actually goes on, quite as if they were laws of impersonal Nature, like gravity and thermodynamics.

But at bottom—so Zipf assured us —such laws work because they describe the situation we create in the course of intelligent coping. Situations like my desktop.

The Making of
the Modernist Canon

A lecture at the University of Chicago, as published in the spring 1984
Chicago Review. *Though "canon formation" has lately come to be
viewed as a sinister conspiracy, it happens in all kinds of ways.*

Your whimsical thoughts, if you live long enough, will be back haunting you. I am now beset by a notion that crossed my mind twenty
years ago. Then it seemed only a mild historical fancy. Now it resembles a cognitive Black Hole. It is simply this: that *no Englishman alive in
1600 was living in the Age of Shakespeare*. For there was no Age of Shakespeare in 1600. That age was invented long afterward.

Partly, I was thinking of Borges's famous statement that writers invent their predecessors; partly, I was pondering angry speculations
rife in those years, when it was held, if you remember, that the Beatles, if you remember them, might be unacknowledged Mozarts. We
were all of us being reproved for not celebrating their genius. Moreover genius, we were being told, never does get properly celebrated.
It goes to a premature and quicklimed grave, after which posterity's
accolades need cost posterity exactly nothing.

We are talking about psychic money: that was the currency bourgeoisiedom denied the Beatles while they were intact. Yes, yes, mere dollars came fluttering down abundantly upon Ringo and George and Paul and John. But not for them a reward that was withheld from Mozart also while he lived: assimilation into the musical canon. It is like the withholding of a full professorship.

I was set to wondering, when did Shakespeare get assimilated into the canon? Moreover, was there any inherent scandal in his not having been assimilated while he lived? And to the second question, the ready answer was no. In 1600 there was no canon, literary history not yet having been invented. Nor, save in theater circles, was Will Shakespeare even so much as a celebrity. Not only no canvasclimber of Drake's, but no learned fellow of the court had any reason to suppose he would some day be envied for having been Shakespeare's coeval, privileged to stand in the pit at the Globe while Burbage, reciting words about seas of troubles, sawed the air with his hand thus. The canvasclimber, for that matter, could have told Burbage a thing or two firsthand about seas and trouble.

How did it ever become obvious that in about the year 1600 Englishmen were living in the Age of Shakespeare? And is it even obvious now? Roland Barthes would have said it is not; he would have had us believe that such determinations were reversible, were in fact at bottom political, serving as they did to advantage a custodial class whose livelihood was bound up with the preeminence of Shakespeare: a class apt to be relegated to janitorial status should anyone make college deans believe that in 1600 men lived in the Age of—oh, Tom Dekker. It is, of course, professors such as myself who have a fiscal stake in Shakespeare. One Marxist gambit is to make innocents doubt whether there is any other stake.

Meanwhile such fin-de-siècle Englishmen as thought about it—fin, I mean, du seizième siècle—doubtless thought they were living in the Age of Queen Elizabeth, not thinking to define their good fortune in literary categories at all. I could as well attribute my presence here to the fact that we live in the age of sterile surgery and penicillin.

By the eighteenth century vernacular literature had accumulated a long enough history to be thought about historically. By 1783 Dr.

Johnson had collected his *Lives of the English Poets*, working from a canon established, interestingly enough, not by himself but by a syndicate of booksellers. It included no poet born earlier than 1605: none, in short, whose conventions of spelling, syntax, and image would be apt to strike an Augustan browser as odd. It was possible to wonder about the present state of literature. If that means, to ask with what names posterity might associate one's own time, then it concedes that our posterity will know us in ways we do not.

So in what age did a literate man about 1810 suppose he was living? Why, in the age of Samuel Rogers, Thomas Campbell, Robert Southey. Those are the names that would have come to mind: names we no longer hear. Our present canonical list is Wordsworth, Coleridge, Byron, Keats, Shelley, to which add Blake: and where did it come from? That is unwritten history. How canons are determined is, in general, unwritten history.

Let me, therefore, throw what light I can on one canon I have a little knowledge of. The canon of literary modernism: How did that get made? Is it made yet?

As recently as 1931, a year I can just remember, it was not made, was not even adumbrated. That was the year F. R. Leavis published *New Bearings in English Poetry*, and felt obliged, before he disclosed the new bearings, to dispose of pseudobearings, the likes of Alfred Noyes and Walter de la Mare. Noyes had lately undertaken a long poem about the great astronomers of history, and Leavis even felt required to deal with that; his dealing was formal in syntax but paraphrasable as a snort. Nor was he overcome by William Butler Yeats, whose intelligence he called "magnificent," but much of whose poetry he described as meditation on the events of the poet's life: an *Irish* life, moreover. Leavis identified one *English* modern poet, G. M. Hopkins; one naturalized English one, the American-born T. S. Eliot (who would later advert to Leavis's "rather lonely battle for literacy"); finally one *echt* American, Ezra Pound. Pound was the author of just one good poem, *Hugh Selwyn Mauberley* (1920); the rest, before and after, was enamel and polish and the doing of inorganic will; such "limited interest" as the *Cantos* had was "technical." Dead forty-two years but organic, G. M. Hopkins was okay. Alive forty-three years, T. S.

Eliot was more than okay; the hope of the time, it was clear, lay with Mr. Eliot.

Whatever else *New Bearings* was, it was an intelligent start at canon defining, given the state of knowledge in 1931. Pointless now to iron-ize at the expense of Leavis's later career: his disenchantment with Eliot, his growing obsession with Lawrence, his virtual dismissal of Joyce, his grotesque determination that what, at bottom, had pre-vented Eliot from being a major poet was his American birth. The state of knowledge in 1931, that is the thing to concentrate on. What do you need to know to define a canon?

Wrong question, since there's no generic answer. Better: what did Leavis in 1931 not know? Two things at least of great scope. One was the unprecedented interdependence of prose modernism and verse modernism. Though his magazine *Scrutiny* was later to deal with *Wuthering Heights* and *Hard Times* in a series it called "The Novel as Dramatic Poem," still how *Ulysses* had been the necessary forerunner of *The Waste Land* was something never clear to Leavis, nor how Henry James's habits of diction were refracted throughout a poem Leavis no-where mentions, Pound's *Homage to Sextus Propertius*. That was a cen-tral modernist discovery, that distinctions between "prose" and "verse" vanish before distinctions between firm writing and loose; there is no more dramatic moment in the *Cantos* than the one that af-fixes to the poem's page scraps of so-called prose that have been ex-tracted and Englished, with neither meter nor ragged right margins, from the contents of Sigismundo Malatesta's post-bag. "Hang it all, Robert Browning," commences *Canto II*, and when Robert Browning had processed old Italian letters he'd felt constrained to put them into blank verse, thus marking the frontier across which they were fetched: from "out there," where prose is, into a genuine *poem*.

But we no longer think language must vest itself in measure when it is brought into a poem. "Give me my robe, put on my crown"—that is a formula it need no longer intone. One test of a sensibility that ac-knowledges this new bearing is hospitality to Marianne Moore, who can pick her brisk way through unmetered though counted lines that are open to scraps of actual prose, and not the prose of Gibbon or Pater either, but corporation pamphlets about the Icosasphere. Of her, despite T. S. Eliot's firm endorsement, Leavis could make nothing: a defeat of a great critic so humiliating it has vanished from the Index to the reprinted *Scrutiny*. Another test is William Carlos Williams, who comes as close as any real poet does to validating the philistine complaint that modernist verse misrepresents mere prose by "lines." *Scrutiny* was not alone in ignoring Williams in England; he was not even published there until after his ex-compatriot Eliot had died, and even today so unabashed a British pro-modernist as Donald Davie confesses to making little of him.

And, of course, when we're in Donald Davie's company we may feel sure we're remote from prose/verse naivete. No, it's something else about Williams, his American-ness, the cisatlantic tang of his cadence, that still eludes John Bull.* And now we are ready for the second cardinal fact that was hidden from Leavis in 1931: the fact that the English language had split four ways, leaving English natives in control of but a fraction. No Englishman will contemplate this with any zest, so if you get your literary news from England you'll hear little of it.

Since Chaucer, the domain of English literature had been a country, England. Early in the twentieth century its domain commenced to be a language, English. But about 1925 it was clear that three countries, Ireland, America, and England, were conducting substantial national literatures in this language. Common words had deceptively different meanings in these three different literatures, and divergences of idiom were guaranteed by the fact that the three literatures drew on radically different traditions and on different intuitions of what literature might be for. It was no longer feasible to retain for the canon only what readers in England were prepared to like, the way they had once liked the songs of the Scotsman, Bobbie Burns, and the Irishman, Tom Moore. ("Bobbie"; "Tom"; they condescend when they accept.)

And by mid-century it was also clear, if not to everyone, that the decentralization of "English" was not the whole story: that there was ar-

---

*Not every Englishman is in this sense John Bull. Williams has had no better reader anywhere than Charles Tomlinson in Gloucestershire, who's responded to him as Mallarmé did to Poe. It is pleasant that Williams knew that in his lifetime.

guably a new center, locatable in books but on no map. English was the language not only of the Three Provinces but also of several masterpieces best located in a supranational movement called International Modernism.

Such a modernism flourished in conjunction with other modernisms, painted, sculpted, danced. These in turn acknowledged new environments created by new technologies: notably, the invasion of the city by the rhythms of the machine (subways and the crowds they brought, motorcars, pavement drills like the Rock Drill Epstein sculpted).

Looking back, Virginia Woolf said whimsically that late in 1910 "human nature changed." She meant that by 1910 you could see International Modernism coming, which is true though an observer thenabouts would have expected its literary language to be French. That it proved to be English instead was largely the doing of James Joyce, whose *Ulysses* helps us define the very concept of an International work. To what literature does it belong?

Not to Irish, though its events are set in Dublin. Joyce had explicitly rejected the Irish Literary Revival as provincial, and had not only left Ireland—many Irishmen have done that—but had adduced alien canons of which his systematic parallel with a Greek epic is probably the least radical. Not to English, though most of its words are in English dictionaries and Shakespeare is an adduced presence. No, the parts of *Ulysses* that resemble a novel resemble continental, not Victorian, narratives, and its sense of what business a large work of fiction ought to be about is continuously alien to English expectations. Its fit reader is not someone schooled in a tradition it augments, as the best reader of Dickens will be grounded in Fielding and Smollett; rather, anyone willing to master the book's language, its procedures, its Dublin materials, must do so all on the book's own terms. In Ireland, peevishness about its authenticity is apt to fasten on the claim that most of its devotees are American, and indeed many of them are, though anyone's current list of six *Ulysses* authorities would include one Australian, one German, and one Swiss.

Though the language of International Modernism, like that of air control towers, proved to be English, none of its canonical works came either out of England or out of any mind formed there. International Modernism was the work of Irishmen and Americans. Its masterpieces include *Ulysses*, *The Waste Land*, the first thirty *Cantos*.

After 1910 it flourished for some forty years. Its last masterpiece was *Waiting for Godot*, which an Irishman living in Paris wrote in English after having first detached himself from English by writing the first version in French. One reason Modernism's primary language was English was the emergence in this century of Irish and American self-confidence, affording to no other Indo-European language so rich a variety of social and cultural experience. And International Modernism was not restricted to language; it drew on a variety of twentieth-century activities which transcend the need for translators: on cubist and non-representational painting, which though mostly done in Paris owed little to any specifically French tradition; on renovations in music, inseparable from the impact (enabled by the railway) of the Russian ballet on three capitals; on the fact that the first century of world travel has also been the century of world wars; above all on the popularization, through technology, of a science that knows no frontiers and sets down its austere oracles in equations exactly as accessible to a Muscovite as to a New Yorker.

Via technology, science has shaped our century. Three events of 1895 might have foreshadowed the shape had anyone known how to correlate them. The first American gasoline-powered car was designed; an Italian named Marconi sent messages more than a mile with no wires at all; a German named Roentgen discovered that rays his apparatus was emitting passed clean through materials opaque to light.

The automobile was to end the domination of the railroad, the nineteenth century's triumphant cultural and economic symbol; post-Ford, all men chugged on their own, and a decent car soon meant more than a decent house.

Wireless, transmitting sounds and later pictures, was to terminate printed fiction and live drama as the normative media for entertainment; the play, the short story, in part the novel, became "art forms," art being the name we give an abandoned genre. (So television turns old movies into an art called "cinema.")

And X rays heralded the bending of learned attention on the technology of the invisible, a change with analogies as striking as they are difficult to reckon. When early in our century John Donne's poems began to be revived after more than a century of total neglect, the eyebeams of his lovers in "The Ecstasie" no longer seemed remote from physical reality as they had when everything real was made of brick.

Hard on the discovery of the electron in 1898 came Max Planck's discovery that energy is radiated not in a continuous stream but in discrete packets, called quanta, which are never fractional, always intact, and can be counted like chromosomes. More: when a quantum of energy was emitted, its electron jumped to a new orbit, without occupying even for an instant any of the space between. Mysterious energies, sudden transitions, are as congenial to the twentieth-century mind as they would have been unthinkable to our great-grandfathers. It is pointless to ask whether Eliot, who made Planck-like transitions in *The Waste Land*, did so on any scientific analogy (probably not) or had heard at all of the relevant physics (perhaps). The life of the mind in any age coheres thanks to shared assumptions both explicit and tacit, between which lines of causality may not be profitably traceable.

Before the First World War, the life of the English-speaking mind emanated from London, the last of the great capitals. The skeptical Joseph Conrad, a Pole, walked its streets (and his son became a motor-car salesman). He was England's most distinguished practising novelist in the century's early decades. The principal novelist of an earlier generation was also foreign: Henry James. He lived in Rye and came up to London for the winters. London, he said ecstatically, could always give you exactly what you sought. And England's principal poet was W. B. Yeats, a man who made a symbol of his Irish identity though from 1895 to 1919 he preferred to live at 18 Woburn Buildings, London WC1. That the principal resident talent in those years was foreign in origin and often in allegiance should arrest us: London was attracting world talent the way Rome had in Augustan times when the world had a smaller circumference, and like Rome it was seeing its cultural affairs preempted by the talent it had attracted. (Vergil, Cicero, Horace, Propertius, Ovid: none was native to the Rome that claims them. Ovid had come from wild hills now called the Abruzzi, as alien to Rome as any Idaho.)

And yet another wave came. Ezra Pound, born in Idaho, reached London in 1908 from Pennsylvania via Venice, partly to learn from Yeats, whose skill in fitting the sentence exactly into the stanza was one of the signs of mastery he discerned. His old Pennsylvania class-mate Hilda Doolittle ("H. D.") arrived a little later. In 1914 Tom Eliot, of St. Louis and Harvard, became a Londoner, too. By contrast the na-tive talent is apt to seem unimportant, or else proves not to be native: even Wyndham Lewis, who went to an English public school (Rugby), had been born near a dock at Amherst, Nova Scotia, on his American father's yacht.

So early modernism (say 1910–20) was the work of a foreign cote-rie, the first literary generation to come to maturity in the twentieth century, in awareness of Marconi and radium and Picasso, in aware-ness, too, of the French poetic avant-garde of the 1880s and 1890s. Their work was either written in London or disseminated from there; Eliot brought *Prufrock* in his luggage; Joyce mailed installments of his *Portrait of the Artist as a Young Man* from Trieste as fast as he could have them typed, for serialization in a London feminist paper called *The Egoist*. London was the place to come to: Mecca: the center of the world's sophistication and prosperity, the great inexhaustible settled capital. When Pound and Lewis in 1914 named the whole modern movement "The Great London Vortex," one thing they had in mind was the ingathering power of vortices. *The Waste Land*'s occasion was the failure of that vortex. Eliot wrote in 1921 that London "only shriv-els, like a little bookkeeper grown old." The same year Lewis dis-cerned " . . . a sort of No Man's Land atmosphere. The dead never rise up, and men will not return to the Past, whatever else they may do. But as yet there is Nothing, or rather the corpse of the past age, and the sprinkling of children of the new."

A while back we left F. R. Leavis, from whom was hidden, all his life, the truth that England had become, linguistically speaking, a province. Thus American literature was no longer English literature that had happened to get written somewhere else. And the history of England, its climate, its customs, its local pieties, no longer afforded, by sheer impalpable presence, a test for the genuineness of a piece of writing in the language called English. And the capital, a "torture" for Wordsworth, was a magnet for polyglot talent including Polish and American talent. As late as the 1930s, Faber & Faber's letterhead was designating one of the firm's directors, T. S. Eliot, as "U.S.A. Origin." He was also known as "Tom (Missouri) Eliot." The capital had lured him but not whelmed him.

As the capital ingathered, the provinces stirred. Poems were mailed to *The Egoist* by William Carlos Williams from New Jersey and by Marianne Moore from New York. Williams had known Pound at college; Miss Moore revered the example of James. Though they stayed settled in America all their lives they were never tempted to make easy rhymes for the natives. Their generation, aware of emissaries in London—Pound, Eliot, H. D.—could look toward London for contact with more than mere Englishness. The next American generation, that of Hemingway, Fitzgerald, and Faulkner, also drew profit from the transatlantic example. By the time of its apprenticeship there were modern masterworks to study, notably *Ulysses* and *The Waste Land*. However rootedly local, American writing, thanks to some twenty years of looking abroad, has enjoyed ever since an inwardness with the international, the technological century. Today young poets in Germany or Norway expect that it will be Americans who will understand them.

Analogously, in England, Virginia Woolf, hating *Ulysses*, still made haste to exploit its riches. She is not part of International Modernism; she is an English novelist of manners, writing village gossip from a village called Bloomsbury for her English readers (though *cultivated* readers; that distinction had become operative between Dickens's time and hers, and Bloomsbury was a village with a good library). She and they share shrewd awarenesses difficult to specify; that is always the provincial writer's strength. And she pertains to the English province, as Faulkner and Dr. Williams to the American: craftily knowing, in a local place, about mighty things afar: things of the order of *Ulysses*, even. It is normal for the writers of the Three Provinces to acknowledge International Modernism and take from it what they can; normal, intelligent, and wise. Seamus Heaney and

John Montague would not be the authentic Irish poets they are but for International Modernism; Montague is especially instructive in having absorbed it, for his Irish purposes, at second hand from Williams, who had learned from Joyce and Pound and had also innovated, locally, on his own. Montague has learned the way of that. A thing writers can learn from one another is how to learn.

I have been describing the view from 1983. I have also been describing it as seen by myself. Other people have seen it quite differently, and from earlier years it has looked almost unrecognizably other. I can next enlighten you best by being personal and specific. It was in 1947, under Marshall McLuhan's informal tutelage, that I first became aware of my own century. Such a lag was perhaps possible only in Canada. By then an American movement called the New Criticism was enjoying its heyday. Like most critical stirrings on this self-improving continent, it was almost wholly a classroom movement. Stressing as it did Wit, Tension, and Irony, it enabled teachers to say classroom things about certain kinds of poems. Donne was a handy poet for its purposes; so was Eliot; so, too, was the post-1916 Yeats. Thus Eliot and the later Yeats became living poets, and a few Americans such as Richard Eberhart, also a few Englishmen, e.g., William Empson. The Pound of *Mauberley* was (barely) part of the canon, 1920 having been Pound's brief moment of being almost like Eliot, tentative and an ironist. But when Pound was working in his normal way, by lapidary *statement*, New Critics could find nothing whatever to say about him. Since "Being-able-to-say-about" is a pedagogic criterion, he was largely absent from a canon pedagogues were defining. So was Williams, and wholly. What can Wit, Tension, Irony enable you to say about "The Red Wheelbarrow"? "So much depends . . . ," says the poem, and seems to *mean* it; for a New Critic that was too naive for words. I can still see Marshall chucking aside a mint copy of *Paterson I*, with the words "pretty feeble."

In those years we couldn't see the pertinence of *Ulysses* either. *Ulysses* had been blighted, ever since 1930, by Stuart Gilbert's heavy-handed crib. Nothing as mechanical as that could be organic. Frank Budgen's 1936 book, which might have helped, was too biographical to survive New Critical scrutiny. (The tears Old Critics dropped in

Keats's Urn got prompted by his tuberculosis, not his words. So a pox on biographers.) Richard Kain's *Fabulous Voyager*, the first book about *Ulysses* in more than a decade, looked like brave pioneering; as, in the circumstances, it was. Not that it took us the distance we needed to go, if we were to see *Ulysses* as pivotal.

Nor to see Pound as the central figure he was. The chain of accidents that brought Marshall McLuhan and me into his presence on 4 June 1948 I'll detail some other time. The *Pisan Cantos* were then newly published. Later I reviewed them for the *Hudson Review*, another connection masterminded by Marshall. I'd read them, ecstatic, with Pound's remembered voice in my ear. Soon, thanks to New Directions' well-timed one-volume reprint, I could read to the surge of the same spoken cadences the rest of the poem he'd begun in 1916 or before. Its authority, after what my Toronto mentors used to call poetry, was as if great rocks were rolling. I was twenty-five, and about to become a Yale graduate student under Cleanth Brooks's mentorship. That fall the dismal Bollingen fuss broke—a forgotten minor poet named Robert Hillyer assembling three installments of invective in the equally forgotten *Saturday Review*—and literati in pulpit after pulpit would do no more than affirm the purity of their own political motives. Enthralled by the master, I resolved that if no one else would make the case for Ezra Pound the poet, then I would. Having no reputation whatever, I had nothing to lose. I was naive enough not to guess that I was mortgaging my future; it is sometimes liberating not to know how the world works. So in six weeks in the summer of 1949, on a picnic table in Canada, aided by books from the University of Toronto library, I banged out on a flimsy Smith Corona the 308 typescript pages of *The Poetry of Ezra Pound* . . . which to my wonderment was instantly accepted by New Directions and by Faber & Faber. By 1951 they got it out. Though most of the reviews were put-downs, Pound before long was a stock on the academic exchange: a safe "subject." What that means is not that I'd "discovered" him, or been magnetically persuasive concerning his virtues. What I'd done, unwittingly, at the threshold of two decades' academic expansion—people peering under every cabbage leaf for "topics"—was show how this new man with his large and complex oeuvre might plausibly be written about. Whether that was a service to him or to anyone I have never been sure.

In 1956, *annus mirabilis*, I visited Williams, Lewis, and Eliot, with introductions from Pound. He had told me that you have an obligation to visit the great men of your own time. Amid those visits and conversations a book to be called *The Pound Era* first began to shimmer hazily in my mind. Its typescript would not be complete for thirteen years during which nothing stood still. Many were making the place of *Ulysses* clearer and clearer; Beckett was defining the trajectory of International Modernism; much attention to Pound was bringing one thing clearly into focus: that what he had always demanded was old-fashioned source-hunting scholarship, the very kind of thing the New Criticism had made disreputable for a generation. Part of a canon is the state and history of the relevant criticism.

For a canon is not a list but a narrative of some intricacy, depending on places and times and opportunities. Any list—a mere curriculum—is shorthand for that. The absence of Wallace Stevens from the canon I use has somehow been made to seem notorious. I account for it by his unassimilability into the only story that I find has adequate explanatory power: a story of capitals, from which he was absent. Like Virginia Woolf of Bloomsbury or Faulkner of Oxford, he seems a voice from a province, quirkily enabled by the International Modernism of which he was never a part, no more than they. His touch is uncertain; fully half his work is rhythmically dead. The life of the live part is generally the life of whimsy. And when, as in "Idea of Order at Key West," he commands a voice of unexpected resonance, then it is a voice unmistakably American, affirming that it finds around itself a wildering chaos in which minds empowered not culturally but cosmically can discern (or make) precarious order. Whence order may stem, how nearly there is none, is Stevens's obsessive theme. Some splendid poems affirm this. They get lost in the shuffle of *Collected Poems* and *Opus Posthumous*, where, "ideas" being close to every surface, the seminars find gratification. His proponents seem not willing, perhaps not able, to distinguish his live poems from his stillborn: a sign, I think, that he is rather a counter on their board game than an active force.

The rumor has been put about that Pound despised him. Let me place on record therefore that the night Stevens died, Ezra Pound, having gleaned the news from the blurry TV in a recreation lounge at St. Elizabeth's, wrote an urgent letter to *Poetry*. In those days I was his contact with *Poetry*, so he addressed it to me. "*Poetry*," he said, "owes him a memorial issue." He hoped that someone, preferably ol' Doc Wms, would explain in that issue what Stevens had been writing *about*. I passed the word to Henry Rago, who solicited Doc Williams, who complied. Williams did not say what Stevens had been writing about; sick and old himself, he was content to affirm a commonality with Stevens in being mortal.

The question, though, was characteristically Poundian. In the story I have been elaborating for thirty-five years, everything innovative in our century was a response to something outside of literature. Pound's way of putting that is famous: "It is not man / Made courage, or made order, or made grace." Nor was it Joyce who made Dublin, nor Eliot London. Nor I, for that matter, the canon. I have tried to reconstruct an intricate story, continually guided by my judgment of six people I saw face to face, and listened to intently, never taking notes. They were Pound, Williams, Eliot, Lewis, Beckett, Miss Moore. I'm aware that I never met Stevens: nor, for that matter, Yeats or Joyce.

Heminge and Condell saw Shakespeare face to face. They subsequently enabled the First Folio of 1623, such a homage, observe, as no other dramatist of the time received. That was the beginning of Shakespeare's canonization. For 350 years this year, we have been confirming the judgment of Heminge and Condell. Something a contemporary can speak to is the aliveness of a man, his power to invest the air with forms. My own testimony, for what it has been worth, is that of a privileged contemporary. Yeats was able to proclaim, of Synge and Lady Gregory, "And say my glory was, I had such friends." I cannot pretend to such intimacy. I can hope, like Spence with his anecdotes of Pope, to have left some reasonably faithful portraits, and remember how, despite the smug confidence of Arnold, Spence's evaluation of Pope is no longer thought wrong.

The Modernist canon has been made in part by readers like me; in

part in Borges's way by later writers choosing and inventing ancestors; chiefly though, I think, by the canonized themselves, who were
apt to be aware of a collective enterprise, and repeatedly acknowledged one another. For our age has been canon minded. One way to
make a canon has been by explicit homages: imitation, translation.
Pound made pedagogic lists of dead authors and translated their
texts. To the suggestion that he tended to list what he had translated,
he replied that on the contrary he translated what he thought alive
enough to list.

Poets translate to get into the language something that was not
there before, some new possibility. In our century they have been especially apt to be incited by a sense of communing, in an ancient author, with otherness: with a coherent sense of the world for which we
and our words are unprepared. If a translation turns out to resemble
the sort of poem we are used to, it is probably unnecessary. Critics and
historians (which all of us are informally, even when we may think we
are simply reading) are similarly guided: we deplore the unnecessary.
Pound discovered that the way for a poet to write the poem he wants
to write, life having prompted some chemistry of desire, may be to co-
opt an alien precursor whose sense of the world, in wholly foreign
words, may guide English words today. Such a poet, the "Seafarer"
poet for instance, became part of Pound's canon. Our canon likewise,
when our eyes are not on pedagogic expedience, is something we
shape by our needs and our sense of what is complexly coherent:
what accords with the facts, and folds them into a shapely story, and
brings us news from across Pound's godly sea, which is also the sea
beside which the girl in Key West sang.

When Academe
Ran a Fever

From The American Spectator, *back in 1977. The last five paragraphs deserve a note. The man who thought "requirements" could sometimes be outrageous was my old friend the late Marvin Mudrick. "The College of Cosmic Awareness" disguises the College of Creative Studies he founded at the University of California, Santa Barbara.*

Ike, "driven to the edge, almost, of a thought," the Keystone Caesar and our last funny president—bliss was it in that fog to be alive, when our only pollution problem was his syntax and after each press conference thoughtful men with push brooms swept the floor clean of disjunctive grunts, still-born modifiers, participial turds.

> The question was whether meetings between the two defense ministers might bring about something I said and of course it well might because what you are constantly testing is statements and then the extent to which those statements are trustworthy carried out and supported by deeds and actions that are provable now as I say at one time I repeat Marshall Zhukov and I operated together very closely I couldn't see any harm coming from a meeting between the two defense ministers if that could be arranged. VERBATIM, UNPUNCTUATABLE

It was masterly, the West Point or Adversary model of language, the asker as enemy to be ever so amiably enfiladed, sudden dummy troops behind every machicolation (hurrah! a shambles), popguns left right and beyond, the *New York Times* man (his pencil snapped) sitting back routed while the general rode off in all directions. What did he say? He didn't say.

And yet, though that was his scenario, Ike conducted it with a sinister up-to-dateness, as though commanding, decades ahead of schedule, the technology of the neutron bomb. His face bespoke popguns, his eyes twinkled with *Beau Geste* romance, but his lips moved through rituals of irradiation, sprayed neutering beams of unmeaning. That was unsettling. A clown is one thing, an insidious disease quite another.

Somewhere overhead Sputnik wheeled. In October 1957—all of twenty years ago now—Lox had flamed white and soil near the Urals rumbled as a sphere with antennae poking out of it was thrust into orbit. (Why didn't it fall down? It was fun to picture Ike's brow furrowing as Wernher von Braun tried to explain.) The Russki owned captive Germans, that much was clear.

Almost immediately a bigger Sputnik went up, cylindrical, with a dog in it named Laika. Laika died as per plan when the oxygen ran out, and from their sinking island in the North Sea overtaxed Britons shrieked indignation. Show me a man, sir, who mistreats a dog and I shall show you a *cad*. Khrushchev's grin displayed little peg-teeth, hippo-teeth.

Laika's cold tomb re-entered the air, turned fiery; "re-entry" was a sudden vogue word. At Cape Canaveral *our* Germans rushed onto the pad a grapefruit-sized satellite atop a Viking rocket; not big, but, you see, superior technology. It fell over the instant Mission Control lit the match: "IKE'S SPUTNIK FLOPNIK." For a while nothing Western seemed to get off the ground. As bonfires glowed round the base of a cartoonist's Washington Monument, the wino in the foreground confided, "It'll never get off the ground."

What got off the ground, hoisting man moonward with it, was the knowledge industry, Clark Kerr its theologian by default. Clark Kerr was Ike reconstituted in hyperspace. His bald dome shielded a memory bank. Once the sensors behind his rimless glasses had locked on your face, then if you were one of the University of California's tens of thousands of employees his circuitry matched you instantly to the right name. He carried home paperwork in grocery cartons. Late at night, while seals barked offshore, he marked memoranda with his tiny green script, for action or inaction. (The top man's powers of inaction are formidable. No one understood that better.) He was top man in a new kind of fief, the Knowledge Factory. Growth was its watchword. It was, among other things, the world's largest breeder of white mice: a Multiversity.

Four paws per mouse, a lot of paws; still by writing Washington it wouldn't have been impossible to finance booties for all of them. Mice were Science, and Science was the West's Response to the Challenge of Sputnik. (Arnold Toynbee, Mr. Challenge-and-Response, was still around, more bewildered than he let on.) At the University of Virginia a white rodent named Robert E. Lee ran mazes faster than any rodent known: faster, surely, even, than any conditioned by Pavlov, the Master Conditioner. Hurrah for a free society! Washington's checks totalled millions, millions.

Hybrids of old sciences, notably biochemistry, altered all lab curricula. Biochemists' offices acquired air-conditioning, and papers were no longer baled in grocery cartons. Lockable filing cases paid for by grants housed the grant applications, drawer on drawer. Savvy administrators threatened the scalps of mere scholars who weren't drafting proposals. The sap of growth ran through questing roots that had found the Potomac.

And grantless, devoid of proposals in the national interest, powerless to orbit however cheap a beep, the liberal arts floundered. Yet they grew wealthy too, willy-nilly. No longer did English professors hover near the poverty line, their soles patched with old pawn tickets. Thousands of twenty year olds, having matched their teachers' skills against those of the checker in the neighborhood Safeway, noted that while the demands were comparable it was the teacher who was now the better paid and elected to get themselves hired as teachers. Teaching, for the first time in history, had become attractive for the money that was in it. Thank you, Sputnik.

Or no thanks. It wasn't teaching, it was sheep herding much of the time, many places. The law of demand that had sucked those salaries skyward and vacuumed into the profession all those eager beavers with their jargon of Job Security, responded to the milling of a million sheep, plodding through Requirements: required English, required Art History, required Frog Dissection. Some gazed with wide eyes, some lay back and hiccuped. What are we supposed to be doing here? The Computer put us here. (That was a sixties syndrome: blame the computer.) Suddenly, late in the sixties it became clear that the roof was falling in.

In California Ronald Reagan got blamed, in New York Vietnam. As well blame the sun-eating devils. Iron laws eclipsed that sun, brought down that roof. Academe, 1977, looks back to that brief golden age when everything on campus seemed to prosper, and looks round at a bleakness of small colleges going broke and overruns in the Ph.D. supply forcing young Doctors of Philosophy into cabdriving. There are devils aplenty to be blamed: Vietnam, Richard Nixon, Republicans, OPEC, color TV, the fickle national mood, inflation, Wall Street, materialism. The recourse to devils is comprehensible: Things were going so well they ought to have gone on going well. But try, just for size, the hypothesis that things weren't going well at all: that the time of warmth wasn't sunshine, it was fever.

One symptom of fever was the zany dependence on Washington, zany because it was a piecework dependence, whole academic departments living in cardhouses of grants. Grants came for projects, and projects had to be supported before they were undertaken. It had to be demonstrated that they would yield important results in the necessary absence of any evidence whatever that they would yield any result. A Senior Investigator was a man adept at writing up projects, in the sort of triplicate doubletalk that affirms significance while stopping just short of promises. Touch up the punctuation of a choice slab of Eisenhowerese and you have a pretty good model for a grant application. Ike was an intellectuals' Zola.

The propriety of Washington's benevolence is another question entirely. A purist right-wing argument runs as follows, that since the principal beneficiary of an education is the student, the student (assisted, if necessary, by loans) should be liable for its costs. The counterargument holds that people at large benefit sufficiently from the existence of an educated elite to justify a deflection of their tax dollars toward that education. Outright grants, on that principle, are justifiable. Project grants are something else entirely. They encourage two fallacies: the division of indivisible human curiosity into budgetable entities called projects, and the need to sell each project on its own.

These distortions may seem at first sight to affect only the universities' scientific establishment, and only a portion of that. Not so: They enshrine the assumption that underlay every part of the academic prosperity of the 1960s, and rendered that prosperity perilous. The assumption is that here, as in a hardware store, the payer deserves a breakdown of what he is paying for.

What was being paid for was (symbolically) an Answer to the Challenge of Sputnik: in short, an improved technological establishment. We needed to know more than we did about numerous things hitherto granted low public priority: rocketry, satellites, re-entry, instrumentation, space medicine, telemetry, weightlessness, solid-state devices, propellants, nuclear drives, the solar wind, on and on. And in a hurry. The universities were (1) to conduct research in a hundred such conceivable areas and in many inconceivable; (2) to teach young scientists; (3) to go on, of course, being whatever it was they were, which was doubtless a good thing to be, though Sputnik seemed to have shown it wasn't enough. As Ike said of something else entirely, "I don't believe I ever spoke out against it, I said this, it was just from— since I have never made a deep study of this thing, because what was the use, from my viewpoint, I said I thought on balance it was unwise." That about summed up the plight of the liberal arts, which found themselves justifying their own relevance quite as tendentiously as any piece of research got justified on a grant application.

Now research, until it's been done, always sounds like a joke, one reason, undone, it's so difficult to justify. Arthur Koestler has argued that the mental faculty that can frame jokes and the faculty that can frame scientific hypotheses work identically and may even be identical. Both a joke and a new hypothesis entail bringing together what hasn't been thought of in one mental act before. When is a human being like a cat? When he's in free fall, for instance adrift outside a spacecraft, and needs to alter his position with nothing to push against. And the better to train astronauts, countless cats were dropped, and how they contrived to always land on their feet was studied by high-speed photography. The dynamic analysis is very tricky. Imagine writing the Grant Proposal for that, and you grasp the usefulness of Eisenhowerese to keep the Granting Body from just busting out laughing. (I don't know if a proposal was ever written; maybe NASA simply rounded up some alley cats and dropped them quietly in a back room.)

So the surreal enters, and the rhetoric of disguising surreality. And once they've entered, they commence to valve the flow of everything fluid: words, ideas, cash.

As curiosity was subdivided into projects, so teaching was subdivided into departments and programs and courses, each dependent on reams of justification. Department chairmen wrote to the Administration the way Senior Investigators wrote to Washington, in quite the same idiom, and with quite the same high-minded but semi-obfuscatory intent. As programs multiplied, their hold on reality diminished, and quite sensible innovations went into gobbledegook disguise because administrators had lost all capacity to evaluate good sense.

As for the liberal arts, they were soon subserving Objectives, their capacity for growth and their right to a slice of the enlarging pie connected with their demonstrable ability to further the Whole Student. A student raising tired eyes from a semi-dissected frog ought obviously to rest them on slides of the Sistine Ceiling; Art Hist then, 3 credits, MWF at 10, and lest we discriminate against the color blind make it interchangeable with Mus Apprec, also 3 credits. And if the number of Student Contact hours in Art Hist and Mus Apprec becomes thereby a function of Biology enrollment—ultimately, of the capacity of a frog farm to produce—still the Art and Music Departments aren't really complaining. They're expanding. Who doesn't want that? From a Chairman and two kindly old Profs to a vortex of ranks, a phalanx of T.A.s, an Administrative Assistant and a Typist, an Audio-Visual budget, very likely soon a Building, at any rate for now a space on the Architects' Master Plan. . . . Meanwhile, so much paperwork there's need for an Assistant Chairman. And anything growing as healthily as all that merits a Graduate Program, with Ph.D. seminars and orals and a bigger slice of the Library budget.

That was what collapsed toward the end of the sixties. I leave as an exercise to the reader the filling in of details: the role of Student Revolt in the collapse; the pertinancy of the cries for relevance, which commingle activist mindlessness with a sane response to officialese; the question of state vs. federal largesse, and of procedures for bestowing it without strings. I'll conclude with a Multiversity anecdote.

The Multiversity grew and prospered, and within it sundry Departments grew and prospered, thriving each one on Requirements. Requirements, being interpreted mean: If you will force your students to take courses in my department, I will force my students to take courses in yours. Thus we shall jointly thrive.

And lo, it became observable that students, a few of them, were solemnly sitting through courses in what they already knew, and that this was especially true of the very best students: Young prodigies, for example, who having for recreation in their high-school years worked clear through texts on calculus and group theory were now being required to enroll in Algebra I.

There was a man who thought this was outrageous. But he had colleagues who seemed to think it more outrageous that students should presume to know so much already, and other colleagues so inured to the profitable system they would even extol the virtues of drudgery; so this man went to the Administration and proposed that incoming students, particularly in mathematics and sciences, should be exempted from elementary courses in those subjects if they demonstrably had no need of them. But that was too simple.

But he was persistent. And after much thought and much writing of proposals (the purpose of a proposal, as we have seen, being to conceal its real thrust behind screens of high-minded obfuscation) a huge budgetary entity was created, indeed a separate College in which such exceptional students could be enrolled; and that College could draw up requirements, and dispense with requirements, as it saw fit. (That was administratively feasible; a mere rewriting of the general requirements was not.)

And that College, in compliance with inexorable law, acquired a name meant to obscure its purpose (which, be it remembered, was merely the abrogation in certain cases of certain Mickey Mouse requirements). Removing requirements looks like a step back, and so must be disguised as a great step forward: hence what we may call the College of Cosmic Awareness. It was allotted a modest building, and budgets, and secretaries, and appurtenances; and after a little while was inscribed in the Master Plan, with land reserved for its eventual Edifice.

And one day the Administration noted on its Table of Organization a College of Cosmic Awareness of which no administrator could any longer recollect the use. Was it the same thing as an Honors Program? Did it offer to make young folk cosmically aware? Had it even a curriculum? The one way to find out was to appoint a committee, which means designating some high-salaried people to drop what they were paid for doing and write a report. A tricky report, since it needed to skirt its recipients' idiocy. Ike's Collected Press Conferences contain a possible model: "We found no place where we were in opposite camps, and we—someone made the observation as we left, whichever wing we all belonged to, it was the same one, and was not different ones." But that style takes a lifetime's mastering, and the committee's report lacks much of being memorable because its chairman had not that mastery. I was the chairman.

Earth's Attic

Another "Inside Story" from Art & Antiques, *this one from December 1986.*

Young Saul, as we learn from the First Book of Samuel, went seeking his father's strayed asses and found a kingdom. A prophet anointed him and sent him home to be greeted with harp and tambour, with flute and zither, and enjoy his people's hosannas as their first king. That would have been about 1025 B.C.

And about A.D. 1947, south of Jericho and just west of the Dead Sea, a boy named Muhammad ed-Dhib (Mohammed the Fox) went seeking one lost goat and found what the Met now calls Treasures from the Holy Land. A stone he'd idly thrown into a cave—one cave of hundreds in that wracked earth—had clinked. A clink, from earth's heart? The sound a stone makes against pottery? Yes, pottery: ancient jars, crammed with rolled-up writings. (He'd had hopes of pieces of gold.) A dealer in Bethlehem gave him, it's said, twenty pounds (British) per scroll.

Those were the first Dead Sea Scrolls, found, as often, by one of a frayed time's irregulars. When his father's asses strayed, Saul's land was a chaos beset by Philistines. Mohammed the Fox lived by smuggling in the Jewish-Arab turmoil of a British protectorate. And Stukas

were plaguing France in 1940 when a dog named Robot chased a rabbit down a hole into the cave we now call Lascaux; the boys who res-
cued Robot (and later the rabbit) gaped by torchlight at polychrome
horses, buffalo, bulls—images unglimpsed during 20,000 years. That
sacred place next served as a stash for Resistance guns.

Another dog, decades earlier, had found Altamira, the finest cave
before Lascaux. The man who'd followed it in liked to come back and
scan the floor for celts and flints. It was his little daughter who
chanced to look at the ceiling: "Papa, los toros, los toros!" Local
tongues spread news of the bulls. In 1902 a young Barcelonan named
Picasso came to see.

Earth, then, our attic, shrouding ancestral treasures. Attic? from
French *attique*, the space enclosed by a spareness nigh a grander
structure; so named for its austere ("Attic") modesty, as from Grecian
Attica. And "Attica"? Likely from Athena, she of Wisdom. Everything hereabouts is shaky, notably that last derivation, where even
the impulsive Eric Partridge says "perhaps." Much that we now hold
certain has had to make its way. UNESCO denied funds to record the
Lascaux bulls (manifest fakes). Altamira's, before that, were hooted
at. And experts rejected the Dead Sea Scrolls for years: never mind
how implausible would be a faker who'd inscribe so much on old
leather sheets sewn together, wrap the rolls in linen, coat them too
with pitch, before prompting an itinerant bedouin to "find" them in
that near-unfindable cave.

No, the scrolls are certainly genuine; but the skepticism is instructive. For no longer can we easily imagine people like ourselves—we
can imagine no other—as sure as the Essenes were that some one
treasure merits entrusting to earth's attic. Valuing their scriptures
above all else, they consigned them, wisely, to Athena, whom they
knew by some other name, expecting to retrieve them when a trouble
had passed, a trouble they didn't foresee outlasting them all.

Trouble to outlast us all we've no trouble conceiving. But what do
we rate as those writings were once rated? To fancy what we might en-
cave, think what we collect. The Mona Lisa? An Andy Warhol Mari-
lyn? A BMW? Or perhaps 1,373 assorted pop-bottle caps? In making
a case for any of these or none, we may learn how we value alike both
everything and nothing.

Where Every
Prospect Pleases

From the April 1978 Harper's, early in a heady period of writing the lead review every other month. Alas, a re-formatted Harper's has since dispensed with the book-review category.

A PATTERN LANGUAGE: TOWNS, BUILDINGS, CONSTRUCTION, *by Christopher Alexander, Sara Ishikawa, Murray Silverstein, with Max Jacobson, Ingrid Fiksdahl-King, Shlomo Angel. Oxford University Press, 1977.*

THE OREGON EXPERIMENT, *by Christopher Alexander, Murray Silverstein, Shlomo Angel, Sara Ishikawa, Denny Abrams. Oxford University Press, 1975.*

Thoreau is perhaps our first instance of the builder as philosopher-king. He was also first with a Utopian literary genre that goes through the motions of imparting technical advice while it sponsors fantasies of a world sprung loose from time and turmoil, where either there are no other people or they're all on your side. *Walden*, where the mass of men lead lives of quiet desperation, commences with the author solving his housing problem as the key to all the others. Invoking the rhetoric of spec sheets, he totals his costs to the nearest half cent: $28.12½ in 1845 money, or 19¢ a square foot, for a house that would last him as long as he needed it, when undergraduates at Harvard down the road were being charged $30 for a single year in the dorm.

His cabin built, the builder settled into the life it made possible, two satisfying years as inspector of snowstorms and forest paths, and you'd never guess to read him that anything stressful was going on in the world. Thoreau had built himself into a private Utopia.

He has fed the daydreams of improbable readers. Fancy W. B. Yeats, of the flowing locks and the pince-nez, lifting an ax! Yet Yeats was early fascinated by Thoreau's "tight-shingled and plastered house" near an acreage planted "chiefly with beans," and soon fantasized for himself a hermit's good life on an island called Innisfree in an Irish Walden Pond called Lough Gill; a small cabin indeed he proposed to build there, "of clay and wattles made" (local materials). As for diet, Thoreau's beans gave the cue: "nine bean-rows will I have there, and a hive for the honey-bee"; unreal, of course, but *Walden* is not seldom unreal in a similar way, the sentences gliding into metaphor just when particulars grow gritty, weaving their filaments back to particularity as the metaphor turns insubstantial.

Cabin building takes up only a few pages of *Walden*. Succeeding fantasists have been much more explicit in proposing that the house-building problem is intrinsic with all else that perplexes us, and that attacking it may be the place to begin. Gazing balefully on Victorian London, Sir Ebenezer Howard dreamed green dreams. His *Garden Cities of Tomorrow* (1902) has been feeding town planners' fantasies for seven decades. It proposed (says Jane Jacobs, acidly) "the creation of self-sufficient small towns, really very nice towns if you were docile and had no plans of your own and did not mind spending your life among others with no plans of their own." Quiet desperation might as well be tranquilized by greenery.

In the twenties Le Corbusier proposed *vertical* Garden Cities, 1,200 people to the acre—ten times the population density of central Paris—all housed in skyscrapers but sharing plenty of grass. By the thirties Lewis Mumford was grumping that cities as they existed were perfectly awful, Frank Lloyd Wright was dreaming up Broadacres

City, and Buckminster Fuller was uttering 7,000 words per hour on mass-produced dwelling machines, to be installed just anywhere like telephones. (Disengaged from realtors, garbagemen, and crabby neighbors, people couldn't help but get a lot nicer.)

In the late sixties Lloyd Kahn's *Domebooks* took Fuller's designs into the woods for one-by-one countercultural fabrication. Subsequently his *Shelter* has rejected the whole geodesic trip and gone back to native crafts. And all these writers have attracted many thousands of readers who have no intention of living that way at all but love to read about it.

Now comes Christopher Alexander of the Center for Environmental Structure in Berkeley with a cluster of coauthors and a trio of interdependent books, one still being born. Alexander may aspire to be the Melville of the genre. Certainly, at 1,171 pages, beautifully produced on Bible paper to weigh a mere 28 ounces, and priced 62½¢ less than Thoreau's whole cabin, *A Pattern Language* emulates the white whale's freakish copiousness, and if its tone never rises to the apocalyptic, its preachments and fantasies are nevertheless enticingly labyrinthine. With its aid you can dream about the weaving together of whole cities, or excogitate your private shelter for the good life, or think how to do something about the back porch, and maybe even do it—sensibly, too.

Each of 253 "Patterns" is a focused meditation that moves from a stated problem to a one-sentence solution, generally under the aegis of a key photograph. They are arranged in rough order of comprehensiveness, from large-scale desiderata like Agricultural Valleys, Mosaic of Subcultures, Local Transport Areas, to minutiae you can implement almost at once, like Small Panes, Half-Inch Trim, and Climbing Plants. Each begins with cross-references to related larger patterns, and ends with cross-references to smaller ones.

The idea is to scan the list for a key pattern that comes closest to what you have in mind to do, meditate on its few thousand words, then let its cross-references lead you to related patterns, till you have a cluster of relevancies and can be thinking clearly before you pick up a hammer or a pencil.

For instance, Outdoor Room (163), Six-Foot Balcony (167), and Dif-

ferent Chairs (251) are all relevant to the back-porch problem. The
first says, "Build a place outdoors which has so much enclosure
round it that it takes on the feeling of a room, even though it is open to
the sky." The second notes that balconies or porches less than six feet
deep are hardly ever used. The third decries any tendency to fit
people of different sizes and sitting habits into identical chairs.

These ramify. Different Chairs leads down the list to Pools of Light,
because you'll want to draw those sitters together with coercions of
shade, and Six-Foot Balcony leads down the list to Sitting Wall—
make minor boundaries with low walls wide enough to sit on. You
stop when you sense that you have your project surrounded.

Patterns higher on the list than your key pattern touch, probably,
on degrees of generality you're powerless to do much about. You ignore them for now.

Or more likely you fantasize about them. Thus, 158 (Open Stairs)
proposes that life in upstairs apartments has a disconnected feeling
when access to the street is controlled by inner stairs and a guarded
lobby; if the latter is not tyrannical, still it's "the precise pattern that a
tyrant *would* propose who wanted to control people's comings and
goings." Nudged by photos of Mediterranean diversity, you can drift
into easeful reveries about social decentralization and the free comings and goings in Greek villages, putting clean out of mind the primary big-city reason for that locked lobby, which is to keep out muggers.

When you come awake you may even get around to reflecting how
unlikely are weeks of browsing among this book's half-million words
to turn up any allusion to thugs or slums or hopelessness. (Psychosis
does turn up in 68—Connected Play—but only for the sake of proposing that you can reduce its future likelihood by ensuring enough
playmates for each child; by a dazzling calculation this entails struc-
turing neighborhoods to put each household within reach of sixty-
four others.)

Perhaps in an ideal city there would be no muggers? And there
would surely be Pattern 58, Carnival (a continuous opportunity for
people to work out their madness); Pattern 81, Small Services Without Red Tape; and Pattern 63, Dancing in the Streets. It's the hidden
premise of *A Pattern Language*, as of early Fuller and of Mumford pas-

sim, that a wholly remade environment, the right boards and bricks in the right places, will depressurize the optimization of everything else.

An explicit statement of premises, an initial volume called *The Timeless Way of Building*, is still in production as I write this. What has held up its completion, I can't say. What would have held *me* up if I'd been trying to write it is the chicken-egg problem of drawing the design decisions out of a community that is (by hidden premise) unlikely to exist till a couple of generations after the decisions have been implemented.

The blurb promises a post-industrial version of "that age-old process by which the people of a society have always pulled the order of their world from their own being," which maps back onto history Thoreau's wish to ascertain "what foundation a door, a window, a cellar, a garret, have in the nature of man." Alexander is commendably negative about master plans that turn obsolete overnight and master planners who assault the chaos of forms like Beethoven navigating a sea of sound, shaping, at best, egocentric majesties of order to which we give thrilled assent (but you can't *live* in the *Eroica*); at worst, the numb portentousness of Skidmore, Owings & Merrill, whom Chicago wit dismisses as the Three Blind Mies. No, he thinks, users of environments are the people who should shape them, as they have throughout most of human history. "Many of the most wonderful places in the world, now avidly photographed by architects"—here a photo of an idyllic Swiss town—"were not designed by architects but by lay people."

Those people, it's conventional to note, worked within a slow-changing traditional culture, bound by shared assumptions about what everything they built was for: the church, the market square, the rows of balconies. We've lost most of that. Hence the Pattern Language, which is meant to "play the role that tradition played in a traditional culture." Alexander and his fluctuating group of associates have been working it out for years, making ingenuity do tradition's work and beset by at least three interrelated difficulties they nowhere acknowledge unless in that unpublished first volume. I'll give them names:

(1) The Esperanto Fallacy: recalling another high-minded effort to

confect a universal tongue from smoothed-out features of existing ones. Alexander & Co. have not always avoided the trap of extolling in seductive prose the nicer features of sundry European towns (Local Town Hall, Bus Stop as a vortex of interest, Cascade of Roofs) and pretending they make a deep-rooted unity, mastery of which will elicit spontaneous expression.

(2) The Sansculotte Fallacy: the tendency to assume that you or the people you're talking to are in charge of whatever matters; that legal and financial difficulties aren't there, or aren't serious, or answer to no one's wishes save an exploiter's.

(3) The Pelagian Fallacy: the assumption that uncorrupted men will profess just this inventory of common needs, pellucid, naïvely clear.

Put all three together and you get some oddly touristy visions. Pattern 157, Home Workshop, commences with a calm avowal: "We imagine a society in which work and family are far more intermingled than today." Since we haven't such a society, what ensues is sheer fantasy, but let's follow it.

In such a society, the Pattern goes on, the home workshop loses triviality; it becomes "an integral part of every house." Moreover, "we believe its most important characteristic is its relationship to the public street." Anyone who has traveled will detect the base of this Esperanto: the streetside carpenters in Taipei, the Swiss carver on his porch. Sansculottism next: "change the zoning laws," bring each workshop into the neighborhood's public domain, with a workbench in the open, maybe a small meeting room. . . .

And a final Pelagian sigh of contentment: the worker has a view of the street, passersby are enriched, children enchanted. But if we envisage a workshop "as central to the house's function as the kitchen or the bedrooms," that implies an out-front shop attached to every house, and every street looking like a street of small trades. But the method of incremental exposition dissuades you from thinking about that; from asking whether you really want the street on which you live—your retreat, perhaps, from a clangorous job—to be so very busy; or (supposing it's *your* workshop) from reflecting that you may not welcome the attentions of every passerby as you struggle with your glassblowing.

In isolating its many themes for separate attention, and in prescribing that the context you seek for any pattern shall be found among other patterns, *A Pattern Language* is more of a closed system than it claims to be, and for all its look of openness to common experience it abounds in hidden persuaders. You don't read it through, you're not meant to; you browse, and the browsing is at first enchanting. But after the book has been around a few weeks you may find two voices going in your head every time you open it. They are the surly unredeemed you, and a new self growing glib in Pattern Language.

"I like my isolation," you may suddenly hear yourself retort to yet another page of communal romanticization. "Out of habit," responds the voice schooled by the book. "You cling to it because you've always had it." "No," cries the old you, "I do not thrill at all to the prospect of tumbling out of my front door into a web of sixty-four other families." And the pattern-self replies, "They are your neighbors, your brothers and sisters, your in-laws, your communal siblings. Be open to their humanity." And if you hear your old self quoting Robert McAlmon's "People are not charming *enough*," you will also hear the new voice raised in extenuation: "Granted, granted, but they would be less damn dull if they had known a different environment. So build a better one, if not for your sake or theirs, for your children and theirs." (Children are a trump card in this sort of game. Being both Absolute Good, to be heeded, and Absolute Potential, to be shaped, they can assume any value the player requires.)

Egg-chicken-egg, round and round. Much of the Pattern Language entails, for lasting conviction, the leap of faith, the faith we all have in good things that are not disproved because they have never been tried.

But wait, here's *The Oregon Experiment*, which seems to be telling us how the Alexander team rode north and lifted the consciousness of the University of Oregon at Eugene. "It's all been tried," this little book keeps telling us between the lines. "It all works."

What it tells us word by word, though, is less definite: two readings of its 35,000 words leave me utterly uncertain whether any structure ever did get built at all, or whether anything happened except a number of conferences of which some of the conferees retain ecstatic memories. The whole tends to be couched as a memo of recommendation, in the optative mood. The authors, when you come down to it, are hoping this is how the university will go.

I hope so, too. There's no worse process than the one by which university buildings are normally commissioned, though it dents one's faith in the Alexander alternative to reflect that the best part of the country's most architecturally successful campus reflects the master plan of one man, Thomas Jefferson. Lacking a Jefferson, though, the Alexander principles—organic order, participation, piecemeal growth—offer more hope than any other procedure that comes to mind. And a campus, which understands better what it's trying to achieve than a neighborhood or a city, seems the ideal place to try them out.

Oregon, moreover, may be the appointed crucible. In my efforts to find out, by telephone, to what extent Eugene was implementing Alexandrianism, I was several times reminded that if anything of the kind was going forward—bull sessions, user input, modest incremental projects, lots of emphasis on bikes and sun and rapping—no one would be likely to notice it, so natural to every Oregonian is fussing about the environment and attending meetings to guard its destiny. It seems no accident that *A Pattern Language* was written in Berkeley, near the southern boundary of the region which Ernest Callenbach, in *Ecotopia*, imagines seceding from the United States to pursue by inner consent an ecology-minded, no-growth destiny.

Ecotopia, which was also written in Berkeley, is a West Coast bestseller still hardly heard of in the East. The year is 1999, and since 1980 Chinese-style isolation has sealed off what was formerly Washington, Oregon, and Northern California. A "crack investigative reporter"—not a brilliant fictional contrivance, but this isn't *Moby-Dick*—is finally there, sending back dispatches, keeping a diary. He finds pretty much the society Alexander envisages, though the Alexander version is less feisty, indeed middle-aged, studied chiefly from the less industrialized patches of Europe.

There's much wisdom and much crackpottery in both men's books. My considered recommendation is that you read *Ecotopia* first, to imagine a possible world, and then keep *A Pattern Language* by your bedside for several weeks, absorbing a few pages a night to substantiate it all. And when the two voices finally start going in your head, forget that you're reenacting the climax of *Ecotopia*. Consider that you're on the verge of creative possibility. Neither Alexander nor Callenbach is, alas, a novelist, but if you are, then it may be your moment to rise up and write, out of the division in your soul, this century's *Moby-Dick*.

Fuller's Follies

Saturday Review, *early 1981, and their title, not mine.*

CRITICAL PATH, *by R. Buckminster Fuller, adjuvant,*
Kiyoshi Kuromiya. St. Martin's Press, 1981. 488 pp.

Others look at plywood and see the wood. Bucky Fuller sees the glue. Plywood is "a plastic material reinforced by wood fiber," and as such is one key (he wrote in 1943) to bringing the economy of wood-rich Brazil into the twentieth century.

More recently, while habit-conditioned eyes were discerning brown pollution over industrial cities, Fuller's eyes perceived sulphur mines. "The amount of sulphur coming out of all the chimneys around the world exactly equals the amount of sulphur mined from the ground and purchased by industry to keep its wheels turning," so trapping it at the smokestack need not be dreaded as a "cost" but welcomed as an opportunity to help balance the world's books by recirculating the world's resources.

For the world is a metabolic system (as are you, and as am I), and our activities are successful in the long run only insofar as they minister to the larger system's ecologies. Success in the short run, which is what is measured by money, seems to Fuller considerably easier.

Thirty years ago he would make this point with talk of a corporation called Obnoxico, contrived to "exploit the most sentimental weaknesses of humanity." Obnoxico could not fail to turn huge profits from such services as silver plating your baby's contoured and safety-pinned last diaper for you to fill with ferns and hang in the back window of your car. That was a good joke in 1947. Today, casting his New England eye on the contents of airport gift shops, Fuller entertains a horrible suspicion that Obnoxico is actually in business.

Bucky Fuller, as everyone knows, invented the geodesic dome, and many know too that he coined the phrase "Spaceship Earth" and organized an activity called the "World Game." But these are details, and in *Critical Path* he marshals his best expository energies to tell us what his life has been all about. Making the world work, that's one short way of putting its theme; and if the whole shebang is not to bog down in Obnoxico or disintegrate in nuclear clouds, making the world work had better be the theme of as many other lives as he can reach.

Fuller's way of reaching audiences and readers is myth. A myth is a story, not necessarily true but not necessarily not true either, which sorts out a bewilderment of facts. Obnoxico makes perverse sense of quite a clutter. A dragon that tried to eat the sun and a ritual to deter it made one strategy for not being paralyzed by eclipses. Today's science is more consistent in its ordering of *more* facts, but doing science and postulating dragons are in some profound way the same kind of human activity.

One of Fuller's most engaging myths, directed at the question why we are here, is the creation myth in the first chapter of *Critical Path*. It draws on many facts: the fact that we are 60 percent water, the fact that "in common only with water-dwelling mammals such as whales and porpoises, humans shed saltwater tears," the fact that selective breeding leads only to specialization, and the fact that people get born naked, with a desperate need to conserve a body temperature of 98.6 degrees.

The regnant myth is that we started with fur coats, like the apes, and evolved. Though near hairless now, we've also evolved tailors, and there was an intermediate stage when we skinned bears. But Fuller starts from a doubt that our kind of omnicompetence could evolve. Breeding makes specialists, and it is central to his thinking that we are not specialists. He'll guess we were *brought* here: "tele-scanned from elsewhere in Universe," as smart on the first day as any Einstein now, but with everything to be learned.

So how and where did our naked ancestors manage? They man-aged as water creatures in South Pacific coral atolls, where lagoon water was so warm you could stand in it continuously. "Crystal fresh waters poured down the mountainsides, and coconuts full of milk fell on the ground around the humans. Fruits were plentiful, and there were no wild animals threatening to eat the helpless baby humans."

That is the memory the Eden story preserves. And the dolphins? Listen: "We can comprehend how South-Sea-atoll, lagoon-frolicking male and female human swimmers gradually inbred pairs of under-water swimmers, . . . and after many . . . outbreedings of general-adaptability organic equipment, the progeny evolved into porpoises and later into whales."

So the dolphin, whose linguistic efforts fascinate, is indeed our cousin, and, with his demonstrable inability to build airplanes or use typewriters, is an object lesson, too, in over-specialization. (So, for that matter, is the curriculum at Harvard, from which Fuller managed to get himself expelled twice. He still sees academe as a dolphin-training enterprise.)

Next, technology grew up around boats; fibers made ropes and cloths for sails and coats; eventually a sailing-into-the-wind people spread forth from the vicinity of Bangkok to colonize the globe and reach the moon. Having walked on the moon only yesterday, we have demonstrated that we have the technical ability to achieve "an un-precedentedly higher standard of living for all Earthians than has ever been experienced by any." Already, says Fuller, 60 percent of us live better than any king did prior to 1900. What we now need to un-derstand is that the plight of the deprived 40 percent is no necessary cost of this partial success.

Not understanding that, we deem scarcity normal. We burn up our savings account (fossil fuel) and our capital account (atoms)—"a spending folly no less illogical than burning your house and home to keep the family warm on an unprecedentedly cold midwinter night." We even threaten Mutually Assured Destruction (MAD) over supplies of oil: this despite a cosmic energy income ("gravity- and sun-distributed cosmic dividends of waterpower, tidal power, wavepower, windpower, vegetation-produced alcohols, methane gas, vulcanism") that pours in on us 400 million times faster than we succeed in consuming energy of any kind. Unhappily, "tax-hungry government and profit-hungry business" won't tolerate any energy transactions on which they can't hang a meter, complete with a man to come and read it and make out a bill.

This brings us to a less successful myth, the long chapter called "Legally Piggily," which purports to detail how governments and multinationals have since World War I euchred the United States into a bankruptcy that only waits to be publicly declared. The villains of this narrative are astute Wall Street lawyers, cartooned from all the starchy noncomprehenders Bucky has met in his lifetime.

The chapter has the defect of all conspiracy theories: It depicts a sequence of deliberate and fully conscious acts conceived by a hidden group with a rationale known only to them and to the theorist, who leans on glib assertion. "I know what I am talking about," he assures us; "[I have been] studying and working for a half-century on the assumption that this present state of affairs would come about at this moment in history." (He *knew all along*.)

You hear there, alas, not the mythmaker but the crank. It's the crank, too, who asserts that the wise rulers of Russia (so unlike our own) intend nothing less than the controlled demilitarization of the world. The Communist mission? Pish tush. "I have discussed this point with the Russians. They admit that a *party* dictatorship is not 'democracy' and, at the same time, also admit that it is for *true* democracy that the Russians, the Chinese, and most of the people of the world aspire."

Those tame Russians at Dartmouth Conferences! He will believe ill of no one. And they no doubt deferred to him.

But let the mythmaker have the last word. "Now, in June 1980 at 85 years of age, I have consumed over 1,000 tons of food, water, and air, which progressively, atom by atom, has been chemically and electromagnetically converted into all the physical components of my organism and gradually displaced by other income atoms and molecules. . . .

"Each one of us is a unique behavioral pattern integrity. The metaphysical you and I are not the coarsely identified 'cornflakes' and 'prunes' that we ate in the days before yesterdays. . . ."

The metaphysical you and I "qualify for continuance in Universe as local cosmic problem solvers," and as we design our critical-path deliverance of all humanity from "fearfully ignorant self-destruction," we have the obligation "to assume as closely as possible the viewpoint, the patience, and the competence of God."

For God "seems to wish Earthian humans to survive," in part, it would seem, by learning to cherish a good myth and reject a wishful or peevish one. As more than physical beings we live on myths, must have them or perish from confusion. The fallible eighty-five-year-old performer of *Critical Path* is with all his vagaries the best mythmaker alive.

A Geographer
of the Imagination

Harper's, *August 1981. It drew a sniffy letter from a man at* The New
Yorker *who denied that J. C. Penney ever manufactured overalls.*

Guy Davenport is grateful for "having been taught how to find
things": all that he has ever done, he's willing to hazard. He learned it
during a whole childhood of looking in fields.

> Every Sunday afternoon of my childhood, once the tediousness of Sun-
> day school and the appalling boredom of church were over with, cor-
> rosions of the spirit easily salved by the roast beef, macaroni pie, and
> peach cobbler that followed them, my father loaded us all into the Es-
> sex, later the Packard, and headed out to look for Indian arrows.

So commences a magical account. The day I first read it, on pages
copied from a magazine called *Antaeus*, I resolved that if it ever appeared in a book of Guy Davenport's nonfictional writings I would
lose no time commending that book to the world. So this review was
scheduled when *The Geography of the Imagination** was announced,

**The Geography of the Imagination*, by Guy Davenport. North Point Press, 1981.

and it was not to be aborted by the discovery, when the review copy arrived, that the name on the book's dedication page was my own. If having known a man for twenty-five years is to disqualify one from talking about his work, then our literary culture will have to be left to hermits.

The eye that found Indian arrowheads on Sunday afternoons in South Carolina is by now the most astute eye in America. What can it not find! Two thousand trimly ordered words defile to bring news of what is findable in a single picture so familiar we have never learned to see it, Grant Wood's *American Gothic*. Here are fifty-seven of those words:

> She is a product of the ages, this modest Iowa farm wife: she has the hair-do of a mediaeval madonna, a Reformation collar, a Greek cameo, a nineteenth-century pinafore.
>
> Martin Luther put her a step behind her husband; John Knox squared her shoulders; the stock-market crash of 1929 put that look in her eyes.

Such prose is as packed with information as the picture, which contains "trees, seven of them, as along the porch of Solomon's temple," "a bamboo sunscreen—out of China by way of Sears Roebuck—that rolls up like a sail," and sash windows "European in origin, their glass panes from Venetian technology as perfected by the English."

The farmer's eyeglasses even, which Phidias would have thought a miracle, are fetched from deeps of history. "The first portrait of a person wearing specs is of Cardinal Ugone de Provenza, in a fresco of 1352 by Tommaso Barisino di Modena," and "the center for lens grinding from which eyeglasses diffused to the rest of civilization was the same part of Holland from which the style of the painting itself derives." This is precisely relevant. Grant Wood once thought he would be a Post-Impressionist; discovering "this Netherlandish tradition of painting middle-class folk with honor and precision" was what sent him back to Iowa from Montparnasse.

American history is a story of bringing and of leaving behind fateful choices. What was brought has imprinted the New World with strange traces of prior origins. On an old road through the Santa Ynez

Mountains in California, certain rock surfaces are scored with ruts spaced exactly as were the wheels of Roman chariots. The stagecoaches that marked them were built to Spanish measurements, and the wheels of Spanish coaches had been spaced to fit the ruts of Roman roads in Spain. Such transfer of patterns is wholly automatic; no one involved need know that it is happening. In a similar way, Grant Wood's vision, learned from Dutch and Flemish masters, came to register in America, in Vermeer's or Memling's way, the mute pieties enshrined in *things*.

Thus "the train that brought her clothes—paper pattern, bolt cloth, needle, thread, scissors [none of these visible in the picture, but all implied by it]—also brought her husband's bib overalls, which were originally, in the 1870s, trainmen's workclothes designed in Europe, manufactured here by J. C. Penney, and disseminated across the United States as the railroads connected city with city."

Every glimpse in America includes artifacts bearing such tales. Most of us, though, resemble most of the time certain people who used to tag along on the Davenport family's Sunday expeditions: people "who would not have noticed the splendidest of tomahawks if they had stepped on it, who could not tell a worked stone from a shard of flint or quartz."

Likewise there are people who draw pay for being art historians and do not think to inquire into the credentials of a pose that displays man and wife side by side. That, too, is Flemish—Rubens used it, van Eyck—and before that it was an Etruscan convention, and before that, Egyptian. Though in Iowa it alludes to the Brownie box camera, it also remembers something Wood need not have known—an Egyptian prince beside his wife, "strict with pious rectitude, poised in absolute dignity, mediators between heaven and earth, givers of grain, obedient to the gods." Prince Rahotep would be holding the flail of Osiris. Our man holds something Mediterranean, a pitchfork, descended from the trident of Poseidon.

So the theme the picture states—a tension between the growing and the ungrowing, wheat and iron—is the theme of Dis and Persephone: he the lord of metals with his iron scepter, she the corn-girl he has captured and adorned with a metal brooch. *American Gothic*, the title of which, by the way, does not sneer at rigid souls but denotes the architectural style of the farmhouse, is finally "a picture of a sheaf of golden grain, female and cyclical, perennial and the mother of civilization; and of metal shaped into scythe and hoe: nature and technology, earth and farmer, man and world, and their achievement together."

Has so much ever been found in what we tend to dismiss as a pointlessly elaborate caricature? And are these findings embarrassed by the information that Grant Wood was thinking not of husband and wife but of father and spinster daughter, prowling males held at bay with that pitchfork? Can a picture know far more than its painter meant, or knew? Certainly, as he spreads out his trove of arrowheads for our inspection, Davenport is apt to incur the suspicion that time past did not deposit them in the fields where he gathered them, that they dropped there rather through holes in his own pockets. Is it perhaps the knowingness of a Kentucky professor that Davenport generously attributes to Grant Wood? We have extraordinary difficulty believing that poets or painters really know very much. This implies that the only way to signal the possession of knowledge is to deliver a lecture.

In Poe's "To Helen" we encounter a "perfumed sea," and have two options. We can dismiss "perfumed" as a typical bit of adjectival silliness. Or we can remember, with Davenport, "that classical ships never left sight of land, and could smell orchards on shore," moreover "that perfumed oil was an extensive industry in classical times and that ships laden with it would smell better than your shipload of sheep." And as for the pertinence of classical times, "those Nicaean barks of yore" in Poe's verse get their adjective from "the city of Nice, where a major shipworks was: Mark Antony's fleet was built there."

Yes, yes, but did Poe really know all that? He knew enough, certainly, to make the ships "Nicaean" and to mean something by it. Beyond that nothing is provable, unless someone can show us a letter of Poe's remarking on the odors that wafted to Mediterranean ships from Provençal orchards. The skill of locating such documents and the strategy of citing them make up what is called scholarship. When the document is lacking, literary explication can appeal only to plausibility. Poe wrote "To Helen" when he was still a boy, and we don't know at all what lore floated through schoolrooms then. Davenport's Poe can scarcely be read by Americans, who have systematically forgotten everything he thought they knew.

Whitman likewise. "Things vivid to him and his readers, such as transcendentalism, the philosophy of Fourier and Owen, the discovery of dinosaurs in the west by Cope and Marsh, phrenology, photography, telegraphy, railroads, have fused into a blur," rendering a great deal of his poetry meaningless. For this state of things the only remedy is information. "Outlines for a Tomb (G.P., Buried 1870)" is retrieved from blather by a note on the millionaire philanthropist George Peabody, who left a museum to Harvard and a museum to Yale and is nowhere mentioned in the *Britannica*.

It helps also to be reminded that "Of the delights celebrated in 'A Song of Joys,' most are accessible now only to the very rich, some are obsolete, some are so exploited by commerce as to be no longer joys for anybody except the stockbroker, two are against the law (swimming naked, sleeping with 'grown and part-grown boys'), and one is lethal ('the solitary walk')." Also that "the largest American business is the automobile, the mechanical cockroach that has eaten our cities; that and armaments."

That Whitman would have shared Davenport's present distaste for the auto is something we're left to divine, forgetting as we do so those magical autos now obsolete as the dinosaur—"the Essex, later the Packard"—that facilitated the expeditions after Indian arrowheads. There's no getting around the way Davenport's poets and painters, as we get to know them, come to resemble Guy Davenport: a special case, no doubt, of something he draws our attention to, "Ernst Mach's disturbing and fruitful analysis of science as a psychological history of scientists. . . . The theory of relativity is in the genius of its conception and in the style of its expression as much a projection of the uniquely individuated mind of Einstein as *Jerusalem* is of Blake's." If that's true of science, and it probably is, then a century's effort to deliver the study of literature from mere accidents of personality by rendering it "scientific" lies inert now, dissolving in ironies. Around its corroding wreck Post-Structuralism, Interpretation's current craze, dances a rite of barbaric despair.

I've just opened a package of books that include Barbara Johnson's *The Critical Difference* ("How does a text mean?" asks the blurb; "How can the same text trigger a history of militantly incompatible interpretations?"), Geoffrey Hartman's *Saving the Text* (subtitled *Literature/ Derrida/Philosophy*), Robert Young's anthology *Untying the Text* (subtitle: "A Post-Structuralist Reader"), and can recommend none of them for a Sunday afternoon. These are nine-to-five books, for the days when you're very alert. Young cites Roland Barthes: "Reading is a form of *work*." Certainly, reading Post-Structuralist prose is a form of work, like jogging with a nail in your shoe. It enjoins us to remember that there is no nontheoretical criticism, only a kind that doesn't confront its own theories and is free to suppose them "natural" and theory free. That's for blithe spirits only, naïve ones.

Bearing theory in mind, though—what really goes on, as we seek to release some meaning from strings of words?—can induce the kind of paralysis that overtook the centipede when he tried to give thought to which foot moved after which. How to write readable Post-Structuralist critical prose is a problem so far unsolved, though Barbara Johnson has moments when something almost moves. For if there are no arrowheads in the field, only ways of persuading yourself that you know they're not there but also know how to mimic the motions of seeming to seek them, then in making it clear that you know your motions are a mimicry, yielding only a highly significant *absence* of arrowheads, if you follow me, then you either write very long sentences indeed or abridge them with the aid of technical terms that the unkind are apt to call jargon. You also find yourself detained by similarities among your own words (this is in part because classic Structuralism, which we're now beyond, discerned meaning only in differences), and games with "text" and "pretext" and "pre-text" signal your awareness that reading, though *work*, is after all a game.

You'll forgive me if I don't illustrate; it's unkind to quote even jargon out of context, though I'm tempted by Paul de Man's whimsy that makes Archie Bunker an arch debunker (of the Greek *arche*, or "origin"), whose impatient "What's the difference?" doesn't ask for a difference but says, "I don't give a damn what the difference is." Thus "the literal meaning asks for the concept (difference) whose existence is denied by the figurative meaning," and Archie is Deconstructionist *malgré lui*, as you'll grant if you know what a pother Jacques Derrida, the arch-Deconstructionist, makes with "difference" and his own coinage, "differance."

It's pleasanter to linger with Davenport, a sweet mind and a fructive. Certainly he can't be convicted of not having a theory, though it is not a theory of reading but a theory of history. It is very likely untrue, but it got his book written. It says, I was happier at ten than I am at fifty-four, and a like pattern is discernible in America. As the fields where we sought those arrowheads are now under an immense lake, so oblivion has engulfed American consciousness, and artists vainly array particulars hardly anyone can command the knack to read. Hence these pages, in which I take pleasure in my own bright arrays, culled in homage from Poe and Pound and Grant Wood and Whitman and Joyce and Zukofsky and Eudora Welty and as many other sly but masterful spirits as I've had occasion to pay attention to.

It may very well be the import of our age, that literature is not the text, does not contain its meanings, is merely what happens in some mind in the presence of a text. If so, then the choice of another mind to spend time with is crucial to your wellbeing. The mind that conceived *The Geography of the Imagination* and executed its elegant meaty sentences is one I'll commend.

Up from Edenism

From the October 17, 1980, National Review, *preserved here chiefly for the first four paragraphs and their footnote. A Poetics of the Frontier awaits its formulator.*

PARADIGMS LOST: REFLECTIONS ON LITERACY
AND ITS DECLINE, *by John Simon. Penguin, 1981.*

In the origins of every language, we may discern a horribly mangled way of speaking some previous one. French began as the saloon Latin of an empire's frontier. In a transalpine Texas where grammarians did not venture, vulgar folk (Lat. *vulgus*, the no-accounts) lost the habit of calling what might get sliced from your shoulders your *caput*, *testa* being more playful and playfulness in isolated places being habit-forming. *Testa* meant "pot" and was slang for "head," like our "noggin," which also means "pot." It got mispronounced *teste*, and the French still say *tête*.

The French also say *cheval*, and we say "chivalry," because legionaries who had gone native in Gaul were less apt to be familiar with a prancing *equus* than with the kind of nag you'd call by the local slang word, *caballus*. So *la tête d'un cheval*,* a horse's head, was formerly a nag's noggin, and if roustabouts who talked like that thought they were talking Latin there were seemingly no John Simons to disabuse them.

Not that it mattered. Whether it was Cicero's Latin was never an issue. Cicero was dead, and all memory of his usages sealed away in a few manuscripts. What mattered was shared understanding among the living, and all the time the Gauls were (as we can now say) preparing the tongue of Racine and Cocteau, their habits of speech were doing what speech always does, binding together a community of speakers who by the tenth century A.D. were no longer in any ascertainable way Roman.

A Gaul understood anyone he was likely to talk to as long as he stayed north of the Alps. Meanwhile south of the Pyrenees, Latin was degenerating into Spanish and around Rome itself into Dante's vulgate Italian. These diverged because there was little traffic across mountain barriers.

Such are the conditions of radical linguistic change: isolation and an absence of written controls. They are Dark-Age conditions, and nobody wants them back, least of all, one supposes, the pundits with whom John Simon is properly impatient—the ones who assert that since language, the property of its speakers, normally changes, and such change has been demonstrably creative, therefore anything goes, even the floating "hopefully."

"Hopefully it won't rain"; "Between you and I"; "Here at the *Times* we're disinterested in grammar": such barbarisms Simon assails with the vigor of an ecologist combatting pollution particle by particle. (Padlocking all the nation's press and half its larynxes would effect control at the smokestack.) Whole chapters of *Paradigms Lost* deserve circulation as schoolroom pamphlets.

Unlike, say, Edwin Newman, who is apt to be tortuously witty about instances, John Simon has a zest for stateable principles, not unconnected with the fact that, like Conrad and Nabokov, he came to

---

*And the Romans used no articles; *la* and *un* are from *illa*, "that," and *unus*, "one": literally "that there head of one horse." Cf. "That's one fine hoss, pardner."

English relatively late (it was his fifth language). For perceiving whatever system a language affords, the lifelong learner is apt to be better placed than the native speaker; no one that I've known knew English half as minutely as the late Louis Zukofsky, who began its acquisition at twelve and kept the habit of looking up everything including "a" and "the."

Not custom but accessible knowledge will be such a man's criterion. The absence of knowledge is called ignorance, so when linguists prate of normal linguistic change, John Simon responds that linguistic changes "are caused by the ignorance of speakers and writers." Let us, therefore, rebuff their ignorance before it infects sound custom.

Let us rebuff it indeed. Let us marvel with him that Rex Reed and Vincent Canby get paid, for gosh sakes, to *write* (do paraplegics get paid to play ball?), and let us rub our hands, too, while the guilty twist and blacken in the heat of a Simon tirade: memorably, the college division director who fired an instructor for the elitist sin of thinking students ought to seek out the right word, whereas, quoth the director in a memo, "Very few English words, usually nouns, have less than two meanings." Simon does not rest with correcting "less" to "fewer"; he offers a helpful list of counterexamples: "nincompoop, numskull, cretin, ignoramus, division director."

Quotation leads me to quotation; though it digresses from our theme I can't omit Simon's deadly demurral when one man likens Gore Vidal to Matthew Arnold, another to Oscar Wilde. Simon, though not quite convinced, is willing to allow Vidal "some very good pieces, as weighty as anything in Oscar Wilde and easily as witty as the best of Matthew Arnold."

And on another page—no, this must stop, lest the space fill with no more said than that *Paradigms Lost* is a zesty, commendable book. And something more does need saying: that accurately though Simon directs his polemic energies, he tends to locate the battle lines imperfectly. There's a defect in his paradigm of linguistic fixity. You'd think a man with at least five Indo-European languages including Serbo-Croatian would allow for the process by which they all came into being. But history is something he tends not to allow for.

Let's run a paragraph through in freeze-frame. "Ignorant, obfuscatory, unnecessary change, producing linguistic leveling and flatness, could be stopped in its tracks by concerted effort." (True; and the concerted effort would bespeak a community concerned with the distinctions that are being leveled.) "The fact that this has not often happened in the past is no excuse for the present." (One thing that didn't happen in the past was the contraception of Simon's five languages.) "We have acquired a set of fine, useful, previously unavailable tools, culminating in the *Oxford English Dictionary* and a number of excellent treatises and handbooks on grammar. We now have the means to slow down changes in language considerably if not to stop them altogether."

The last fascicle of the *OED* appeared in 1928, not long before John Simon (b. Subotica, Yugoslavia, 1925) commenced acquiring English, a synchrony perhaps not unconnected with his implication that the *OED* is a terminal moraine of linguistic evolution, indeed usable for stopping it. Far from being a monument of fixity, the *OED* is a magnificent piece of historical lexicography, a documentation of centuries of semantic change.

In 1400 Chaucer's Knight's "Trouthe and honour, fredom and curteisie" denoted respectively fidelity, chivalrousness, magnanimity, and the knightly code. The story of five centuries of civilization is entailed in the evolution of those four words, and it won't suffice to remark, as Simon does in connection with "nice," that nothing has ever governed such a story save ignorance.

And as for stopping change: far from being a prospect only now available, fixity was a famous eighteenth-century dream. Swift dreamed it, the sensible Sam Johnson dreamed it; in Europe academies were founded to implement it. For in the first century to be dominated by the printing press, the editing of "old authors" such as Shakespeare (as old then as is Tennyson now) left the literate confronted with the scandalous fact of vernacular change, confounding their hopes of writing vernacular classics, things to endure. "For such as Chaucer is, shall Dryden be," wrote Pope in a mood of Stoical resolution; what hope, he meant, for Pope?

And yet, Dryden, who has been dead for 280 years, wrote an English we still recognize as "modern." His language as it happened *was* effectively fixed, and by the very thing that had made change apprehensible, the printing press. Spelling settled down; there is nothing like print to make people anxious when a word's appearance changes. So did grammar and so did punctuation. Since 1700 the major languages of Europe (I don't know about Serbo-Croatian) have been regulated not by ear but by eye. In effect there are two Englishes, the spoken and the published, the latter governing.

John Simon himself tells us how at about sixteen in Yugoslavia he consolidated his command of English by reading novels with a tutor. No matter that the novels were by Edgar Rice Burroughs, their idiom was far more formal than anything you'd hear spoken, even at Oxford. Burroughs and his publishers inherited the syntactical and other conventions of printed English, worked out by two centuries of copy editors.

So where Mr. Simon sees an unaccountable slippage of literacy setting in about two decades ago, I see two related causes: our increased electronic exposure to the spoken language, which has always been somewhat anarchic, and a lapse in the competence of publishers' staffs, an anonymous workforce on whose literacy the whole system of stabilization hinges.

A newspaper editor once told me why proofreading standards in Canada declined in the 1940s. Reading proof—a dull underpaid job—had once kept retired clergymen from starving. It was when the aged clergy commenced to draw pensions that papers had no recourse save to hire less literate drifters. Where book publishing gets its serfs today I've no idea, but a glimpse of their quality can be obtained from the caption on a publicity photo Simon's own publishers are circulating to reviewers of his book. It identifies him as "author of *Paradigm's Lost*." By at least not going on to write "Literacy and It's Decline," the caption writer managed to bat .500 against the apostrophe. That's not good enough. And it's merely by luck that he's not a copy editor.

Copy editors used to clean up untidy writing: hence our illusion that writers were formerly literate. Now, in my experience, they routinely make good enough worse. Simon sniffs, as do I, at the construction "critic X," yet the phrase "Critic Marvin Mudrick" appeared under my byline in the August *Harper's*; that was thanks to a copy editor who stuck in the word "critic" for the guidance of someone out there who's ignorant of Marvin Mudrick. And the only time the construction "It looks like there's . . ." has ever appeared over my signature, the sentence had been rewritten in a New York office.

How the system works that escorts sentences toward print is something a man as knowing as John Simon ought to be telling his readers. If he'd focus his attack on the present state of that, he'd be zeroing in on a plague spot. Meanwhile the spoken language, where every thousandth barbarism merits attention, might be left to its Sam Goldwyns and Yogi Berras, and its purveyors of words like "smarmy" (not in the *OED*). "Smarmy" has uses. It's the word for Barbara Walters, who doesn't merit what she gets in *Paradigms Lost*, eight thousand demolishing Simon words. Enough to be grateful that she doesn't edit copy.

Colonial Lexicon

Harper's, *February 1981. How seldom books of reference get coldly looked at is amazing.*

OXFORD AMERICAN DICTIONARY, *edited by Eugene Ehrlich, Stuart Berg Flexner, Gorton Carruth, and Joyce M. Hawkins. Oxford University Press, 1980. 816 pp.*

The sea, we know, is wine-dark, but how do we know it? That most familiar of Homeric phrases turns out to be a lexicographers' fiction. *Epi oinope ponton*, says the Greek, "upon the [something] sea." Unriddling the middle word was patient work for many decades of scholarship, and entailed at least five crucial decisions: (1) It is a Greek word, not merely a Greek effort to spell some word the Greek poets inherited from pre-Greek peoples. (2) It can, therefore, be dissected into Greek components, *oinos*, "wine," and *ops*, "face" or "appearance." (3) In saying "with the look of wine" the words point to wine's color, not, for instance, to its sparkle. (4) We are to think of a "red" wine, not a "white." (5) The salient quality of this wine's color is *darkness*.

Each decision on this list has been challenged. We trust a shaky card-house, indeed, when we try to read what no speaker is alive to set us straight about. The Reverend Henry G. Liddell and his collaborator, the Reverend Henry Scott, were the first to put English "wine" next to English "dark," a deed recorded in their *Greek-English Lexicon*, published in 1843, early in the great age of methodized lexicography. Like other coinages of theirs ("rosy-fingered," "ox-eyed"), it soon became part of Victorian writers' vocabularies, and of everybody's solemn thrills at the mention of ancient Greece. Within twelve years "wine-dark" had found its way into a novel called *Westward Ho!* A decade more, and it was a classy way to name the color of a marquise's dress. We may want to rank Liddell and Scott among the more influential creators of our ancestors' fictions, and savor the friendship of Dean Liddell's daughter Alice with her father's Oxford colleague "Lewis Carroll," one of whose durable imaginings was a fragile Humpty Dumpty who sat on a wall and explained the meaning of words. That order of explaining has been an Oxford specialty.

Intricate, precarious guesswork, by contrast, was not exacted from the team that has just finished the *Oxford American Dictionary*. This is not a dictionary of Americanisms but a dictionary for Americans if they want one, and like all lexicons of spoken tongues it purports to tell us about matters we can check for ourselves. Unlike Homer's Greek, which you'll not hear even in Athens, "American" buzzes right here, and we may envisage editors—three of the chief four American—who had only to open a window and let their ears wag.

> cra-zy (kra-*see*) *adj* 1 *insane* 2 *very foolish, not sensible. this crazy plan.*
> craz'i-ly *adv* craz'i-ness *n.* crazy quilt, a quilt made from pieces of fabric
> of many colors, sizes and shapes. like crazy, *(informal)* like mad, very
> much.

Observe several strengths: the accessible typography, the no-nonsense phonetic respelling, the adroit italicized examples, the openness to spoken idiom ("like crazy"), the willingness to take this "informal." But then wonder how the still commoner "crazy about" got missed, and end by reflecting on the plight of a user whose reading has turned up the phrase "crazed porcelain." That reader, the most likely consulter of this page one can imagine, will find no help either in the "crazy" entry or in any adjacent one. (For "crazed" we get only "driven insane, *crazed with grief*.")

But one thing "crazed" cannot uncommonly mean is "covered with a pattern of fine cracks," and why is that information missing? I don't know the official answer, since neither in the prefatory matter nor anywhere in the copious reviewers' press kit is there anything about principles of inclusion. Still, phrases like "not intended to be comprehensive" lead one to speculate that someone may have thought crazed = cracked altogether too unusual for inclusion. Ask the first one hundred passersby about "crazed" and your chances of hearing "cracked" are vanishingly small.

And in representing only the most likely senses, haven't the editors produced a handsome listing of all that is least likely to be looked up? If so, history is being repeated as farce, since it took centuries for lexicographers to confront common words at all.

The first "dictionaries" (places you found diction, as "apiaries" were where you found *a-pes*, bees) were simply Renaissance lists of hard words, deemed worthy of attention *because* they were uncommon. Common knowledge took care of the rest. Samuel Johnson's great work of 1755 duly wrestled with such elements as *cow* and *poker* ("The iron bar with which men stir the fire"), but remained heavy on entries like *assuefaction, minorate*, and *inspissation*. It was left for the great *Oxford English Dictionary*, the *OED* of 1884–1928, to dispose of *antidicomarian* in four crisp lines and devote twenty-three heroic, labyrinthine pages to the verb *set*.

Rare words are the easiest to define, their sense being technical and specific. Readers of William F. Buckley who seek the *Oxford American*'s help with *irenic* may reflect that the definition will have been as easy to write as it is to understand: "tending toward or promoting peace." (The editors were even brisker with another Buckley favorite, *eschatological*, which they dealt with by leaving it out.) *Crazy*, being more used and having more uses, is harder. *Set*, with its myriad idiomatic functions* and its prepositional compounds *(set out, set by, set to)* is virtually impossible.

---

*E.g., "resting," used of a rabbit; "rung so hard it pauses inverted," used of a bell. Neither is in the *OAD*.

The *Oxford American* does a clean job with *set*, making nothing harder than you thought it was going to be. Its nineteen senses for the verb include things people do with a broken bone, with hair, with type. There are seven more for the noun (a tennis set, a TV set, a stage set) and three for the adjective. For a bonus we're enjoined against confusing *set* with *sit*. Seekers are conceivable who might want any of the senses, and many who stand in need of the injunction.

And whether you have a practical need or not, the list repays browsing. It performs one of the most bracing services of a dictionary, placing you for a moment outside a familiar node of the language, to ponder its workings with clarifying detachment. Why we *set fire to* is something we may never wonder till we see it under the second main sense of *set*, "to put in contact with," and reflect that, indeed, the flame gets touched to the fuel.

Such clarifications are muffled in the great *OED*, one ambition of whose makers was to be absolutely comprehensive. There *set* promised trouble as early as 1881, when James Murray, the chief editor, came to doubt if the language contained a more perplexing word. An assistant had already spent forty hours on it, and Murray anticipated forty hours more. *Set* (the verb) was completed more than three decades later, and the time its final arrangement took Murray's chief associate, Henry Bradley, was something like forty days, in the course of which he improvised twelve main classes with no fewer than 154 subdivisions, the last of which (*set up*) required forty-four further subsections.

The result, a treatise two-thirds as long as *Paradise Lost*, is from most points of view a triumph of ingenious uselessness, reminiscent of Yeats's *A Vision* in being nearly impenetrable through sheer complexity of classification. Someone who had heard of hunters "setting" to fowl would toil long and hard through those columns en route to his quarry, low down in the final clause of #110: "*set*: to get within shooting distance by water."

Nor was *set* unique. In 1895–96 *do* occupied Murray himself off and on from Christmas till the end of June, though when he finished the *D*'s on Christmas Eve 1896, he exemplified the Law of the Ease of Hard Words by polishing off *Dziggetai* while his wife watched. In 1909 a vis-

itor to the office reported every surface in sight snowed under with
put. Browsers in his granddaughter K. M. Elisabeth Murray's *Caught
in the Web of Words* (1977), one of the most endearing biographies in
the language, may read the letter that begs a friend to realize what the
entries for *penguin* and *pelican* cost: "I could have written two books
with less labour."

Penguin seems to have given the *Oxford American* no trouble at all:
"a seabird of the Antarctic and nearby regions, with webbed feet and
wings developed into flippers used for swimming." Murray's agonies
stemmed from the need to ascertain whether the bird to which the
word was first applied (and by whom?) was the same one we now
think of. Like Liddell and Scott with their almost wholly conjectural
"winedark," he was groping in poorly documented mazes to which
he'd been consigned by the *OED*'s cardinal principle, historicity. His
earliest "penguin" example dates from 1578 and seems, as he notes
wanly, to have pertained to the Great Auk. The *OAD* has life much
easier in starting from Now. It has only to state what *penguin* means to
us, and everybody knows that.

Or what *crazy* means now, and we've noted a problem with *crazy*,
namely that its applicability to porcelain can drop out. But turn to a
fair-sized "collegiate" dictionary, such as the 1978 printing of *Webster's
New World*—the one I happen to have handy—and you will find "1.
having flaws or cracks; shaky or rickety; unsound. 2. unsound of
mind. . . ." This unpretentious work arranges meanings in order of
etymological development, and *cracked* was what *crazy* first meant.
The crack-pated sense came later.

Here we may discern the unadvertised cardinal principle of the
OAD, its total repudiation of the idea that dominated lexicography
from 1812 (Passow, a German) until quite recently: that the meanings
of words unfold from a root sense, still obscurely alive in the remotest
application. *Arrive* is related to *river*, something with banks, and to *Ri-
viera*, the Mediterranean's shore; when you arrived you came by
water, and reached land with a relief still present in the most casual
use of the word, which seems never to connote reaching an *unwelcome*
destination. "He has arrived," they said of the peanut farmer when he

became governor of Georgia, as though, like a tenth-century seafarer come to shore, he had left featureless coping at last behind him.

This principle, pertinent to Darwin's century, when they felt you understood man better for grasping his simian origins, wholly dominated the *OED*, which commenced its dealings with each word about A.D. 1150 if possible and did not mind if the earliest senses it cited were long since obsolete. It persists in most of the dictionaries you can buy, which, however perfunctory about etymologies, still follow the prompt of origins in ordering their definitions.

But the *OAD* starts with the sense judged most current. "*Art:* 1. the production of something beautiful. . . ." Never mind that "art" for centuries had nothing to do with the galleries or connoisseurship, simply with human activity as distinguished from the workings of nature, a sense *Webster's New World* follows history in placing first. *WNW* gets around to "beauty" by sense 5. But the primal meaning enters the *OAD* as though by afterthought, in sense 3 (of three)—"any practical skill, a knack"—and would not enter at all, not even debased to a knack, were it not for usages like "the art of sailing." What you'll find first in the *OAD* is what just anybody thinks of first, hence such clunkers as *poem*: "a literary composition in verse, especially one expressing deep feeling or noble thought in an imaginative way." These three requirements—verse, depth, nobility—are hopelessly entoiled in boozy sentiment. "An arrangement of words," commences *WNW*, remembering Gk. *poein*, "to make," and putting the emphasis where it still belongs.

Poem displays *OAD* at its weakest, its populist base being shakiest. Turn to something the folk are at home with and behold admirable economy. "*Pop* (n.) 1. A small sharp explosive sound. 2. A carbonated drink." And for *Pop* (v.), . . ." 3. to put quickly or suddenly, *pop it in the oven*. 4. to come or go quickly or suddenly or unexpectedly, *pop in for coffee*"; also pop fly, pop off, pop out, pop the question. A second *pop* (n.) is (*informal*) father, and *pop* (adj.) leads into pop music, top of the pops, pop group, pop festival, pop art.

Pop art is "a style of art that relies on images in posters and comic strips": that doesn't essay metaphysics but states an essential. At its best the *OAD*'s strength is in seizing gists. "*Poker*, a stiff metal rod for poking a fire," would rival Johnson save for the inelegance of poker/ poke (Johnson's verb was "stir"). "*Horse*, a four-legged animal, with a flowing mane and tail, used for riding on or to carry loads or pull wagons, etc." is at a rhythmic but not a semantic disadvantage beside Johnson's "a neighing quadruped, used in war, and draught and carriage."

Yes, Johnson is the model to evoke, the one great lexicographer whose work preceded the dominance of etymologies, and who therefore confronted, like the *OAD*, the challenge of stating not the word's origin but what it now said. So, for *poetess* he wrote "a she poet," speaking for a time when a poet's sex could cue eyebrows. In a later time, *poetess* appears in the *OAD* as "*fem.* of *poet*," chaperoned by a caution: "Many regard the word *poetess* as objectionable, and prefer to use *poet* for women as well as for men." That would have pleased Marianne Moore, who was also pleased by Johnson's biscuit-plainness.

Much of the *OAD* would have pleased her, too. *Red* is "the color of blood." *Post* (2) is "the place where a soldier is on watch." *Lost* is "strayed or separated from its owner." *Orgy* is "a wild drunken party." Such concision can do nobody anything but good; the *WNW*'s "any wild, riotous, licentious merrymaking; debauchery" brings nothing so specific before the mind. (*Orgy* was not yet English in Johnson's time; in checking I noticed *orgasm*, for which he gives only "a sudden vehemence.")

The *OAD* might help teenagers learn to talk straight, might also greatly assist non-native speakers, might—alas, that's all I can think of. Of course it will confirm spellings, but any paperback word list will do that. Most of what is in it, if you're alive now, you know, though you may not know it with such concise forthrightness. Not only is etymological arrangement abandoned, there are no etymologies whatever. Not only is *crazy* (cracked) absent, so are numerous still more demotic usages. *Gee* is here but not *haw*, *crap* is defined only of dice, *follies* receives no showbiz inflection, *bed* (v.) is accorded no sexual overtone (likewise *tail* and *piece*, and the *do* entry omits *do it*).

Numerous hobby terminologies are ignored. *Bindings* have no ski connotations. *Audiophiles* are present but bereft of their special intentions for *distortion* and *frequency response*. There are no *sine waves* or *square waves*, and the entry for *audio frequency* is utterly wrong (it says "between 15,000 and 20,000 cycles per second"; the first figure should be merely 20). *Hang gliders* made it, and golfers are authorized to *birdie*, but surfers can't *hang ten*, and you can *dribble* a ball but not be a *cager*.

By way of perfunctory Americanism, every president is included, every state, every state capital, though who would look up *Iowa* in a book that says only "a state of the U.S." is someone I can't imagine. There's no Winston Churchill (inclusion requires an American passport) and no William Shakespeare, though *Shakespearean* is present, mysteriously defined as "of Shakespeare." There is no *aardvark*, but for some reason a *peccary*.

None of which is surprising. This seems a provisional job, chiefly an attempt to sell books, partly a first attempt since 1755 to base a dictionary boasting prestige of sponsorship on any principle save the historical. The straightness of many definitions deserves commendation. So, as far as they go (not far), do the notes on usage, though empiricism deprives them of their potential bite. You might rebuke the floating "hopefully" on historical grounds, but these are inaccessible when you have abandoned history. The best that can be managed is a flaccid appeal to the verifiable, not a linguistic fact but a forensic: "Many people regard the second use ['it is to be hoped'] as unacceptable." So they do, yes, so they do, and some are vocal; and John Simon will get you if you don't watch out.

Most misusers of "hopefully" prattle out of range of Simon; for them the *OAD*'s sanctions are as futile as Emily Post's. Piping its puppydog maintenance of standards ("Careful writers avoid *back of* in the sense of *behind*") with nothing discernible back of its gestures save a hope of avoiding the abuse that got heaped on *Webster's Third* (1961), the *OAD*, for all its virtues, would have made Sir James Murray weep. The most important word it has redefined, he would have thought, is "Oxford."

Bouquets from Your Bureaucrats

From the April 1983 American Spectator.

**THE HAZARDS OF WALKING, AND OTHER MEMOS
FROM YOUR BUREAUCRATS,** *edited by Carol
Trueblood and Donna Fenn, introduction by Charles Peters.
Houghton Mifflin, 1982.*

From the Department of the Army (San Francisco), for A- B- C- Distribution: ". . . 2. The hazards of walking. . . . (b) This inattention coupled with reading or reviewing documents while walking; going up or down stairs with both hands occupied (not holding the handrail); and wearing footwear of unusual design are responsible for the great majority of mishaps. . . ."

From a Section Chief, Illinois Department of Labor: ". . . On April 30, . . . at 8:25 in the morning, I noted that you had again plugged in the coffee pot. When I pointed out that you were aware that I had asked you not to plug it in, you replied that it is not 8:30 yet. I then told you that I am in charge of the section, even though it is not 8:30 yet. . . ."

Internal Revenue Service, to all agents: "Recently an employee received and apparently answered a telephonic request for information. Calls from taxpayers for Information Requests should be referred to the Freedom of Information Reading Room at National Office. . . ."

On and on: Government talking incessantly to itself. Its larynx is Selectric, its resonant sinuses are Xerox. For bureaucracy's days are enabled by expensive mechanical toys, three in particular. One is Mr. Carrier's air-conditioning, which in defiance of God's express intentions has rendered the Potomac Basin habitable year-round. A second is Mr. Edison's dictating machine, which affords the year-round inhabitants something to do there. And the third is Mr. Carlson's copier, which in defiance of human sloth enables any Selectrified mumble to, no, not trickle down "channels of distribution" as in the old days when its scope was contained by the illegibility of the sixth carbon, but instead to be flushed through those channels with hydraulic force, ending up on as many as a thousand desks, miraculously multiplied, a pristine turd.

There deposited, it requires a response. The bureaucrat's categorical imperative is simple: *Don't just sit there, dictate something*. He may even dictate his manner of "routing" what he dictates: "The above drafts come to me first for review, and I give them to Mr. Gregory for typing. The typist returns them to Mr. Gregory for his record of typing completions. Mr. Gregory will return the typed copies to the originator for review for typing corrections and/or sign off. The originator, after corrections and sign off, will route the typed report or letter to me for sign off and routing to Mr. Clemens. Copies of mailed letters come back through Mr. Gregory for recording." That is from a Coordinator, Title IX Team, in HEW's Region IV-Atlanta. Mr. Gregory's version is not preserved, but it is evident that he and incalculable numbers of others have little time to dream up public harassments.

Less busy folk have proved less harmless. H. R. Haldeman's most famous memo, "The President would like to have the bowling ball man come in and fit Mrs. Nixon and Tricia for balls as soon as possible," went to Colonel Hughes, copy to Mr. Chapin. Colonel Hughes will have responded, Mr. Chapin also, and conceivably Haldeman responded to their responses, but that was merely a three-way exchange. It grows lonely near the top. An insufficient paper empire to occupy him is something historians may wish to connect with Haldeman's later difficulties. Staffs should never be lean, nor distribution channels scant. Could Tricia's balls have generated a proper gale-force Washington blizzard of memos we might all have been spared Watergate.

Thus, one reason the Chief, Office Services Section, Facilities Management Branch, Internal Revenue Service has never done time in the jug is that memo writing keeps him harmlessly busy. His evaluation of Suggestion 42-EP/EO 132 was routed to an E.O. Specialist through the Incentive Awards Coordinator, to advise the recipient that something he had suggested could not be approved since action was already initiated in its area. The suggestion pertained to the location of windows in envelopes, an aspect of "the Envelope Program" that was even then occupying an "Envelope Task Force," its target date for completion a mere six months off.

That incredible numbers of these papers have to do with paper itself—its sizes, its grades, its orientation in the heaps into which filers gather it—is something we should be grateful for, since it normally bodes no action whatsoever. Indeed we should wonder if the IRS man was altogether wise in withholding the envelope window suggestion from the Task Force. He no doubt did not want to derail its progress toward its target date, undervaluing the fact that when target dates are met something really expensive may happen.

Washington's most momentous event of 1979, the conversion of all official paper from 8 by 10.5 inches to 8.5 by 11—a mere 11 percent increase in area and a gross underestimate of bureaucrats' verbal inflation—was not only missed by every political observer but came to pass no thanks to a Task Force insufficiently torpid. And once it had been effected, not even Temporary Regulation B-5 ("dated September 21, 1979, copy attached"), on "Procedures for Conversion," could ward off such consequences as confronted the Agency for International Development, when the new, larger GSA-approved paper proved "too large to fit the stationery drawers of many standard GSA desks," and AID was driven to such measures as "exchanging desks for others in stock." (True, people had to *carry* those desks, which created blue-collar jobs.)

Haste, you see, makes waste, and it is alarming to notice, here and there, tremors of some bureaucratic itch to get moving. Up at the New York State Office of Mental Health, someone even completed a Time Management Course, from which he came away with the insight that "certain times of the day must be 'meeting-free' if work is to be accomplished." The Director of the Bureau of Capital Operations* accordingly proposed to keep weekdays, 9:00–10:00 and 1:30–2:30, "meeting-free," and advised all staff to "keep these times open for actual work." Ten hours "actual work" a week! That would be ominous, save that he requested "feedback" at subsequent meetings, which can be expected to ooze into the meeting-free hours. For a few years yet, New York taxpayers may enjoy unregulated access to their own minds.

Another omen is the fitful lust after clarity. Someone writing for the Commander, Wright-Patterson Air Force Base, re "Dog Patrol, Explosive (Your ltr, 17 Oct 73)" protested lax words that would promote "a tendency toward confusion."

"AFLC cannot identify any FSN to Dog Detection-Explosive or as WRAMA puts it in 17 Oct 73 letter, Patrol Dog/Explosive. We cannot determine whether they want a dog or an explosive." Any bureaucrat who can frame so clear a question may even find out what he wants to know. Such a man should not be trusted with paper. His memo being nearly ten years old, the clarification it witlessly proposed may now occur any day, and Exploding Patrol Dogs become routine hazards.

Ponder, by contrast, the example of President Reagan. "We inherited a mess," said he on 20 January 1983, "but we're turning it around." Now *there* is a man who has grown into his job. Nothing

---

*By etymology these would pertain to the head, where mental health, such as it is, is situated.

should ever be done with public messes save turn them around. Let future administrators turn them round yet again. Meanwhile let them on no account be *shifted*. Try to shovel them away and people get hit. Ron came into office all gung-ho for action, but his current phraseology holds out hope for us yet. He's learning to talk just like a bureaucrat writing.

DARE to
Make It Known

The Times Literary Supplement *not only commissioned this, but afforded adequate space in its May 9, 1986 issue. I wish I could find the charming letter it drew from Dr. Cassidy.*

A century ago Mark Twain prefaced *Huckleberry Finn* with the claim that he'd preserved distinctions among no fewer than seven dialects: "the Missouri negro dialect; the extremest form of the backwoods South-Western dialect; the ordinary 'Pike-County' dialect; and four modified varieties of this last." The shadings, he further asserted, had not been done at haphazard but painstakingly, and not by guesswork but "with the trustworthy guidance and support of personal familiarity with these several forms of speech." So readers were not to suppose "that all these characters were trying to talk alike and not succeeding."

Being a notorious joker, Twain was quickly and widely doubted, but in 1979 a scholar named David Carkeet succeeded in isolating all seven dialects and assigning them to their speakers. One thing that made this feat difficult is that the dialects in *Huckleberry Finn* are not set off against a "Standard English" narrative; the entire book is non-standard, in fact challenges the assumption that "Standard" has ascertainable meaning. The opening sentences run,

> You don't know about me, without you have read a book by the name of "The Adventures of Tom Sawyer," but that ain't no matter. That book was made by Mr. Mark Twain, and he told the truth, mainly. There was things which he stretched, but mainly he told the truth.

That is the book's narrative voice, Huck's own. Now listen as the voice of Nigger Jim rises clear of it: "Ole Missus—dat's Miss Watson—she pecks on me all de time, en treats me pooty rough, but she awluz said she wouldn' sell me down to Orleans."

Here, by contrast, is "the extremest form of the backwoods South-Western dialect": "My very *words*, Brer Penrod! I was a-sayin'—pass that-air sasser o' m'lasses, won't ye?—I was a-sayin' to sister Dunlap, jist this minute . . . ."

Listen, finally, to one of the four Pike-County modifications: "Two years ago last Christmas, your Uncle Silas was coming up from New-rleans on the old Lally Rook, and she blowed out a cylinder-head and crippled a man. And I think he died, afterwards. He was a Bab-tist. . . ."

The distinction between Negro "Orleans" and Pike-County "Newrleans" is the sort of painstakingness Twain took rightful pride in. So is the "b" in "Babtist" and the comma between "died" and "afterwards." One problem he couldn't surmount, though he tried to outflank it by letting Huck himself narrate, is that what he meant for unselfconscious speech comes to rest on the printed page looking like a tangle of illiteracies. In an 1889 letter, Twain acknowledged the limitations of a twenty-six-letter alphabet, augmented only by italics and marks of elision. So constrained, the writer often "follows forms which have but little resemblance to conversation, but they make the reader understand what the writer is trying to convey." His aim was, above all, to make you *hear*.

He passed over the kind of reader who, refusing to listen, can perceive nothing save orthographic effrontery. Mark Twain never condescended to the regional, never offered to brand it sub-standard. A country that throughout its history has lacked a capital in the sense of London or Paris—Washington is merely where the government is kept, and by American tradition government is comic—the United States supports densely overlapping speech communities. Twain's view of any wish to standardize them is evident in the reason he has Huck give for electing flight to "Ingean" (outlaw) territory: "because Aunt Sally she's going to adopt me and sivilize me and I can't stand it. I been there before."

Splendidly edited by Walter Blair and Victor Fischer, the new University of California Press "Mark Twain Library" edition of *Huckleberry Finn* (with maps, notes, and glossary) has appeared almost simultaneously with Volume I (A–C) of the *Dictionary of American Regional English* (DARE). Both are installments of huge and majestic projects. The Works and Papers of Mark Twain, on which the Mark Twain Library draws for the texts of its inexpensive trade editions, has been in preparation for years and envisages seventy volumes. As for DARE, its roots go back almost a century, to the founding of the American Dialect Society in 1889, the very year Joseph Wright commenced work on his *English Dialect Dictionary*, another project that ventured to use the alphabet as its filing system for the saliencies of regional speech.

Wright's fieldwork could be confined to a smallish island. But America, as even Americans do not always fully realize, confronts any such project with a nearly intractable vastness. From Los Angeles to New York is about as far as from Barcelona to Moscow. Three million square miles: 200 million people: overlaid waves and dispersals of immigration: even though in 1889 some of the numbers were smaller, that challenge wasn't to be met by haphazard funding or by happenstance collecting. For decades the society stumbled at random, publishing word lists and helping with a dictionary or two. It wasn't until 1962 that DARE got seriously framed, with Professor Frederic G. Cassidy appointed Chief Editor.

Professor Cassidy, now seventy-nine, is reportedly still very much in charge while production of the remaining four volumes proceeds. Meanwhile, he has every reason to be pleased with both the volume in hand (over six pounds, beautifully arranged, produced, and printed) and with the huge project of which it betokens the consummation.

DARE draws both on printed sources (some 5,000, including diaries, small-town newspapers, and, of course, *Huckleberry Finn*) and on living informants, 2,777 of whom, in 1,002 communities, gave oral answers to 1,847 questions posed by eighty field workers who'd been coached not to alter the wording nor to prompt responses. Informants had to have been born in or near where they were interviewed, and not have traveled or stayed away long enough for habits of idiom to be contaminated. To obtain a pronunciation profile, they were also taped as they read "Arthur the Rat," a grim little tale tessellated out of several hundred test words (hoarse/horse, morning/mourning, greasy, business, out, roof, room . . .). Over a century ago Henry Sweet was using it for similar purposes in England.

The long questionnaire was shrewdly designed. It begins, Professor Cassidy tells us, "with the neutral subject of time in order to allay possible suspicions of some hidden purpose. Next come weather and topography, equally neutral and safely concrete; houses, furniture, and household utensils follow, with dishes, foods, vegetables, and fruits. And so the questions continue to more abstract topics: honesty and dishonesty, beliefs, emotions, relationships among people, manner of action or being. . . ." And when someone said, "I shouldn't have said *snuck*; *sneaked* is the right word," the self-correction was noted.

A sequence of typical questions:

What do you call a dog of mixed breed?

What joking or uncomplimentary words do you have for dogs?

To make a female dog so that she can't breed, she must be_____.

Ditto for cat

A cat with fur of mixed colors.

A cat that catches lots of rats and mice—you'd say, "A good _____."

To tell a dog to attack an animal or a person, you'd say, "_____."

To tell a dog to lie down on the ground and keep still, you'd say, "_____."

To tell a dog to stand without moving, you'd say, "_____."

To call a cat to make it come, you say, "_____."

You see at work there the inevitable bias of any dictionary; what the questionnaire is fishing for, all the time, is DARE's element of reference, the isolated word or phrase. That's not the way speakers think, but it's the way a lexicographer must think.

The resulting database, coded for computer access, runs to 2.5 million items. (A compressed presentation of all the answers is promised for Volume IV.) One thing the computer did was generate the maps that show you at a glance how "buttonwood" (= sycamore) is primarily a Northeastern word (not a single instance west of Indiana), while "chughole" (a hole in the road, elsewhere "pothole" or "chuckhole") seems virtually confined to Kentucky and Tennessee. All over the country, it seems, you hear "crazy bone" (for the point of the elbow, which you don't want to bump), though least often in the deep South and in New York City. And they call grandmother "Big Mamma" in only eleven states, all of them southern, and even there the usage seems predominantly black.

Though DARE offers hundreds of such maps, they need viewing with caution, what they tell us being inextricable from how the question of the moment was worded. Fortunately, DARE's users can consult the full set of questions; here are the four that elicited the information above:

(T13) What other names do you have around here for these trees: [list of nine, including "sycamore"].

(N27b) When unpaved roads get very rough, you call them _____.

(X33) The place in the elbow that gives you a strange feeling if you hit it against something.

(Z4) What words do people around here use for "grandmother"?

So what the "buttonwood" map seems to show is not the range of the word "buttonwood" but the range of informants *who also knew the same tree as "sycamore,"* and could in effect translate between two idioms. The "chughole" map locates totalitarians who call the whole mess a "chughole," not people for whom such a hole is an incident in the mess (as is "pothole" in Maryland, where I live). Neither question seems elegantly enough framed to draw a border around the usage it's after.

In what spirit a word is used, and how exclusively, is another question dictionaries are poor at answering. It seems evident that in "Big Mamma" territory "grandmother" remains the standard word, "Big Mamma" a playful variant; and that's different in principle from "crazy bone," for which there *isn't* a standard word, medicine, so far as I know, having no term for that brief surfacing of the ulnar nerve. Volume II of DARE may be expected to show us where "funny-bone" is the name of choice. The *Oxford English Dictionary*, which gives "funny-bone" as "the popular name for that part of the elbow . . ."— finessing the fact that it has no names save popular ones—also deigns to notice "crazy bone (U.S.), the 'funny-bone.'" I'd guess that "funny-bone" is natural to me because I grew up in an anglophile region of Canada, though we're left with no explanation for the rarity of "crazy bone" in polyglot New York City.

Mention of the OED may serve to remind us that the Great Work, as William Empson used to call it, relied by definition on printed sources. But any dictionary of regional usage must rely heavily on fieldwork with living informants, and we've seen how the framing of questionnaires can be tricky. Professor Cassidy cites a 1915 French enquirer who noted that the time to refine a questionnaire was *after* the fieldwork had been done. Late in the game, and in just a few communities, DARE solicited the names of wildflowers with the aid of color photographs instead of words. Why this "greatly increased the fieldworker's burden" is unclear, also why it couldn't also have been done with trees, birds, insects, bushes. It might have eased problems of the buttonwood = sycamore class.

A second obvious limitation of living informants is that they confine investigation to a present-day lifetime. Not even informant MD001, a Baltimore teacher born in 1877 and aged ninety-one when the interview took place, could lead the inquiry more than a short way back into the nineteenth century. Though each interview took about a week to conduct, the net harvest of them all is simply what 2,777 Americans knew about local idiom in the years 1965 through 1970. A typical DARE entry presents its information in historical sequence, like the OED, and sometimes commences with the sixteenth century. To such an entry, often many inches long, the questionnaire results, when they figure at all, contribute little save a present-day footnote. They are frequently disposed of in a single line of type.

In short, despite the emphasis its front matter gives the questionnaires, most of what DARE puts on show has been drawn from printed sources. The system by which those were scanned is not clearly specified. "In the early years a reading program was launched in which volunteers marked possible examples of regionalisms in more than two hundred American novels, short stories, plays, and poems." Later, as the enterprise found its bearings, we have DARE's staff casting its net into seas ateem with letters, diaries, travel journals, regional fictions, newspapers. While we learn much about caveats that attended selection from the catch, we could wish to have the weave of the net described.

Perfection, though, is a direction; the continent is vast, so is the time span, and the criteria are provisional. Toward the end of his Introduction, Professor Cassidy reflects with reluctance that the task of covering all the regional variation in American English is "beyond human accomplishment." In a project like this the things you do find out help define what you'd ask about in that second lifetime the gods never grant. In this life DARE's staff performed prodigies, and accumulated wonders for our delectation.

> Bock beer, n. chiefly Nth: A relatively sweet dark beer brewed in winter for consumption in the spring. "Called 'bock'—in English buck or goat—because of its great strength in making its consumers prance and tumble about like these animals." (Illinois, 1856).

> Bodacious, adj, adv. [prob blend of *bold* + *audacious*] chiefly Sth, S Midl: Audacious. "He . . . jes' plum bodacious hipped an' ruinated her." (reported from the Ozarks, 1929). [About "hipped" we may guess while we wait for the "H" volume.]

> Bubble and Squeak: "Most recipes have no similarity to the English dish of the same name. In Maine it's a leftover contrivance: cold cooked beef, cold smashed [*sic*] potatoes, cold cabbage, shredded onion, etc., browned in pork fat and served with vinegar. It's hearty, and cleans out the refrigerator."

We learn, too, that the "buck" in "pass the buck" abbreviates *buckhorn knife* (i.e., knife with a buckhorn handle), once used as a token in poker; that in saying a horse "bucks" (leaps upward with arched back) we're remembering its maleness (hence "buck", to oppose;

"buck", to push); that "buckaroo" however derives not from "buck" but from Spanish "vaquero," cowboy.

You learn, in fact, so much that, like Eric Partridge's splendidly cranky *Origins*, DARE can hold you for half an hour when you'd intended merely a purposive visit. Look up "coffin nail" (a cigarette, reported from every state but Nevada), and you find yourself lingering over "coffin varnish" (whiskey, esp of low quality), "coffin-carrier" (the great black-backed gull, *Larus marinus*), "coffee-worm" (the common worm used for fish-bait, from the custom of attracting them with used coffee-grounds). . . . Note that what creates such surreal groupings (fag, booze, gull, worm) is simply the alphabet.

We'd give much to hear the quality of the talk from which "coffin-varnish" and "coffee-worm" are natural ebullitions. Alas, one inevitable lack in DARE's word-by-word treatment is what no word-by-word treatment can respond to the drive of living rhythm. A fallacy all dictionaries tend to foster, for all their usefulness and fascination, is that speech is made of conjoined words. But it's writing that proceeds by choosing words. It is even sustainable that in living speech there is no such thing as a word. Far from being elements we use to speak with, words are units of attention we dissect speech into, DARE-wise, for analytic convenience. Humans had been speaking for millennia before that was feasible; the "Word," a string of letters flanked with spaces, seems a by-product of the great Phoenician discovery that speech could be mapped onto phonetic symbols. That is why it is only with written materials that lexicography is really comfortable.

Which brings us back to Mark Twain's observation that he was attempting, by alphabetic means, to convey the effect of pre-alphabetic phenomena. "Whoo-oop! bow your neck and spread, for the pet child of calamity's a-coming!"—there we have Twain busy at his difficult, deceptive task of somehow imitating the streams of utterance from which lexicography seeks to pick its "words." The raftsman who emitted such a wonder likely couldn't have said what "spread" was meant to mean. Nor, I'll guess, for all its industry and its awesome erudition, will the final volume of DARE.

The Impertinence
of Being "Definitive"

From the Times Literary Supplement, *December 17, 1982; and it lifts some paragraphs from the opening of my book about Irish writers,* A Colder Eye, *which was still in typescript. I'm sorry such observations as I make here got me thought of as an "enemy" of the late Richard Ellmann's, but I'll have to stand by them. Biography, it's to be feared, is not a science but a modest sub-genre of fiction.*

JAMES JOYCE: NEW AND REVISED EDITION, *by Richard Ellmann. Oxford University Press, 1982.*

This is intricate business. A way into it leads past the Irish Fact, definable as anything they tell you in Ireland, where you get told a great deal. Last summer, amid James Joyce symposiasts, meeting in what had been the old University College classrooms, I amused myself between sessions with repeatedly asking where the fireplace might have been beside which Stephen Dedalus had his talk with the Dean of Studies. "Why, right over there," was each Irish informant's reply, with a gesture toward the fireplace in the room of the moment. *A Por-*

trait records that it was in the physics theatre. Substantiations you'll get with ease in Dublin, but you'd best be wary lest they be Irish Facts.

I commenced to learn this lesson as long ago as three years before Richard Ellmann's *James Joyce* was first published. In 1956, something I had written drew correspondence from a Dubliner who signed himself "W. P. D'Arcy." Embedded in the first of his letters was an arresting phrase: "My father, the late Mr. 'Bartell' D'Arcy. . . ." Bartell D'Arcy! As Joyce's "The Dead" moves toward its climax we read,

> The voice, made plaintive by distance and by the singer's hoarseness, faintly illuminated the air with words expressing grief:
>> *O, the rain falls on my heavy locks*
>> *And the dew wets my skin,*
>> *My babe lies cold . . .*
> —O, exclaimed Mary Jane. It's Bartell D'Arcy singing and he wouldn't sing all the night.

So I was in touch with the son of "Bartell D'Arcy," whom I hastened to compliment on the presence of his father in the greatest short story in the English language. His crisp reply was that his father—a man who had sung with Jim Joyce's father on Saturday nights—had not been pleased at all. For as to why he wouldn't sing all the night of the story, Joyce has him saying "Can't you see that I'm as hoarse as a crow?," moreover saying it "roughly," which was none of it true. He immediately went round to his solicitor. It was when the solicitor told him he had *no case* that D'Arcy Sr. took to narrating, again and again and at length, the real events of that fabled Christmas party. He'd drink while he talked, which may have been what ended him.

There's an interesting premise here, which pursuers of Joyce's shade will meet often. In Dublin writing has a special and precarious status, no allowance being granted for "imaginative" genres. They are apt to tax the penman for not meeting his chief obligation, which is to put down events the way other people remember them. Thus in his 1953 memoir, *Silent Years*, J. F. Byrne was cross about a *Ulysses* sentence that situates Bloom's missing latchkey "in the pocket of the trousers he had worn on the day but one preceding." Since, so Byrne tells us, it was Byrne's misadventure with a key Joyce built this on, the sentence is nonsense because on the day preceding the misadventure he—Byrne—was using his key, and never mind about Bloom.

The solicitor was another interesting touch. (The English love a lord, the Irish a lawyer.) In another letter Mr. D'Arcy was persuasive about the commencement of Joyce's lifelong exile only after his books started to be published. For had he once set foot on the green sod, people he had mentioned by name in print would have detained him in courtrooms until doomsday, demanding redress over points of detail. There were more such people than anybody guessed. When the BBC heard from "Reuben J. Dodd Jr.," after broadcasting some pages of *Ulysses*, they thought it was a joke and at heavy cost discovered it was not.

So fortune seemed to have put me in touch with an oracle, and my first visit to Dublin (November 1956) included a rendezvous with Mr. W. P. D'Arcy. We met at dusk and tramped Grafton Street while he discoursed. He was soon elucidating something Joyce wrote in 1906 to his brother Stannie. Jim had been planning a new *Dubliners* story, about "Mr. Hunter," someone Stannie would know: a story to be called "Ulysses." So who was Hunter? Herbert Gorman in his 1939 biography of Joyce had doubted if we'd ever know.

"Hunter," Mr. D'Arcy stated, "was his name, or rather it was not his name, if you follow me." I did not follow him, and he drew together his cheeks to expel the elucidation, "Jew." Hunter's wife, everyone knew about his wife and about the men she entertained and more than entertained, and Hunter knew about them, too, but was unable to control her. She was part Spanish, and she sang. The singing was a handy pretext, what with the traveling.

Molly Bloom, you are thinking. Yes.

"Her special man, the one who organized her tours and more than her tours, the one Joyce called Boylan, was a man named Creech. He worked in the post office with my father. And to help you with him I have brought along a photograph." In the sepia rectangle, he then produced the purported Creech/Boylan, moustachioed, stared at a lens, hence at us, over (I seem to remember) folded arms. If this was "Blazes Boylan" he looked like what he had become, a man in a photograph made about 1900.

"I was present one day when Hunter was walking along this very path [by now we had crossed to Stephen's leafless green] and from around the bushes came Creech. They drew face to face. And I heard myself Hunter's very words to Creech."

Note, "I heard myself," moreover *on this very spot*. Those, are formulae to beware of, notwithstanding that the son of "Bartell D'Arcy" was narrating how "Bloom" confronted "Blazes Boylan": an event outside the scope of *Ulysses* itself, truly something to have come to Ireland to hear. He was facing me to make sure I heard it, and his voice dropped to a stage snarl: "You and your fuckin' concert tours!" A high-pitched laugh, and he savoured the line anew. "You and your fuckin' concert tours!"

Of the Irish Facts in this kaleidoscope, some at least appear to be reliable. Thus, when Ellmann Mark I appeared three years later, you could read what Stannie, by then himself an old man, remembered of Mr. Hunter: ". . . a dark-complexioned Dublin Jew . . . who was rumoured to be a cuckold." Professor Ellmann had a different original entirely for "Bartell D'Arcy," on he did not say whose information, and he listed several for Boylan, none of them called Creech, which is only to say that his researches led him through a different array of Irish Facts entirely.

As for Hunter's wife being part Spanish, I could have been hearing about the factual nudge that gave Joyce's Molly Bloom her Spanish mother, or else Joyce's book could have been nudging my man toward a little anecdotal creativity.

As for the concert tours and their epithet: here a 1904 memory seems far less likely than a 1956 improvisation, meant to clinch to my satisfaction ("on this very spot!")—Bloom's equivalence with Hunter, Boylan's with Creech. For what happened in Stephen's Green that November dusk in 1956 was like many such Dublin happenings, an inextricable mixture of reminiscence and performance.

Though of Dubliners who had known Joyce—the only one I met was Mr. D'Arcy—the city at that time still contained numbers of them. Had I been contemplating a biography, as I was not, I should have had to sift dozens of such performances for what substance they might contain. The copious Ellmann notes cite many an "interview," but in time one learns caution, great caution, and trusts he was cautious, too.

One's natural question, turning through Ellmann Mark II, is what Joyce's biographer has learned in a quarter century. The answer reduces to this, that his files have grown ampler.* What was best about Mark I is now still better, notably the establishment of a firm grid of dates, events, addresses. No one who remembers how futile was recourse to the Gorman book for even simple chronology will underrate that accomplishment. Many details in the grid have been refined. Thus the book now (correctly) has Joyce born in Rathgar, not Rathmines—that got fixed, indeed, in Mark I's second printing—and baptized in St. Joseph's Chapel of Ease, Roundtown, instead of in a church that had not been built in 1882.

Many more details have been added, and what they are added *to* can repay inspection. Thus to the discussion (page 246) of "Bartell D'Arcy" we find a new footnote appended: "A friend of Joyce's father, P. J. D'Arcy, an overseer at the General Post Office, sang sometimes under the name of Bartholomew D'Arcy, and may have contributed to the character." (The source is "Letter to me from his son, W. P. D'Arcy.") Alas, scrutiny of that for meaning yields only blur, so little "character" was there to contribute to. "Bartell D'Arcy" in "The Dead" is a walk-on part, a narrative contrivance to get a song sung: no more than a name, a tenor voice, and a brusqueness. Dublin abounds in voices, and anyone can be brusque. What there was for P. J. D'Arcy to contribute was simply the name.

Yet Ellmann's "may have contributed" sticks to his Mark I assertion that there was a more central contributor. The Mark I sentences are still present, and they run,

> Bartell d'Arcy [*sic*], the hoarse singer in the story, was based upon Barton M'Guckin, the leading tenor in the Carl Rosa Opera Company. There were other tenors, such as John McCormack, whom Joyce might

*We now know, for instance, Joyce's height—nearly 5'11", as measured (page 212) by his brother in 1907; not a trivial datum, since the "tall" of report is apt to reflect psychic stature. Ezra Pound, for instance, got routinely described as tall, though he wasn't.

have used, but he needed one who was unsuccessful and uneasy about himself; and his father's oft-told anecdote about M'Guckin's lack of confidence furnished him with just such a singer as he intended Bartell d'Arcy [*sic*] to be.

His father's often-told anecdote? Here a note directs us to page 14 (though that pertains to the old edition and should have been emended to 15–16). There we find a story in which I discern no trace of "M'Guckin's lack of confidence," only a handsome compliment he's said to have paid to a young singer, Joyce's father. (If you praise a comer, does that connote lack of confidence? These values are scrutinizable.) On Ellmann's pages, the story is told as (we are assured) Joyce's father "told and retold" it, in rich Dublin idiom. Was a tape recorder present? Where did the biographer get it? The apposite note (page 747) still says, "Interview with Mr. John Stanislaus Joyce, in Maria Jolas, ed., *A James Joyce Yearbook* (Paris, 1949)."

By now I seem to be picking knots from a tangle of wool, half-doubting if the result is worth the labor. Bear with me. "Interview with Mr. John Stanislaus Joyce": that has become a minor *pons asinorum*. "The authenticity of this interview has been questioned," as the fine print rightly says; "A Dublin writer (Brian O'Nolan) is said to claim he invented it."

So he did; he is better known as "Flann O'Brien," author of *The Third Policeman* and *At Swim-Two-Birds*, and when he was alive he'd double up with laughter when mention of that "interview" let him boast of how he'd hoodwinked the professors. (I never met him; my authority is Harvard's Professor John V. Kelleher, who heard the claim made.) Mme. Jolas has told me the unsigned typescript turned up among James Joyce's papers after his death, and if it was a Brian O'Nolan fabrication, then how it got there remains to be explained. We are deep amid Irish Facts.

Ellmann, dismissing the fabrication theory, asserts that the "interview" is "one of several transcripts of his father's conversation which James Joyce had friends make during the 1920s," but he doesn't tell us where the others are (Southern Illinois University has a few, bare fact lists) nor where, that one time, among his Dublin correspondents, bald writers, however well they may have talked, James Joyce found someone with so miraculous a gift of idiomatic transcription: page after page of vivid monologue. Save with the help of creative endowment on a par with O'Casey's or O'Nolan's, I find I cannot conceive of so rich a flow getting fixed on paper. It's a fishy, though fascinating, document however regarded.

Ellmann rejects an O'Nolan fabrication because he wants to use the "interview." I can sympathize with that; I used it myself, for its color, as long ago as 1956, before I'd commenced to learn about Irish Facts. And no great harm is done the biography? None, save that our confidence in the biographer's criteria may be a trifle dented.

And finally—I draw a long breath—what emerges from this cat's cradle, the one assertion really based on that suspect "interview" that has anything to do with our experience of reading Joyce, is the assertion that "Bartell D'Arcy" was "based upon Barton M'Guckin," because both display lack of self-confidence. But try a more plausible scenario: (1) What caught Ellmann's eye in the "interview" long ago was the likeness of "Barton" to "Bartell." (2) He then needed to justify a pointless allusion Joyce seemed to be making. Reading lack of self-confidence into both the man in "The Dead" and the man in the "interview" was an effort to do that: never mind that both readings are forced. (3) After his book came out he heard from W. P. D'Arcy, a man with a habit of writing to authors of books on Joyce. By Occam's Razor, what W. P. D'Arcy contributed makes the whole elaborate detour unnecessary, including its stubborn defense of the "interview." But (4) all of it is still here, with, courtesy of D'Arcy, a superfluous sticking-plaster affixed. Mark II is billed by the publisher as "the first new edition, thoroughly revised and expanded, of his classic work." At Oxford they know a classic.

If I do not apologize for the small size of the mouse that has emerged from such mountainous heaving, that is because biographies—certainly this one—are made of minutiae, and one needs to watch how they are handled. Mr. Ellmann's handling obeys certain imperatives, as that no good story should be rejected. If many of them are discreditable to the subject that does not mean they are untrue, but one notes of Irish stories as a genre that they tend to be discreditable. Another of his working hypotheses is that James Joyce, whose method of composition was "the imaginative absorption of stray material" (page 250), put down little he'd not actually seen and heard: indeed possessed so little imagination that "imaginative" becomes a word of courtesy.

These principles have midwifed a far bigger and more colorful life of Joyce than we might have thought possible. The second one is especially convenient in licensing the biographer to borrow freely from the fictions when details are needed, secure in his confidence that if they got into Joyce's fictions they were originally facts. Thus, when little Jim was deposited at Clongowes Wood College in 1888, we are told (page 27) how "His tearful mother begged him not to speak to the rough boys; his father reminded him that John O'Connell, his great-grandfather, had presented an address to the Liberator at Clongowes fifty years before. He gave him two five-shilling pieces, and told him never to peach on another boy." When these sentences were first published in 1959 no witness to that occasion survived at all, so the four details can come only from *A Portrait*, to which, sure enough, a note (page 749) seems to attribute one of them.

That one, though, is the address to the Liberator, which *A Portrait* does *not* say was recalled by his father at the college door; it also specifies "granduncle," not "great-grandfather." So the one item of four that's footnoted isn't quite so. Meanwhile the three that are not footnoted slide without notice straight from Joyce's *Portrait* into Ellmann's *Joyce*, there to help out the accumulating impression that James Joyce had not much imagination at all: if only when, in rereading *A Portrait*, we dimly remember those details being in *James Joyce*. (By the way, the five-shilling pieces are a splendid touch in *A Portrait*. Families were living on a pound a week, so "pocket-money" of that order, bestowed on a six year old, would be analogous today to twenty-pound notes.)

So effectively did Mark I project its image of the impressionable drudge that by 1968 a new and startling allegation could pass with no notice at all. That was in Mr. Ellmann's afterword to the Penguin *Ulysses*, where we read on pages 708 to 709:

On the night of 22 June 1904 Joyce (not as yet committed either to Nora or to monogamy) made overtures to a girl in the street without realizing, perhaps, that she had another companion. The official escort came forward and left him, after a skirmish, with "black eye, sprained wrist, sprained ankle, cut chin, cut hand." Next day Joyce lamented to a friend, "For one role at least I seem unfit—that of man of honour." He did not mention what in retrospect evidently became the most impressive aspect of the fracas: he was dusted off and taken home by a man named Alfred Hunter in what he was to call "orthodox Samaritan fashion." This was the Hunter about whom the short story "Ulysses" was to be projected. Presumably that story would have shown Hunter circumnavigating Dublin and, in the end, offering a lifebuoy to a castaway resembling Joyce.

Presumably? Never mind that on a story about a man offering a lifebuoy the title "Ulysses" would have had no point.* Pay heed to the sheer assertion, "he was dusted off and taken home by a man named Alfred Hunter"; note also the dig at Joyce, who (devious fellow) didn't mention it. Now where did that assertion come from? It is not, as casual Penguiners may have supposed, something documented in the Mark I biography. It is not even present there. Yet so persuasive has it been that it's enshrined on a plaque next to Bloom's salvaged front door in The Bailey, Dublin.

So why was it plausible? Partly, because Mark I seemed to have established that what Joyce wrote Joyce had experienced; also because reviews of Mark I ("definitive"; "masterly") made it seem that what Richard Ellmann asserted of Joyce was *so*. And where did it come from? For fourteen years Penguin readers have been content with a byline: Ellmann, the man who knows. But Mark II finally tells us: "If Dublin report can be trusted" (page 161)—a rare concession to the quality of Irish Fact—then we are to believe . . . ah, but our longtime Hunter expert, the ubiquitous W. P. D'Arcy? The note says, "Letter to me from W. P. D'Arcy," who "heard the story from John Joyce" (Jim's father). Also "Other confirmation is lacking" (page 762). I'm sure it is. "You and your fuckin' concert tours."

*Surely the story was to deal with the husband of an unfaithful Penelope, wandering, as Bloom does in episodes four through ten, in the knowledge that he is being cuckolded.

It happened or it did not, and Ellmann has been willing—is still not unwilling—to sponsor the titillating notion that it happened. In two hundred years they will believe it happened. Never mind today's sales, we have our obligation to our posterity. Who, in A.D. 2182, will have the patience, or the resources, to pick this cat's cradle apart? And whoever may try it will surely be assailed for assailing something its own time judged "definitive."

"Definitive," in 1959, was a word that got thrown around rather thoughtlessly by reviewers stunned beneath an avalanche of new information. But there can be no "definitive" biography. Biography is a narrative form: that means, a mode of fiction. Many narratives can be woven from the same threads. Biography incorporates "facts," having judged their credibility. Its criteria for judgment include assessment of sources (here, often, oral sources—Irish Facts) and, pervasively, assessment of one's man.

If one's man was a writer with little imagination, then testimony, however shaky, to an event that turns up in his writing acquires high plausibility. If he was silly and vain, then when he has a stab at medical studies you indulge an otherwise unbottomed sentence about "The daydream of himself as Dr. Joyce, poet, epiphanist, and physician, surrounded by fair women . . ." (page 111): never mind that in 1902 medicine was one of about three available uses for an Irish degree. Earlier (page 97), we were told "The writer, who had Ireland for patient, to anatomize and purge, might plausibly be physician, too. Such a conjunction helped lure Joyce on to what did not prove 'a brilliant career' in medicine." Dissection of motives is not our author's forte.

Was Joyce silly and vain? That judgment seems enforced by many little touches. Mark I, discussing the completion of *A Portrait*, reported a bee Stuart Gilbert had put in the Ellmann bonnet: that "In bringing the book together [Joyce] found unexpected help in Balzac, who made Lucien de Rubembré say in *Splendeurs et misères des courtisanes, 'J'ai mis en pratique un axiome avec lequel on est sûr de vivre tranquille: Fuge . . . Late . . . Tace.'* These Stephen translates as his own watchwords, 'Silence, exile, and cunning.' " Mark II rewrites this (page 354) to insert newer information, that "Fuge, Late, Tace" (= Flee, Hide,

Hush) is the motto of the Carthusians, hence available to Joyce (if indeed he used it; the match is not really good) from a nearer source than Balzac. The Balzacian provenance, though, isn't abandoned; rather, it's newly enforced by a ritual kick at Joyce's ingratitude: "This did not keep him from telling Stanislaus that all the ten novels of Balzac he had read were 'the same formless lumps of putty.'" Since he'd told Stannie that six years before, what didn't prevent what gets a little hard to follow.

Even in accommodating counterevidence, Ellmann seems unwilling to abandon old positions, particularly when they pertain to his subject's insouciance. Mark I told us that in 1914 "The necessity of meeting deadlines for the *Egoist* installments of *A Portrait* spurred Joyce to try to finish that book," and that is something Mark II still says (page 354), though the claim is no longer made "that Joyce, in spite of his good resolutions of 1909, had not yet written the fourth and fifth chapters." One reason for dropping that claim would be the painstaking demonstration by Hans Walter Gabler (nowhere cited) that the book was substantially completed in 1912–13: indeed that, far from struggling to write Part V while the *Egoist* was setting Part I in type, Joyce had in fact recast the Part I they were setting to align it with an already-written Part V.

So what does "spurred Joyce to finish that book" mean? If we let the phrase pertain to small revisions made while the thing got typed, we do not diminish its rhetorical effect. What it does for the casual reader—and after 350 pages *all* readers grow casual—is augment by one further increment the impression of a feckless fellow indeed, one jump ahead of the printer the way his father kept a jump ahead of the bailiff.

Yes, oh dear yes, this is the best Joyce biography we are likely to see. There is no use anyone's thinking of starting over. Ellmann commenced his researches in the nick of time, and has earned our gratitude for all he has preserved. By now hardly any witnesses, save to the last years, are left alive.

No, oh dear no, it is by no means "definitive." It was skewed from the start, for one thing, by a prime source, Stanislaus Joyce. Delete what didn't come from Stannie—from interviews, from his Dublin and Trieste journals, from his cranky *My Brother's Keeper*, from the innumerable letters of his brother's he preserved and made available to the biographer before they were published—and the crucial first half of the book grows thin indeed.

Feckless, sponging, wholly egocentric, mooning after women, cavalierly putting off till tomorrow: that was James A. Joyce as Stannie (understandably) saw him: Stannie with his iron sententiousness and his soul of a tax accountant, who disliked "Circe" and was "bored and repelled" by "Penelope." "The greatest master of English since Milton," was T. S. Eliot's judgment, but it's Stannie's Joyce who shoulders his way to the foreground.

Tone is a delicate matter; we don't want a hagiography. We'd like, though, to feel the presence of the mind that made the life worth writing and makes it worth reading. Ellmann knows well what his predecessor Herbert Gorman seems not to have grasped, that his subject was a very great writer. "This bizarre and wonderful creature," he even calls him in the Mark II preface, "who turned literature and language on end." That seems insufficient, as, regrettably, does Mark II.

Joyce on the Continent

New York Times Book Review, *mid-1979. Joyce using the* Irish Times *to keep his body warm may have prompted Beckett's Molloy, whose insulator of choice was the* Times Literary Supplement.

PORTRAITS OF THE ARTIST IN EXILE:
RECOLLECTIONS OF JAMES JOYCE BY
EUROPEANS, *edited by Willard Potts. Illustrated.
Seattle: University of Washington Press, 1979. 304 pp.*

First witness: "He drooped like a rag. He looked around as if he were lost. He was as passive as a repentant sinner and exuded humility. Walking the streets with his head in the clouds or entering the classroom with a pious bow, pinched face, and sheep's eyes, he looked like the Grand Black Knight in the Lodge of Benevolent Death."

Thank you. Next witness please. "He was always hastening from house to house to give their hour of English to all the Triestines. Energetic and punctual in his work, devoted to his wife, his children, and his house, he was remarkable for his sobriety."

Recall the first witness please. "I had to watch helplessly the spectacle of a good man reduced to nothing . . . I had to accept the situation and smell Joyce's alcoholic breath, while in chorus with the other drunkards he roared a high-pitched, out-of-tune,

> Ancora un litro di quel bon
> Che no go la ciave del porton.

Roughly translated:

> Of the good stuff let's have more
> Because I've lost the key to my door.

Not, as you might suppose, reports on three different men, but three views of the same man, James Joyce, at the same period in his life. Parallax, you see. Observed from different angles, Gestalts alter. And Joyce not only employed the parallactic principle in his books, he seems to have found a way to incarnate it. Look at five different photographs of Joyce and you may feel unconvinced that they show the same man. And if he could bewilder a lens, it is unsurprising that to different human observers he presented aspects as divergent as any two of the contours we get on Leopold Bloom in *Ulysses*.

In *Portraits of the Artist in Exile*, Willard Potts has collected seventeen accounts by thirteen authors of half-a-dozen nationalities: an exemplary job of selecting, annotating, and indexing. (Connoisseurs of the index should study this one, which seems able to retrieve from the text any piece of trivia you remember having noticed.)

Some of these eyewitnesses reconstruct conversations from careful notes, some from a memory colored by the discovery that the long-ago Irishman was somebody important. Some write from affection, some from curiosity. One or two simply perform, with clownish abandon, while down at the foot of the page the harried editor issues correction bulletins.

In some minds facts mutate like Silly-Putty. "Marvellous Joyce!" Louis Gillet exclaims. "Not long since a friend showed me on the heights of Dublin, in a shabby and triangular square decorated by a puny linden tree, the shanty where he was born sixty years ago. A sad

cradle, conveying a recent downfall, a shameful distress, the most lu-
gubrious of all miseries. . . . " On and on.

But not so fast. Writing in 1941, Gillet has his friend's age wrong by
a year. And Brighton Square, Rathgar, is not situated on heights of
any description, and neither "shanty" nor the French word Gillet
used (*bicoque*) applies to what we may find at No. 41, a two-story brick
row house with a bay window, in a district that is still genteel and in
1882 was a bright, modern subdivision, by no means to be associated
with "shameful distress."

The "Square" is indeed almost triangular, and I'm not sure about
the linden tree. Otherwise, every fact in this effusion is wrong. The
editor's footnoted correction—"a 'modest and comfortable' house in
the Dublin suburb of Rathmines"—is wrong, too: Rathmines is not
Rathgar, and the social difference goes deeper than the orthographi-
cal. The editor's attempt to set Louis Gillet straight was indebted, by
bad luck, to an early printing of the Ellmann biography, another book
permeated by hearsay: (In the current printing the hero is no longer
born in the wrong suburb, but he's still baptized in a church that
didn't then exist).

Our chance ability to correct the biography here should alert us to
the innumerable occasions when there's no way to check it at all. "The
unfacts, did we possess them, are too imprecisely few to warrant our
certitude," as Joyce wrote in *Finnegans Wake*. Picked apart into molecular facts, human testimony about anything whatever is apt to yield
little save contradictions, only rarely to be settled by so decisive an experiment as going to look at a brick building.

Seventeen testamentary performances, though, have more to offer
us than a buzz of unfacts. Out of the very contradictions a kind of hol-
ogram of Joyce emerges. For we get a sense of different people talking:
of who they are, of how their memories work, of what they respond to
and how scrupulously. Though Louis Gillet's official credentials included membership in the French Academy, it's an enthusiast's voice
that emanates from his pages; the voice of a riser to rhetorical occasions, and what we learn about Joyce is chiefly that Joyce could inspire
such paroxysms of enthusiasm in a mind so generously inexact.

Jacques Mercanton, by contrast, soon earns our trust in his recreation of tones and nuances, as on the day he remarked Joyce's blackthorn cane: "Whenever he seated himself, he slid it between his legs; then he remained motionless, like a bird hooked onto a branch, his eye on the lookout and yet distracted. One never knew what he was looking at or what he saw." That's the aging Joyce of 1936, and so is this, also recorded by Mercanton: "One evening, while we were waiting for him in the hotel lobby, Mrs. Joyce described Joyce to me as he was when she met him for the first time in Dublin, many years before: his expression strange and severe, an overcoat that hung down to his feet, shoes down at the heel, a big, white sombrero. She drew his portrait with tender irony, astonished that a long life together, every instant shared (for they were seldom apart), had not effaced that fleeting image. 'He is old,' she said gently, 'but he has not changed much. In so many ways, he is a little boy, as you have noticed.'"

The man who once faulted Goethe's "no-age Faust" had himself aged ambiguously. Mercanton's "little boy" is the Joyce of the final harsh years, 1936 to 1941. A decade earlier, Nino Frank met "an old man" (of forty-four!) who got strangely younger ("a blind adolescent") upon acquaintance.

He could be aloof when he wanted, everyone agrees. Frank recalls him addressing "perfectly interchangeable remarks" to grandmasters of literary politics who came to pay their respects. They would leave "shrugging their shoulders." Callers who had won his trust were permitted to see whimsical customs. One day Joyce (who, according to Frank, kept in practice as a polyglot by "daily skimming through four or five of the most important European newspapers, among others the *Osservatore Romano*") despatched Mercanton on an errand. They were in Lausanne, and he wanted the *Irish Times*. By some miracle, one turned up.

"Rather proud of myself, I took it to him at once. His face lit up.

"'You will see how indispensable that paper is to me.' And half unfolding it in one supple gesture, he slid it under his coat, against his back. 'Nothing will keep you warmer than that. Provided it's a good newspaper.' Then he reassured me. 'It doesn't hurt the paper. When you are ready to read it, you will find that no harm has been done.'"

It was the ads he meant to put to use. *Finnegans Wake* needed the addresses of some Dublin laundries.

Dublin. "Every day in every way," he wrote a Dublin friend in 1937, "I am walking along the streets of Dublin and along the strand. And 'hearing voices.'" His exile has been much exaggerated. Of the 707 months he spent on earth, a surprising 275—some 39 percent—were passed in Ireland. Though data for a Yeatsian computation are not accessible, I'd be surprised to learn that the poet of "The Tower" lived as much as a third of his days in the country where he was at pains to get himself thought of as the National Poet.

Yeats kept popping in, and, by continuous brief returns to Ireland, created the illusion of continuous presence there. Joyce seems never to have thought of returning after the 1914 publication of *Dubliners*. He was being eminently practical; when he said "I am not taking any chances with my fellow countrymen if I can possibly help it," he was surely reflecting that he had peopled his books with countless identifiable people, many under their actual names, and that Irishmen, living amidst strict libel laws, dearly love the theatrics, and the vengeance, of bringing suit.

Practical always—"it was he who took charge, who settled things," Mercanton reports—he settled as if for keeps into various countries, mastered languages, read papers; was never merely the displaced Irishman, impressed several witnesses even as not acting especially Irish: inconspicuous, rather, self-restrained, not "Celtic." He seems to have been happiest in Trieste, and it's a pity that it's from Trieste that we have our scantiest testimony: nine austere pages from Silvio Benco, forty of tedious clowning from Francini Bruni. In these images of the "European" Joyce, it's the Paris Joyce that bulks largest, naturally, since men sought him out there after his fame.

The Dublin Joyce is well known. So is the Zurich Joyce, thanks to Frank Budgen's magnificent forty-five-year-old book. The fullness of the Trieste Joyce may elude us forever. The Paris Joyce, though, and a needful sense that whatever the Joyce of the moment there were always other Joyces, *Portraits of the Artist in Exile* brings home as never before.

Classics by the Pound

Harper's, *August 1982. And the Library of America goes* on.

Late this spring, tense in their cubicles, lips moving carefully, American book-page editors and their proofreaders were learning to spell "Pléiade," a word that kept jumping out at them from the flackery while forklifts trundled toward stockrooms the first four volumes in the Library of America.

The book I have just taken from my jacket pocket is Volume II of *Oeuvres de Flaubert* in the esteemed French series Bibliothèque de la Pléiade. Seven-eighths of an inch thick, it weighs twelve ounces. The pages are four inches wide, six and three-quarters high, and there are a surprising 1,008 of them. Anywhere I open it the book lies flat, to display forty-three lines of highly legible text on a page that doesn't look crowded. Despite the extreme thinness of the sheet, what is printed on the reverse side doesn't show through. The gathering? Neatly sewn signatures, with a woven, green marker attached. The binding? Flexible plastic-coated green leatherette, gold-stamped. The paper? I see no sign that it has discolored in thirty-four years. When I paid twelve Canadian dollars decades ago there was also a dust jacket, long since lost.

Flaubert's fiction consists of just six books, and Pléiade's Volume II contains three of them complete, in texts specially established for the series by two expert editors, who have also supplied historical and biographical introductions, textual and explanatory notes, appendices, and bibliographies: everything you'd want for serious reading. Volume I, all the rest of Flaubert's oeuvre, is somewhere upstairs.

That there was no American Pléiade seemed a scandal to the late Edmund Wilson, who as long ago as 1962 drew up a project for "bringing out in a complete and compact form the principal American classics." He did not envisage gestures of commemoration, just simple availability for books not to be found. "The only collected edition of Melville," he wrote, "was published in England in the Twenties and has been long out of print; and there is not, and has never been, of Henry James and Henry Adams any complete collected edition at all." A book here, a book there, and a long silence in between, was the best America did for the authors it claimed to be proud of.

"The kind of thing I should like to see," said Wilson, "would follow the example of the Editions de la Pléiade, which have included so many of the French classics, ancient and modern, in beautifully produced and admirably printed thin-paper volumes, ranging from 800 to 1,500 pages. These volumes, published by Gallimard, have evidently been commercially successful, for they are to be seen in every bookstore in Paris."

After two foundations had said no, the National Endowment for the Humanities said yes, and then something bureaucratic happened. Somehow, as Wilson understood it, a conspiracy of boondogglers doing business as the Modern Language Association Center for the Editions of American Authors contrived to get his funding suppressed in favor of a project of their own.

This was solemnly denied all round. Honest Injun, nobody at the MLA Center knew where Wilson's money had gone; all they knew was that they and platoons of honest toilers were indeed at work on diligent MLA-approved editions of Hawthorne, Melville, Howells, et al., with results Wilson was quick to deride. The books were whimsically chosen, he charged, outrageously expensive, and bespattered with the flyspecks of a ludicrous pedantry. A page looked like "something between an undecoded Morse message and a cuneiform inscription."

He was especially funny about eighteen Twain editors reading *Tom Sawyer*, word for word, backward, "in order to ascertain, without being diverted from this drudgery by attention to the story or the style, how many times 'Aunt Polly' is printed as 'aunt Polly,' and how many times 'ssst!' is printed as 'sssst!'" Since the MLA had ordained that "plain texts"—books you just *read*—were to await the establishment of "critical texts"—books that with full display of evidence sift out printer's errors and restore lost auctorial revisions—we'd be waiting, he estimated, "a century or longer."

If not exactly what Edmund Wilson envisaged, the Library of America has taken less time than that. "An American Pléiade," cried *The New York Times Book Review* last July, examining a crystal ball thoughtfully provided by the project's board. It seems that in 1979 the Ford Foundation and the National Endowment for the Humanities put up the kind of seed money Wilson had angled for, and the resulting books would be "in every way comparable to their French counterparts." No longer would visitors from abroad have to ask of American literature, "Where is it? And how can I take it home?" A great wrong, said the *Times*, would be set right, "and one of the capstones of American civilization put firmly in place."

Now that the first four titles are available, we can examine the Pléiade analogy. Here are three Melville novels in one volume (*Typee, Omoo, Mardi*), and when I lay down my Pléiade Flaubert to pick it up, I'm aware of hefting something *very heavy*. Thirty-one ounces, says the same kitchen scale that assessed the Flaubert at twelve. A two-pound book is not a thing you hold in your hand to read. You'll want a table. (If your bifocals have the right prescription, a lap will do.)

Where did that weight come from? Part of it from more pages: 1,342 as against 1,008. But one-third more pages would raise the Flaubert to a mere sixteen ounces, still a two-to-one lightness advantage. So what else? Well, the Melville pages are bigger, 4⅞ by 7⅞, and the book is much thicker: an inch and three-quarters. That means (1) there is no way it can be squeezed into a jacket pocket; (2) Melville, to be dankly physical about his fate, has been entombed in a block of acid-free wood pulp that uses up sixty-seven cubic inches of space, as against Flaubert's mere twenty-four. The *whole* of Flaubert—I've just found the second volume—totals fifty-four cubic inches, total weight twenty-seven ounces. You could stick half his oeuvre in each pocket and hardly notice.

But when the Melville part of the project is completed—four volumes—the *Times*'s hypothetical Frenchman who takes it home by air will find that the works of only one author leave him no space for less bulky souvenirs. He (or anyone) will find reading Melville physically uncomfortable for another reason. The excellent typeface has been imposed with scant regard for the "gutter," the center valley where facing pages meet. Those center margins are so narrow for so thick a book that parts of words disappear into the gutter unless you *force* the thing open *flat*.

No Library of America volume will get tossed into a knapsack. Too bricklike. If (speaking of gutters) rain falls onto the binding (imported Dutch-dyed rayon), it will stain; raindrops on a Pléiade you merely wipe off. The paper, however, will last "for generations," so if you don't wear the books out with reading or let them get rained on, you can build an estate, the "personal library" one of the brochures mentions.

An American product just a little too cumbersone for normal maneuvers: that may sound familiar, and lead you to wonder if the Library of America was by any chance designed in Detroit. Scrutiny of the press kit from Gail Rentsch Public Relations, 527 Madison Avenue, leaves me unable to say. The text was laid out by Bruce Campbell, whose past credits include part of the beautiful Bollingen series; the jackets are by Robert Scudellari with calligraphy by Gun Larson (according to my spies, two of the most expensive people in their line of work). But the overall physical package? No one is saying. Possibly a committee.

If so, its collective unconscious envisaged a buyer who thinks the Pléiades rather *light* for the money: someone requiring a substantial object for his twenty-five dollars ($19.95 by subscription through

Time-Life Books), but with no immediate plans to spend hours reading, and certainly no intention of taking Melville along, the way the
footloose in France take a Pléiade, on an airplane trip or a backpacking
weekend.*

But suppose someone insists on reading. Is he offered editorial
help? Yes, some. A five-page Melville chronology, a four-page note on
the texts, seven and a half pages of textual and explanatory notes ("Sabine atrocity: The legendary rape of the Sabine women by the followers of Romulus, legendary founder of Rome"; dig the caution of that
double "legendary"). Introductions, we are told, have been omitted
because they date, and these books are to stay "permanently in
print": it's unclear, though, what need date about the introductions
we get in the Pléiade Flaubert, a compact arraying of facts about when
the novels got written and what they drew on. Melville's three Pacific
romances, which came partly from identifiable source books, partly
from what he saw after he jumped ship in 1842 in the Marquesas,
seem to ask for just such preliminaries.

As for the texts, they are plain text, i.e., "reading," derivations
from one of the projects Edmund Wilson hooted at, the MLA-
Northwestern-Newberry editions of 1968–70, and the "Note on the
Texts" makes it clear that straightening out *Typee* in particular was a
nasty job. It entailed getting rid of second-edition changes Melville
made to calm a nervous American publisher (e.g., "lovely houris" for
"naked houris") while trying to save other revisions he'd have made
anyway. An editor would want to calibrate these changes with the
help of the initial manuscript. But that has vanished, and for their
"control" version of *Typee*—the only source for restoring numerous
cut passages—the editors had to make do with a British edition that,
in the course of being typeset from the lost manuscript, got infested
with British spellings and usages. They persevered while Wilson
grumbled, and the Library of America text of *Typee* is the best we're
likely to get.

---

*A friend writes: "Over the past several years I've put up a number of visitors from
France. They have never failed to have a volume of the series shoved somewhere in the
shoulder bag carried aboard."

The other three inaugural volumes are uniform with the Melville; just as heavy, just as scrupulous. They include a Hawthorne (Volume I of four), a Stowe (three novels, including *Uncle Tom's Cabin*), and—especially notable—a Whitman *Complete Poetry and Collected Prose*, which wisely uses 145 pages to reprint the 1855 *Leaves of Grass*, the anonymous twelve-part poem Emerson thought "the most extraordinary piece of wit and wisdom America has yet contributed." Though *Leaves of Grass* subsequently became Walt's title for his ongoing interminable callithumpian collected poetry (here given in the final 1892 version), the integrity of that first sequence deserves the separate emphasis editor Justin Kaplan has accorded it.

Future volumes will include James in eight volumes, Emerson in four, Twain in six, Poe in two, Henry Adams in four . . . does the roll call sound familiar? It does, despite the inclusion of Jack London (two volumes, and billed as "the most inclusive collection available"). *That*, let us face it, is officially American Literature: something safely embalmed and (with London as wild card) long since defined at Harvard. Dead a mere sixty-five years, Henry James in that company seems ultramodern. Hemingway? Faulkner? Scott Fitzgerald? Pound? Olson? William Carlos Williams? (And what of Tom Eliot? Does he count as American? He abandoned his citizenship, but so did James.)

One difference between Jack London and Hemingway is that London was a storyteller and Hemingway was a "writer," what the French call an *écrivain*. Another is that Hemingway's copyrights were long ago sewed up by Charles Scribner's Sons. One difference between Pound and Whitman is that a legal committee controls every syllable of Pound's that gets into print. A proposal for a university press Ezra Pound, many volumes of texts to be straightened out and annotated, was scrapped a while back when the committee said no.

And one difference between Harriet Beecher Stowe (1811–96) and Ross Macdonald (1915–) is that Macdonald, in devising his fables of modern identity, wrote them as things called "detective stories," handled at Harvard with tongs, whereas Mrs. Stowe's famous eleven-Kleenex tract, sanctified by a testimonial of Lincoln's, soars aloft into the Disneyfied sunsets of Literature. So the matter stands in 1982. But in a hundred years, if this series is still around, it either will have atrophied into total irrelevance or else will have managed to embalm three novels by Ross Macdonald. Just watch. And you read it here first.

So what are our classics? Somehow the canon first got defined in New England, and its epicenter located in Concord, Massachusetts. (Still, in a prospectus that runs to spring 1984 I don't see Thoreau mentioned, or Emily Dickinson. The only edition of Dickinson to consider is owned by Harvard's Belknap Press, who have their own "plain text" version in print. Is that perhaps a problem?)

Ezra Pound thought the Concord canon unconvincing. *Real* American literature, he used to argue, stemmed not from a gaggle of New England clergymen's families and their acolytes but from Thomas Jefferson and John Adams, notably their correspondence. (Jefferson is listed for fall 1983: one volume. No John Adams. Henry, yes.)

But however we define its past, American Literature became an indisputable entity at about the time it entered the international mainstream, first with James and then with overlapping generations born late in Whitman's lifetime: Pound's own generation and its immediate juniors, Pound-Eliot-Williams-Moore and Faulkner-Hemingway-Fitzgerald. Then Oppen-Zukofsky-Reznikoff followed, then Olson-Creeley . . . I've skipped names, but one pattern is clear. It continues to the Beats, e.g., Ginsberg, Michael McClure, Gary Snyder, who like Whitman often pretended semiliteracy as a way of outflanking the professoriat. (For light on Beatdom, see Michael McClure's new collection, *Scratching the Beat Surface*, published by North Point Press. McClure's becoming the Beats' elder statesman.)

The Library of America is perforce a bureaucratic enterprise, and bureaucratizing the realities of the past eighty years confronts it with special problems. One is copyrights. The Pléiade series, to revert to that one more time, includes a number of twentieth-century French writers—Proust, Valéry, Claudel, Gide, Camus. But these are Gallimard authors, and Gallimard publishes Pléiade. One reason there is no Pléiade Beckett may be that his French publisher is Editions de

Minuit. And if so far the Library of America's formal announcements make no mention of anybody later than Henry James or Jack London (who coincidentally died in the same year, 1916), one reason may be that unlike Pléiade/Gallimard, it has no automatic access to any publisher's active list.

Another difficulty inheres in the word "American," which as used on expensive books adorned with a tri-color band connotes something we all agree on without thinking, a remote whole haziness with Lincoln somewhere near the middle and Teddy Roosevelt at the outermost bound. As Jack Kennedy is said to have said of the project back when Edmund Wilson was pushing it, "I know that its fulfillment will do a great deal to display, both to our own people and to the world, the richness of the American literary heritage." That does sound presidential. (And "JFK Supported the Idea," runs a heading in a press release.)

JFK's key word is "display," and once these shelf-fillers are on display, what next? The flack sheets offer come-ons for looking inside, behind which no particular conviction is discernible. Of *Mardi*: "Tracing the quest for the elusive and beautiful Yillah, it remains a timely political allegory and a thrilling adventure." Of Hawthorne: ". . . astonishingly contemporary . . . the reader at the end is left in a kind of awe at the multiple possibilities of meaning." Of racial violence in *Uncle Tom's Cabin*: "some of the brooding imagination and realism that anticipates Faulkner's rendering of the same theme." Of Whitman: "elegiac, comic, furtive, outrageous." Such boiler plate is stamped from the very dies they use at the Classics Club to shill Aristotle, "this wise old Greek." We have brought you the packages, tied in red, white, and blue. They are substantial two-pound packages. We have even told you what thrills lurk within. Now let us all quietly contemplate America.

The trouble with more contemporary books is that, read or not, they arouse passions. Did misgivings leap in your blood when I spoke of including Ross Macdonald? That's what I mean. And the howl over "Howl"—*American?*"; I can hear it from here. There are remarks in *Uncle Tom's Cabin* fit to raise Jewish hackles ("One would think you had taken lessons of the Jews, coming at a fellow so!"), but Pound in the Library of America is what would trigger letters to congressmen. By unspoken consensus, books a century old are safe. Transfer them to acid-free paper bound with the grain and Smyth-sewn, and lo, a capstone of American civilization, firmly in place, Grant's Tomb.

Images
at Random

From the December 1977 Harper's, *which slyly noted how the* Columbia Encyclopedia, *fourth edition, page 276, cites me as "High Kenner." (For how such things grow routine, look back at "Up from Eden-
ism.") I concentrated on mathematical examples because they seemed
exempt from vagaries of opinion. At Random House this piece seems to
have been read, since a later printing corrects most of what I fingered.*

The new *Encyclopaedia Britannica* (fifteenth edition, volume x, page
401) has a caption under a cut of Jules Verne that identifies him as *Au-
riparus flaviceps* (in Texas, the yellow-headed titmouse), photo courtesy National Audubon Society. For to package information is to court
perils. Letterpress printing, for one thing, converts everything it can
process, images and winged words alike, into rectangles of lead
someone's hand can mix up.

Or someone's eye can tire. The newest *Columbia Encyclopedia*
(fourth edition, page 1,434), in the course of updating its entry on
James Joyce, managed to misspell his bibliographer's name once, the
title of his last book twice, the name of his biographer three times.

These aren't blotches like Simth for Smith but errors that look okay if you don't know, and one-volume works of reference (with the notable exception of Eric Partridge's dictionaries) are in general neither written nor checked by people who know. Their millions of words are condensed out of various sources by clerks in a hurry, assailed by the clack of one another's typewriters, beset by deadlines, harried by word counts. The "experts" whose mysterious proximity gets ritual acknowledgment up front have better things to do than fit a selection of remarks about Bach or Wittgenstein into three-and-a-half column inches.

Onto this minefield, bright-eyed and brassy-cheeked, *The Random House Encyclopedia* has now made its bravura entry, propelled by a $1 million ad campaign (324 TV spots in six weeks) and hyped as "a 'family bible' of knowledge for our times" quite as though there were no problems at all. There are plenty.

What they've been doing at Random House, it turns out, is spending $1.5 million to make what can be sold as an encyclopedia out of the American rights to an "art bank" of several thousand four-color visuals, some banal, some stunning in their intricacy, which the transatlantic originators at one time didn't quite know what to do with.

Anyone old enough, like me, to remember G. H. Davis's cutaway drawings of ships in the long-ago *Illustrated London News*, or young enough, like my son, to be thrilled by John Batchelor's loving dissections of planes and tanks in the current *Purnell World War Specials*, can respect a British tradition of visual explication—the right word, since it means "unfolding." The richest of these drawings unfold an object—a layered Roman road, the vaults of a mosque, a locust's anatomy—with patient detail and command over perspectives no eye has ever seen. You can look at, and through, and into; on page 1,738 of the new book you can examine the painted decor of a trireme, its above-deck engines of assault, its warriors in their armor; then study, beneath peeled-off planking, the jointure of wooden ribs, and (deeper inside) the rowers' benches, the black rhythm-keeper with his twin drums, the captain's wine store. It can take a half-hour to fully absorb such a picture, and must have taken the artist a week to execute it.

Whistling up that kind of artist and other kinds was a house skill at Mitchell Beazley, the British publishers of *The Joy of Sex*, *The World Atlas of Wine*, and other feats of biblio-gourmandise. They got ambitious, and a few years ago, with financing from a Dutch firm that envisioned artwork for a twenty-volume encyclopedia, they had close to 275 people bent over layout boards, trying to arrange the joy of knowledge into two-page spreads. Sixty-five percent of all human learning had become visual, somebody involved had been told by somebody.

With a lot of talent and money backing a wholesale commitment to the visual, nobody wanted to reflect that some subjects are more visual than others. Elementary astronomy is chiefly things to look at, and on sixty layouts it comes through brilliantly: star maps, telescopes, a cutaway Skylab, stark renderings of how remote looming planets would look from their inhospitable satellites. Human anatomy in forty-five layouts is another triumph. The novel in the nineteenth century, on the other hand—like it or not, it's words, words, and a painting of Zola can convey no more than a thoughtful dandy with a beard, leaving the caption to make kiddie points ("Naturalists believed writers should portray the brutality of industrial life").

Worse, themes like "Industry and Economics" haven't even faces to offer, yet must be made visual; hence jazzy graphs which would serve to clarify a thoughtful text, dominating a text which must try to make sense of them. By 1975, when Random House bought in, the distinction between what pictures can do and what they can't had simply been wished away, in a package that looked too succulent to question.

Random House sensed difficulties that might lie low if the user could somehow effect entry through the alphabet. Since the alphabet was what Mitchell Beazley had hoped to leave behind, this seemed to mean swinging the whole drifting project around stem to stern, but though you're nudged toward imagining geniuses aleap naked ("Eureka!") from Random House tubs, what got done was simple enough. The 1,750 pages of visuals retained their sequential flow, and a made-in-the-U.S.A. section got annexed: 822 pages of ordinary verbal lookups, more or less haphazardly referenced to the color. Each part, it was hoped, would make up for the other's deficiencies. They were christened Colorpedia and Alphapedia, thus conferring a certain wan glow on a Pyrrhic victory.

What with "Flags of the World," an atlas, a time chart; a bibliography, it all comes to 2,856 pages, four inches of thickness, nearly twelve pounds to lift and flop open on a sturdy table, with a special binding that restrains sag when the monster is stood upright, and a price tag ($69.95) that makes premotivation of the buyer essential.

That, too, has been seen to. The pretested commercial made 60 percent of control groups in metropolitan shopping malls say they felt an urge to head for a bookstore, and since 50 million are expected to watch the commercial you may wonder why only 175,000 books have been printed. That figure reflects, presumably, an estimate of how many copies bookstores can afford to stockpile to meet the pre-Christmas rush TV is meant to churn up. The bookstore is the publisher's unpaid warehouse, and the Random House sales plan (notably the single-volume format, unique among the dozen-odd Mitchell Beazley clients), stakes everything on bookstore sales. Colorpedia, Alphapedia, TV—it adds up to an Archimedean feat of marketing, the earth moved without a demonstrable place to stand on, and Jess Stein, a sometime word-man who edited *The Random House Dictionary* before assuming editorial directorship of the new enterprise, now affirms in a convert's tone, "We all feel that this is how people learn today—visually." They learn, sure enough, that visually is how they learn. That leaves the Alphapedia to one side.

With entries so short they average thirty per page, the Alphapedia—cousin to those one-volume fact books writers use to verify a spelling, fill in a date—is less for learning from than for firming up what you know already. As such it's a quintessential alphabet-keyed resource.

When the notion of alphabetical access crystallized in the eighteenth century, it helped establish the corollary notion that knowledge is assembled out of units called facts. The great encyclopedic minds of antiquity—Aristotle, Cicero, Confucius—wouldn't have known what a fact was. They beheld a kaleidoscope of interacting principles in which no event stays still to have its tail salted, though sometimes process can be caught on the wing with a statement like "Nature abhors a vacuum" or "The good is enemy to the best." Study led to slow understanding, and might entail the study of virtually everything.

But the alphabetized reference book, in permitting you to start reading anywhere and stop almost immediately, is meaningless unless in your skim and dip you can pick up something substantial. What you pick up is a "fact" or several. Fact (from the Latin *factum*, "done") once meant something like "feat," a kindred word, and still does in legal usage; the detective who wants the facts is asking what people *did*. But new customs demanded a new usage, and a fact in a reference book is something over and done with, stuffed, on display, and still; one sort of ultimate fact is a corpse. Since number is our sturdiest rhetoric for the unchanging, a date is a welcome sort of fact; so is a name correctly spelled, a word defined, a bit of genealogy. Look under "Aisha" in the Alphapedia and you find: "AISHA (611–678), the favorite of the 12 wives of the Prophet Mohammed, daughter of abu-Bakr." That's a line made of facts, and when knowledge is reduced to elements of this kind, the meaning of knowledge is substantially altered. Understanding matters less than getting the facts right.

In so compact an array, all facts are of equal importance, since there's no predicting which ones a user will want. Hence all errors are equally catastrophic. The little time I spent spot-checking things I happen to know already makes me wonder if the Alphapedia isn't punctuated with catastrophe, no doubt from having been put together so fast. The reader is told that Georgian Bay has thirty islands (read 30,000); that T. S. Eliot wrote *The Sacred Woods* (read *Wood*); that the date of *Waiting for Godot* is 1956 (French text 1952, English 1954); that two of William F. Buckley's books are *Man, God, and Yale* and *Four Reformists* (read *God and Man at Yale, Four Reforms*); and that his sparring partner John K. Galbraith was born in Iowa Station, Ontario (read Iona). If any of these was the fact you went into the book for, you'd have drawn a wooden nickel from the knowledge bank.

Other stumbles occur midway between fact and judgment. From

the T. S. Eliot entry again: "After the successful reception of his first published poem, *The Love Song of J. Alfred Prufrock* (1917), he devoted the rest of his life to literature as a poet, playwright, critic, and editor." Here not only is the factual peg wrong (the poem was published in 1915; what came out in 1917 was a book called *Prufrock and Other Observations*), the rest would have made Eliot blink with astonishment (in no sense, save among perhaps thirty people, was the book successful, and as late as 1924 he was still slaving in Lloyd's Bank).

Or browse in the forty-six-page time chart. Here are Auden and Spender assigned to "a group of left-wing poets in London in the 20s" (wrong decade; Spender was twenty-one when the twenties ended), and here's Pirandello lending emphasis to the years 1930 to 1932 (wrong decade again: try the twenties). Or check the book's own statements with one another. The commencement date for Pound's *Cantos* is variously given on pages 1,375, 1,869, 2,010; the suggestions span nine years. The birth date of the Victorian computer wizard Charles Babbage depends on whether you consult page 1,672 or page 1,935. Spellings are likewise adrift. The mathematician Fibonacci, right twice, loses a letter on page 1,441; the unit of frequency, hertz, right several times, is herz on page 1,650. Under "Expansion" (mathematics) the series for sin x, an affair of letters and symbols, is several ways wrong.

And so on. Most of the facts are after all correct, but you may feel you'd need another encyclopedia to be sure which ones. Signs of haste are everywhere. Though the Alphapedia was conceived as a finding device for the Colorpedia, it sputters and coughs when asked for that kind of aid. The entry for Buckminster Fuller refers us to Colorpedia page 1,412, where he's nowhere to be found, but not to the Alphapedia entry on geodesic domes, which in turn fails to point to color pictures on pages 1,463 and 1,803 (the latter of which, composed entirely of hexagons, is, by the way, a mathematical impossibility). Numerous goodies, like the beautiful cutaway drawing of the Frank Lloyd Wright Price Tower (page 1,415), aren't cross-referenced from any place I could find. Lacking any general index save the whimsical and spotty Alphapedia, the browser in the color section faces massive frustration of any desire to find something a second time.

Which brings us to the Colorpedia itself, two-thirds of the book, its justification and showpiece, and the locus of its major problems. Pictures, too, are obdurately fact oriented, and between two kinds of commitment to molecular fact whole areas of human experience simply drop out. What to do with Shakespeare? The Alphapedia can give a dated list of his plays, the Colorpedia can show us his face and his playhouse, and neither can really say why he deserves as much attention as the eminently picturable planet Jupiter. The Alphapedia, where a sense of such problems stirs occasionally, does attempt translation of his greatness into fact: he is "the most frequently quoted individual writer in the world."

Where it lacks statistical grist the Alphapedia, still game to try, here and there emits little telltale flatulences. Of Mallarmé: "His style is complex"; of Wallace Stevens: "His work is rich in metaphors and in it he contemplates nature and society" (that won't help you tell Stevens from Rod McKuen). These betray a commendable intuition that some lack in the color spreads wants compensating; that in taking as the unit of presentation two pages with perhaps 1,000 words of text plus ten or so pictures and their captions, the British team made a Procrustean decision, which no amount of talk about user habits (82 percent watch TV, 41 percent read books) can quite justify.

It's true that the spreads offer sequential flow. When you've absorbed "Britain and the Industrial Revolution" (the Crystal Palace, cotton mills, penny postage) you turn the page and find "The Novel in the 19th Century," which makes more sense than turning from Aardvark to Aaron. What makes less sense is the rigid picture-oriented two-page module, over which some themes can be lightly stretched but into which others must be stomped down stunned.

Unpacking such information is a skill not taught by TV. Many pages take more rigorous spells of attention than most reading one can think of, and some are just too compressed to be comprehensible unless you understand them already. The presentation of calculus on pages 1,460–61 would have been a pedagogic triumph if about 2,000 more words had been available. But turn the page for more help and the subject has changed completely. Many earnest students will just give up. Worse, many more will settle for browsing and gaping, and if there's something we don't need in 1977 it's encouragement for yet more citizens to gape as knowledge flows by.

Finally, the decision to keep the Colorpedia self-contained meant fitting many thousand bits of information into the only available spaces, the ones the layout staff had left for captions. This meant, as we learn from the May 9 *Publishers Weekly*, very heavy editing, "to the point of virtual rewriting to fit spaces allotted in the layouts," the artist having determined how many words the writer could have. At *Life*, where the staff faced similar problems weekly, they gradually set up an organization for intricate cross-checking, and rehearsed for years before trying anything really complicated. Starting from scratch, Random House processed 3 million words in less than two years, and the frayed edges show.

Close-checking my way through thirty-odd consecutive pages on mathematics, I found entirely too many snags, each apt to worry the student who, as the text demands, is poring letter by letter: on page 1,450 an apparent misprint in a formula ("fi" for "L"); on page 1,454 a meaningless "right H angles," also a fatal wrong number in the equation for the circle (elsewhere given correctly); on page 1,466. . . . But let's slow down.

"Each word of the encyclopedia," the preface says, "has been read by independent academic advisers." Balderdash. What got read, I'd conjecture, was preliminary drafts, before the cruel space-fitting commenced. If any academic adviser passed what I'm about to quote as it stands, he deserves to have his slide rule broken over Jess Stein's knee at high noon. It's page 1,466, caption 5, attached to a picture of a geometric model, and if you find the subject unfamiliar, what encyclopedias are for is to tell you what you don't know.

> *Uniform polyhedra* can have several different regular polygons contributing to their faces. There are 13 "Archimedean solids" (not counting the infinity of simple prisms allowed by this definition) each of which has a regular polygon top and bottom, joined by square faces around the middle. If faces are allowed to intersect, 53 additional uniform polyhedra result. This one is composed of star-shaped dodecagons and equilateral triangles.

The first sentence will pass. The second, though dead wrong, can be put right if you know enough to move the closing parenthesis down to the end, making "which" refer to prisms, not to solids. The third would be correct if it were clear that the "faces" it mentions aren't the kind mentioned in sentence one (for a good explanation, see Alan Holden, *Shapes, Space and Symmetry*, page 94). The fourth is a disaster. No "star-shaped dodecagons" (twelve-sided figures) are to be discovered in the very pretty photo, and I hate to imagine the misery of the student who thinks he should be finding them. Five-pointed stars, yes. And only some of the triangles are equilateral.

Part of the trouble lies with the model, which seems to have been built for decoration, not pedagogy, and isn't sure whether it's a ditrigonal dodecahedron (none of the triangular faces equilateral) or a small ditrigonal icosidodecahedron (all of them equilateral). The more interesting question is how the words went so wrong. I think I can guess.

There will have been, attached to that photo, an expert page or two on the fancier polyhedra, which will have mentioned that the one illustrated is derived (by "faceting") from the dodecahedron. A non-comprehender in a hurry had to fit bits of this information into twenty-three lines each seven-eighths of an inch long. "Dodecahedron" caught his innocent eye and sponsored the nonsensical "star-shaped dodecagons." And well out of expert eyeshot a caption was born.

If you say "So what?" you don't want an encyclopedia. You want a great big polychromed gee-whiz pacifier sputtering facts and unfacts like a wobbly Roman candle, and this is just your book if you're willing to lift it. It has at least 1,000 good pages, too.

The New Oxford Book
of American Verse

New York Times Book Review, *October 17, 1976*.

THE NEW OXFORD BOOK OF AMERICAN VERSE,
edited by Richard Ellmann. Oxford University Press, 1976.
1,076 pp.

F. O. Matthiessen's *Oxford Book of American Verse* dates from 1950 (Korea, Kaiser-Frazer, the crinoline revival, the ya-ya sound); so a quarter century later we have a new model. That's not as fast as Detroit changes models, but at ten million cars a year, Detroit can exhaust its market pretty fast. Not even an Oxford Book sells at that rate.

Also the Oxford Books have cultivated a kind of Rolls-Royce reputation and can afford a certain indifference to fashion. You still meet the rumor that Rolls seals its engine compartment shut because faults are unthinkable and idle hands shouldn't tinker. *The New Oxford Book of American Verse*, correspondingly, has been welded shut with seventy-eight poets inside, if you count Anon, and seems likely to run till about A.D. 2001. The youngest poet is Leroi Jones, now forty-two, so by that measure the current editor, Richard Ellmann, is a mite less venturesome than was Matthiessen, whose youngest poet, Robert Lowell, was thirty-three and who included an excerpt from the "Pisan Cantos," then only two years in print.

Lowell, fifty-nine, is now an elder statesman, senior to the nearly two dozen poets who populate the last quarter of the new book. And today's anthologist has a Lowell oeuvre at his disposal, whereas Matthiessen had only "Lord Weary's Castle" (1946, the work of a man in his twenties) when he chose eight poems for the old edition.

So it's instructive to check how his nineteen poems in the new anthology correspond to one's sense of Lowell's achievement now. His three decades' effort has been toward a poetic of interaction that rarely stakes everything on the single poem, but pushes single poems to extremes in the knowledge that other poems can qualify them. Representing such a system of tensions in miniature is almost more than one can ask of an anthology but up to a point the new Oxford does it well. Its perspectives have dwindled Lord Weary but not abolished him (three of the eight Matthiessen poems retained). Set pieces of precarious resoluteness ("Waking Early Sunday Morning," "For the Union Dead") seem hollow-cheeked as adjacent poems cross-light them. Sketches of time-trapped eminences (Eliot, Pound, Berryman) consort with the evocations of ruptured domesticity and 4 A.M. weariness that have been part of Lowell's repertoire since "Life Studies."

But what buyers of *The New Oxford* won't find is the Lowell of "Imitations," those phrase-by-phrase Jacob's wrestlings with other times, literatures, languages, possibilities, which invite the reader both to cheer from the ringside and to enter the plight of a poet for whom such encounters offer simultaneously Exit and No Exit from the American Now.

One can think of reasons for leaving them unrepresented. The "Imitations" aren't facile reading. They need the originals to complete them, they are part of an effort Lowell hasn't yet assimilated, many critics didn't like them at all. Having said all that, and said, too, that anthologies are cruelly short of space, one can't help saying something more general, too: that there seems to be an overall system of exclusions: that *The New Oxford Book*'s policy does tend to exclude whatever might furrow a browser's brow or be thought odd.

Thus, the Pound of these pages gets no further than he'd got by 1945 (no "Confucian Odes," no Canto 90 nor 106 nor 110) and is chiefly represented by work that was behind him in 1920. Thus Williams gets only one excerpt that's later than the first book of "Paterson" (1946): none of the "Pictures from Breughel" for instance. Thus, in choosing the poems, one criterion seems to have been entertainment: either an arresting idea ("Johnson's Cabinet Watched by Ants"—Robert Bly) or an amusing texture (Berryman on Wallace Stevens: "Mutter we all must as well as we can / He mutter spiffy"). Poets whose lack of these isn't made up by an inescapable intensity of personal presence (e.g., Sylvia Plath) simply aren't represented. The most conspicuous omissions are Oppen and Zukofsky; it's depressing to find that the most ambitious anthology we are likely to see in this decade is still playing the dreary game of pretending that the authors of "The Materials" and "Anew" don't exist.

"A number of the choices, and of the exclusions, may be controversial," Mr. Ellmann concedes near the end of his introduction. Since (unlike Matthiessen) he has nothing to say about principles of selection apart from a casual remark about "intrinsic merit," controversy has just two options. It can quarrel piecemeal with the anthologist's taste, or it can look for an unstated principle and consider the merits of that. And a principle does seem discernible: Mr. Ellmann, it's defensible to guess, thought it altogether unwise to perplex his reader, a reader far less sure of compass bearings than the reader Matthiessen envisaged in 1950.

And truly, in 1950, certain things seemed altogether clear. There was a major poet living, T. S. Eliot, who had recently finished his major poem, "Four Quartets." And Eliot had created not only a body of work but a milieu. In the process of reintroducing living speech, Eliot had made a seventeenth-century manner accessible, and Donne's way, Marvell's way, shored the procedures of substantial second-level poets like Tate and Ransom. This meant, as Matthiessen formulated it, school-of-Poe, school of craftsmanship, and by defining a contrasting school, school-of-Whitman, school of inclusiveness, he was able to note how Dr. Williams in New Jersey continued Eliot's work, keeping poetry open to "every ordinary fact." Whitman and Poe divided their posterity between them (though Frost was hard to place). The job of the anthologist was to sum and celebrate these clarities.

In 1976, the job of the anthologist is apparently to permit, like the Viking Lander, an introductory look-round at terrain whose contours and geology are far from clear. Whereas Matthiessen's introduction presupposed a reader who had much American poetry in his head and deserved to know how this sampling had been made, Ellmann's appears to address a reader who is blank about the whole subject and needs reassuring that it has identities of any kind.

Though this may reflect Ellmann's long residence at Oxford among people who frown politely and frostily when Americans mention their poets, it reflects also, probably, a lapsing of the consensus here at home. It was Eliot's name, a quarter century ago, that held the consensus together. Now that one man is no longer *arbiter elegantarum*, nor yet the poet new poets imitate, the present is less easy to characterize, and so is the considerable portion of the past, which our apprehension of the present controls.

Looking to Ellmann's introduction for his working historical model of the twentieth century, we find him talking of the first fifty years as dominated by a kind of composite eminence—Frost, Stevens, Williams, Pound, Eliot—and unable to state with any clarity what came afterward. "There was a sense"—when? sensed by whom?—"that the earlier poets of the century had aimed to become modern classics, and in so doing had lost touch with the immediate and unkempt." It's hard to know how to square this with the earlier statement that Williams "celebrated immediacy, 'contact' with 'those things which lie under the direct scrutiny of the senses, close to the nose.'"

Next we are told that Eliot, in later life, "acknowledged with needless embarrassment and humility that 'The Waste Land' was for him only a personal and wholly insignificant grouse against life." It was no longer impersonal, then. It's not clear how Eliot's change of heart (not printed till after his death) changes a 1922 poem, but the incident seems to be offered as a turning point, to introduce some remarks about "confessional" poets (Lowell, Plath).

Then "Pound had spoken of a 'consciousness disjunct,' but Pound was not greatly interested in the unconscious or in the disjunctiveness between it and the conscious mind. For some poets this unconscious is rather the archaic survivals into the present: Olson justifies considering the geological remains that form Gloucester, as Snyder sees the temper of Oxford and Cambridge in terms of the 'strata that underlie them.'" But (1) Pound's "consciousness disjunct" had nothing at all to do with the unconscious, its disjunctiveness being that between intermittent perceptions; (2) the poet of the Oxford and Cambridge strata isn't Gary Snyder but Ed Dorn, under whose name the passage is duly anthologized.

". . . And of course there are excellent poets who resist even these general classifications."

One prods such statements not to mock their paraplegia but to marvel at the introducer's plight. Until we saw it tried we should hardly have guessed how impossible it is to give the naive reader what the naive reader is judged to want, an intelligible, historical account into which the poems he's likely to find appealing will fit. Perhaps the unit of attention is inappropriate: perhaps reader and anthologist should be taking more interest in textures and voices, less interest in achieved poems that begin and end (Charles Olson's sense of things tended that way).

Or perhaps the problem inheres in the reader's state of preparation. Yeats, on whom Mr. Ellmann has written so influentially, remarked long ago on the immense amount of acquired tradition even simple lyrics presuppose: tradition the candlestickmaker hasn't absorbed (so he "doesn't like poetry"). Williams, Pound, and Stevens— to name just three—spent each a long lifetime both learning a way to write and teaching us how to read what was written that way. If we haven't learned—well, anthologists sense our predicament and just leave their late work out, all but Stevens's, which commanded a deceptive tranquility.

If it's true that poets can no longer be read in excerpts before we've mastered their whole systems (and it's certainly not true of all poets: I state the extreme case) then it's useless for anthologies to offer what this one seems to offer, an introductory sampling. A handy compendium of what we already admire, that would be something feasible; but not a *vade mecum*.

And the situation in 1976, when we find a potentially large readership that is unequipped to read the most characteristic poetry of its own time, may be temporary merely. Mysteriously, today's best undergraduates dig what baffles their parents. We may be just between two generations of literary understanding: such generations seem often to be spaced fifty years apart. In that case *The New Oxford Book*, perhaps prompted by Bicentennial doings, got born a quarter century prematurely, and the publishers may take heart at the thought of 2001.

In the Dymaxion Anthology of that year, what thresholds may we expect, what antinomies? Robert Lowell will by then be eighty-four, and the clamorous young will have pushed him clear back to the middle of the book. Book? Will it be a multichromed microfiche? A 3-D videotape? It will surely start anyway, like its two predecessors, with Anne Bradstreet's

> To sing of Wars, of Captains, and of Kings,
> Of Cities founded, Commonwealths begun,

and the commonwealths it will go on to celebrate will be, at a venture, those commonwealths of the mind that lie just outside the 1976 *Oxford Book*'s grasp.

A New Voice

I found this book by chance in a crank bookstore, bought it, and rushed these paragraphs to National Review, *July 19, 1974. Watergate was obsessive then, and the next thing I knew* Time *was on the phone. Could I tell them where to find the book? I could. They found it and cited it: RMN's Finest Hour.*

THE POETRY OF RICHARD MILHOUS NIXON,
compiled by Jack Margolis. Cliff House Books, 1974. Unpaged.

Here are no sonnets for an idle hour. Stark, terse, hard bitten, cunningly disequilibrated—tiptoe, in fact, on the needlepoint of our century's anguish—these poems speak to and for the thwarted Tamburlaine that lurks in the psyche of urban America. Make no mistake, ours are not easy times. Old certainties dissolve. On every front—ecology, government, Russia, Raquel Welch—we face both ways while poet Nixon speaks for all of us:

MIXED EMOTIONS

I still have mixed emotions on it.
I don't know.
I don't know.

> I have been one way one time
> one way another.

By contrast, how quintessentially *English* was Tennyson's "This way and that dividing the swift mind," a genteel stab at a comparable authenticity. Mr. Nixon has nothing for the ear of Queen Victoria: no periphrasis, no effete pentameter. The American idiom beats in his *Threepenny Opera*, which in frank concession to our decade's theme, inflation, is entitled "One Million Dollars":

> We could get that.
> On the money,
> > If you need the money,
> > > You could get that.

> You could get a million dollars.
> You could get it in cash.
> I know where it could be gotten.
> It is not easy,
> > But it could
> > > Be done.

American, this, alike in its unsleeping self-reliance and in its acknowledgment of engulfing reality.

Reality: that is Mr. Nixon's note. He will have us dodge nothing. One of his most laconic lyrics, "Let's Face It," arrays bitter words down the page like bars of iron, bitten off and quietly spat out:

> Nobody
> Is
> A friend
> Of ours.

> Let's
> Face
> It.

> Don't worry
> About
> That sort
> Of thing.

These are poems to read in the subway, in the line at the checkout counter, beside the gaspump, wherever life is lived. No fellow in a quilted jacket confected them. No, resuming the methods of his master, Homer, Mr. Nixon resorted to the wellspring of authenticity, oral improvisation amid real shock, real stress, and his utterances were transcribed for his editor, Mr. Margolis, to arrange into lines. Division of labor, that is the sole modern note. Mr. Margolis is a master of lineation, who had he been available might have saved Homer some awkward enjambments. But the words are all Mr. Nixon's: not one syllable nor (we are told) one punctuation mark tampered with in any way.

And how flexibly his emotions pulse against the skin of language! Once or twice a simple heartfelt lilt breaks through:

> You can say I don't remember
> You can say I can't recall.
>
> I can't give any answer
> To that
>   That I can recall.

—and how subtly this evades the merely ingenious rhyme!

But more often, as in the haunting "Who Are They After?" (a profound reversal of Wyatt's "They flee from me," effected by a student of "The Hound of Heaven"), Nixon will pare away the merely formal core to leave *Angst* freestanding:

> Who
>   the hell
>   are they after?
> They
>   are
>   after
>   us.

The mythic dimensions of this, one leaves to more eloquent pens, content with the resonances a poet can strike from a mere ten words.

Face to face with such quiet mastery, one is startled to learn from the jacket that this is Mr. Nixon's first book of poetry. Surely we may expect much more from his Sony? We have no right to expect better. So consummate an achievement, one is quietly satisfied to remark, certifies to the viability of the Middle-American lifestyle. Yorba Linda has given tongue to Pittsburgh, to Winnetka. Here is no footloose vagrant, no sandaled unshaven bum. Unlike Homer or Allen Ginsberg, Mr. Nixon, a civil servant, is content to reside "in Washington, D.C., with his wife Pat."

Jaina Riddles

This restatement of a favorite theme, the ficticity of historical knowledge, appeared in Art & Antiques *in December 1986.*

Like Yul Brynner in *The King and I*, he knows what he's about. Decision flows upward from those planted feet; the folded arms dismiss nonsense; casually, the head- and chest-adornments confirm status. The hand that shaped him in clay knew its business, too: no rote, no banality, no fumble. That hand was guided by eyes that saw in the round: saw not the contours only but the substantialities of a human form asserting its claim over space.

Naked save for the smartly folded loin-cloth, he betrays no need for externals of command. His is not, in the European way, authority donned with costume. "Give me my robes, put on my crown," Shakespeare made his Cleopatra say, the lass unparallel'd becoming a great queen by the same means the boy-actor used to impersonate royalty. And even the royal can but impersonate royalty. Like actors, as Shakespeare elsewhere lets us know, such rulers must cope offstage with insomnia and night-sweats. Under the regalia shivers "a bare fork'd animal," a common and timorous mortality.

But not here. Nor did his sculptor even feel an Egyptian need to overwhelm with scale. He's not a great deal bigger than a stevedore's fist: seven inches and seven-eighths exactly.

He. Who? Not a clue. Is he human even? A god perhaps? No one knows. Jargon to the rescue: "This type of figure is usually called a standing dignitary." Yes. "This important figurine"—dealer talk. "A classic Maya (600–900 A.D.) Jaina figurine of a standing male"—museum talk. "Very imposing and dignified for such a small sculpture." You can hear the bafflement.

What confrontation does he dominate? We can't even say if it's with the seen or the unseen. Or is he himself the unseen asserting its presence, donning with a certain disdain the look of mortality?

We know this much: that Jaina, in the Gulf of Mexico, was a burial island just westward—death's direction—from the Yucatan coast. There Mayan dead entered Xibalba, the Underworld. Did they cross the water by boat? Perhaps; or perhaps there was once a ceremonial bridge. On Jaina their bones fill tens of thousands of graves, accompanied by figurines of fired clay. Most of those are hollow and came from molds. Death being prodigal with numbers, the human recourse was to mass production.

Hollowness let them double as whistles or rattles. (For gods to call the soul with? This is all guesswork. We don't even know where the mass production was done. Terra-cotta is all but indestructible, so there ought to be dumps of fragments, left-overs, discards, but none has been found.)

The wonders, though, aren't mold-made but are like this one, solid and hand-wrought with a baffling confidence. They were polychromed once; a few traces of red can still be made out on ours. Many look like portraits done from life, the teeming life of a rain-forest civilization that supported cities of 20,000 souls. It collapsed rather suddenly about A.D. 900, again we cannot guess why. The monuments stood, the books went on being recopied. There just wasn't anything new. It's like a detail from the *Star Wars* trilogy.

Except that Darth Vader needs his black robe and his mask, and this figure needs nothing of the kind. It's hard to think of a parallel for such assurance. The ten-inch bronze Poseidon in the Louvre? The other Poseidon, in Athens, six feet ten inches tall, that was fished up from the sea off Cape Artemisium? But both express, and especially the former, the *effort* even a god must exert to intimidate. Olympian calm was never in the Greek repertoire. And in carved Roman heads, Garry Wills has been accurate in seeing masks: "masks that proclaim an exceeding inner busyness, one that eats at them." That clue leads straight to Shakespeare and the crown's uneasiness.

With an ease we can't aspire to, any old Mayan woman likely understood this figure. But she is gone, and her communal knowledge. Did she possibly respond as we do to a bust of Lincoln, by simple recognition? If a competent uninspired sculptor wanted uninformed posterity to think him a master of serene authority, he'd do well to let Lincoln's features guide his hand. Great assurance can stem from a cliché.

Umberto Eco has invited us to wonder what they'd make of our art, of our selves, after two millennia, if all that survived was one episode of "Columbo." That's like our position, confronting the pre-Columbian. Pre-Columbian? That means, before an Italian navigator blundered on Caribbean shores and thought he was in China: a mistake, an irrelevance in the story of the Maya, who were never thinking of being pre-Columbian, but of other things we don't know about.

Rectitude
and Certainty

Jeff Schaire, who'd survived a Night of the Long Knives at Harper's *to become a Senior Editor (i.e., factotum) at the new* Art & Antiques, *called me on the basis of a* Harper's *acquaintance to commission this. It commenced my long association with the magazine, and (I'd like to think) Jeff's propulsion toward his present Editor-in-Chiefship. The piece appeared in the April 1984 issue.*

Art is anything perfectly useless that someone will buy and thereafter remain middling satisfied. The magic of the word "Art" has made money change hands in the vicinity of a stuffed goat with an auto tire round its middle: money for critics, photo-engravers, museum guards, accountants, insurers. Conversely, the jingle of unreckonable money is what validates the tired goat as Art. (Have I waited a quarter century to get excited? No, I've chosen an example aged enough to be "classic.")

Thus Art is the joint creation of buyers and sellers. Its production, like that of stick-on digital clocks, is highly organized. There are even professional sellers, called Art Dealers, and professional buyers, called Museums. There have always been, of course, people to stuff dead goats, and other people to make things like auto tires. We may call these "artisans," and reflect that in 1600 the skills of the tire-moulder would have been deemed miraculous.

There is also a small class of ingenious persons who get visited by such ideas as combining one tire with one goat. These are called "artists," which is one of their rewards, but it is not they who make Art. The whirl of greenbacks, that is what makes Art. The job of artists is to devise opportunities for commerce. That is what they are paid for. And they do have fun.

Ho hum, I know, that has all been said before. I replay it, like a recording of urban noises, to set off the song of an authentic mechanical bird: William Blake (1757–1827), who derided as long ago as 1810 a custom whereby "he is counted the Greatest Genius who can sell a Good-for-Nothing Commodity for a Great Price." Such transactions were apt to be sprinkled with talk of "expression." But expression is a by-product of what Blake called "character," and he asserted that neither character nor expression could exist "without firm and determinate outline." And how do these statements hang together?

"Firm and determinate": that puts the artist in charge. Of the tired goat, the *viewer* is in charge. The "artist" made no assertion save to trundle it out, bedaubed with paint and stood on a daubed base, for whatever response might ensue. Robert Hughes in *The Shock of the New* is one who has obliged, finding *Monogram* (which is what goat + tire + Rauschenberg's fame gets called) "one of the few great emblems of male homosexual love in modern culture: the Satyr in the Sphincter." Blake had different criteria for emblems.

Blake goes on to exalt a "distinct, sharp, and wiry" bounding line. "How do we distinguish the oak from the beech, the horse from the ox, but by the bounding outline? . . . What is it that builds a house and plants a garden, but the definite and determinate? What is it that distinguishes honesty from knavery, but the hard and wiry line of rectitude and certainty in the actions and intentions?"

"Rectitude," that's not a word to use freely near Art dealings. Nor is "certainty" applicable to Art criticism. But skip name-calling and concentrate on Blake's claims for a "bounding line," something "distinct, sharp, and wirey." Like most of his simplistic-seeming terms, "outline" proves a powerful metaphor, rooted, like the best metaphors, in manual experience. Burin in hand, Blake the engraver could leave no line's whereabouts in uncertainty. A Blakean line was *here* or it was *there*, it was straight or it was wiggly. It was what distinguished ox from horse, oak from beech, angel from thug. So it was a *moral* line: exactly what people mean when they say you must draw the line somewhere. Unlike Heisenberg's electron, beloved of sixties explicators, it proclaimed location and energy level together.

And one line it draws is the line around the work of art, absolute as the rectangle of the canvas. That's a line the Duchamp urinal made famous sport of, and a line the tired goat refuses to have drawn. Is it Art? What makes it Art? An Artist's say-so? Rauschenberg found his goat, so the story goes, in a Seventh Avenue typewriter-dealer's window, and what it was doing there is about as inexplicable as what it has since been doing in a museum. I don't know where he found the tire. He made the goat look as though it had been poking its muzzle, goat-fashion, into sundry paint cans, and he gave the tire white treads instead of white sidewalls. But "Monogram" is not exactly painting, nor exactly sculpture, nor exactly anything save a costly curiosity. You could even call the whole thing a metaphor for its own elusive status, the front or painted end of the goat having passed through an arbitrary boundary into Art, while its rear end lingers in the less prestigious cosmos of taxidermy.

Or you could say . . . but that is just the point: *you* could say. If there's to be any saying, it's up to you. And there must be saying. If works of "Art" are sphinx-like, it's the better to compel talk. And nothing describes a culture of high-minded softness like its wordiness about the reciprocal roles of perceiver and perceived. As "Deconstruction," this now infests literary discourse. I'm reminded how, fully thirty-one years ago, Rauschenberg deconstructed a drawing by de Kooning; he did it with numerous erasers, and framed the result. That's emblematic; whatever "distinct, sharp, and wirey" lines de Kooning had assumed responsibility for, it was Rauschenberg's business to get rid of them [lines] totally. And, of course, it is Rauschenberg who gets to sign the non-result. (I hope no one mistakes all this for a diatribe against Rauschenberg; I single him out for his service in defining issues of moment.)

"A little squinting image of zero," wrote Wyndham Lewis a long generation ago, never mind about what. He invited us to see gold dust being sprinkled over it: dealers' and prize-givers' gold dust. Word dust, I think rather. Art exists today in a vortex of talk: of intelligent people finding ways to say something coherent.

"To communicate and then stop," was a Confucian summary of the law of discourse. But art-talk is distinguished by the way it can never stop. "Rectitude and certainty," was Blake's phrase. But much talk is a measure of great uncertainty, not to be dignified by dubbing it "Heisenbergian." To say "conversation piece" was once a way of being kind to amusing trivia. As we poke around the art scene of a quarter century, there seems nothing else for us to say.

One Reel
a Week

This was to have been a Foreword; but when the authors chose to stay un-chaperoned their editor donned an alternative hat to run it as a "review" in his Film Quarterly *(Spring 1968).*

The movies began as a con game, which seems thoroughly appropriate, since the object of the game was to exploit a mechanical illusion. At its heart was a piece of machinery, patented by Edison, for imparting intermittent motion to a strip of perforated celluloid. The Edison patents, though they rested on largely groundless claims, were valid (i.e., enforceable); the effort to enforce them cluttered the Edison payroll with detectives (i.e., "spies"); and entrepreneurs who'd thwart the curiosity of the spies took to hiring very large and big-muscled adjutants, whose job was "to stand by the camera and discourage anyone from getting too close." A suitable entrepreneur "had been around and was nobody's chump": for instance Charlie Bauman, a former streetcar conductor who "liked to boast of putting a nickel in his pocket out of every four fares he rang up."

A young man breaking into such a game in 1905 spent much of his time in his employer's basement, making pirated copies of French films ("It required little intelligence to know that this was shady business, but Mr. Lubin carried on the practice as if it were perfectly ordinary and completely legitimate"). The Frenchmen made life difficult for pirates by imprinting a trademark on every frame; the pirate's apprentice accordingly painted it off every frame, with dexterity that would have done credit to an engraver of the Lord's Prayer. And the economic impetus for such goings-on came from the insatiable delight of cash customers in a flickering illusion capable of deceiving nobody for an instant. Today we hear about the Art of the Cinema.

Much of what passes for cinema history has depended on an allied art, public relations, amid the exuberant woody lianas of which scholars have subsequently had to advance with machetes. Eighty thousand critical words by Gordon Hendricks, honed by more than three hundred footnotes, were required to subdue the tangle of allegations which gives Edison credit for anything more than pertinacity in securing patents (*The Edison Motion Picture Myth*, 1961). *One Reel a Week*, however, seems unlikely to exact corrective vigors. It is neither written from old press releases nor intent on bolstering anyone's claims to priority, and though subject, like all memoirs, to the simplifications of memory, it is pleasantly untainted by flackery.

The authors tell, turn and turn about, their vivid tale of how it was to dodge the spies and grind the cameras and make the prints, and what early actors were like and early sets—how dungeon walls were slowly dipped into tanks that waters might seem to rise around Pearl White—and how as the movies finally settled in Los Angeles a last wave of entrepreneurs, the toughest of all, not amiable peddlers of basement duplicates nor chiselers of trolley-car nickels but big-money dealers accustomed to being paid heed, consolidated the industry out of its handicraft phase. Their day came because the product was from the first so standardized, and so dependent on standardization, that the will that shaped it grew inevitably obsessed with control.

Control, not content; the industry, not the script. And though latterly the key to effective control was a distribution network, in Miller-Balshofer times it was the camera; hence the pertinence of those Edison patents. First came the oscillating claw and the perforated film, devoted to such two-second trifles as *Fred Ott's Sneeze*; only long after-

ward came such intellectual refinements (called "story properties")
as *The Perils of Pauline* and *The Song of Bernadette* (Mr. Miller photographed both of these, thirty years apart).

The history of the movies is reducible to a sequence of efforts to (a)
safeguard the chance of exploiting an illusion-machine while (b) devising things to do with it, given the mysterious fact that a large public
would pay, and pay repeatedly, to watch the shadows flicker. The
public was hooked on the machine, not the photoplay, and was at first
entranced to glimpse, through a hole in the top of the Kinetoscope, a
tiny black-and-white man bowing and raising his hat. Soon batches of
several dozen were sitting in front of a white sheet to watch "The Firemen's Parade on Fifth Avenue" and "exciting stories of the dime novel
type." To collect repeated admissions from the same people, it was
only necessary to vary the scenes represented. Narrative excitement
was not essential; five years after *The Great Train Robbery* we hear of
distributors dickering with Mr. Balshofer for exclusive rights on 2,000
feet of Coney Island sights: a boat splashing into the pool, a car loop-
ing the loop. The fascinating thing was simply movement, reconstituted in that silvery light. Movement came to mean horses, and
horses, westerns; the essential plot line, growing directly out of the
exigencies of the medium, was the impact of motion (e.g., outlaws)
on immobility (e.g., a town).

And yet within a few years we begin to hear of an employee called
the Art Director, whose job, with the aid of elaborate drawings and
trompe l'oeil devices of scale, was to make large sets look utterly realistic.

Films, in short, had begun as early as 1916 to imitate stage drama:
the degenerate stage drama moreover that exacts of its carpenters individual handcrafted leaves on property trees, with for preference a
few pneumatically operated birds, to make the forest of Arden look
botanical. That sort of thing, as we learn from his *Letters*, was exacer-
bating the young W. B. Yeats in 1899, though it seems also to have
spurred his famous interest in clockwork birds for a mental Byzan-
tium. It was a bad turn for the drama, and a suicidal turn, it would
seem, for mechanized moving shadows thrown on a bedsheet.

Such distractions interested neither Chaplin nor Keaton, whose
genius flowered during the following decade; but the great clowns

proved not to be in the mainstream of the industry, which discarded them as soon as sound gave it an excuse. What on earth was the industry thinking of? Money, certainly; respectability, likely—a genteel status, disconnected from peep show or immigrant origins. Hence its subjection, at incredible cost in technical painstaking, to the pretensions of Drama. Hence, concurrent with the heyday of the great comedians, the recruitment of the likes of John Barrymore. Hence shoals of adapted plays, including—what now seem Keatonian in their madness—ventures into silent Shakespeare. Hence, after sound, a dreary procession of adapted books with descriptive passages for the camera to pick up plus dialogue for the microphones, while schoolmarms and librarians clucked approval. The genteel tradition that began in Boston ended its days in Hollywood, a coddled and venerated centenarian, stipulating from its sickbed that a poolroom shyster like W. C. Fields needed putting to decent employment as a supporting player in *David Copperfield*.

Such reflections, a sort of subliminal sound track, are apt to accompany a reading of this unique joint memoir. The book's virtue is that it makes no such points. Its authors are intent, like the primitive camera, on incidents we feel confident no thesis has pummeled. Thesis-spinning is the reader's privilege, amid encounters with Edison spies and energetic grifters, improvised scripts and piano-wired stunts, mummers turned Thespians and taking themselves seriously, mood music on sets and a director's pecking order keyed to possession of the largest megaphone, all in an air rendered heady by bigger and bigger bucks; while gradually about the frenzied improvisation there forms, as though Emily Post had taken the Keystone Cops in hand, a colloidal respectability, setting, thickening. Investments grew simply too large to improvise with, theaters too sumptuous to contain anything less than the Burning of Atlanta. By then the moving shadows had left off jiggling, and were colored as well, and the screen had ceased to waver in strong drafts; and there were very few left in theater or on sound stage to recall the picaresque, far from innocent days of One Reel a Week.

Miltonic Monkey

The harvest of an afternoon to kill in New York, near a theater that was showing the old wonder. It appeared in National Review, *late in 1976.*

Flackery prates of a new improved *King Kong*, with a bigger, hence better, ape and a $22 million price tag. In 1933 Merian C. Cooper brought in the original for one-fiftieth of that, a mere $430,000 plus change. The sound effects cost under $450, including $10 for the squawk of a pterodactyl.

Today, connoisseurship of spray-can excellence is apt to be condescending. The black and white is grainy, the animation jerky, Kong himself of uncertain size (fifty feet according to the publicists; actually eighteen feet in the jungle, raised to twenty-four in New York after the stone canyons dwarfed him in the first tests). It all creaks.

Still, on the Late Show, on campuses, and in art theaters, Kong hypnotizes as he did forty-three years ago. Kong atop the Empire State Building (brand-new when the picture was made), snatching a fragile biplane out of the air with Fay Wray stunned at his feet, is the single most unforgotten image in the history of cinema. At the premiere it overwhelmed *The New York Times* man, whose review, apparently written in a state of shock, ascribed *Gulliver's Travels* to Defoe. At an East Side Manhattan movie house this fall, in what was billed as the positively final showing, it was still pretty overwhelming.

Misinformation about how it was all done quickly filled 1933 magazine columns, some of it planted by the studio, which wanted to protect its investment by leading competitors into expensive blind alleys. *Modern Mechanix* explained that Kong was a man in an ape-suit; later at least two actors claimed the role, and only seven years ago one of them was telling the *Chicago Sun-Times* what his pay had been per week. Guff. No man donned a monkey-suit for any part of *King Kong*. Contrariwise, somebody from RKO fed *Time* a statistics-studded fantasy about a fifty-foot robot ape, its eighty-five motors operated by six men. Also guff, though in the thirties any yarn with a robot seemed plausible, and *Time* bit.

Belatedly, two kong-sized paperbacks now take us behind the scenes: Orville Goldner and George E. Turner's *The Making of King Kong* (Ballantine, $3.95), and Ronald Gottesman and Harry Geduld's *The Girl in the Hairy Paw* (Avon, $5.95). *Girl* is an edited potpourri in which authenticities are uncritically jumbled with myth. *Making* seems reliable as far as it goes, but you'll need to supplement it with details from *Girl*. The prose of both books is uniformly excruciating.

Anyhow, Kong. There was a giant head, for close-ups of natives being chewed, a giant paw to cradle the life-size Miss Wray, a giant foot, crane operated, to stomp victims. But when you saw Kong all at once what you saw was no bigger than a large teddy bear: about eighteen inches. His aluminum skeleton had joints that held their positions, and his latex flesh was covered with strips of rabbit fur.

A young sculptor named Marcel Delgado handcrafted the Kongs: two of them, one for use while the other got repaired (on pages 204 and 205 of *Girl* you can see them both in one photo). They needed much repair because most of the picture was shot frame by frame, consuming hours under hot lights for a few seconds' screen action, and the heat and the constant minute repositioning kept breaking down the latex. Especially, the brow of Kong's mobile face received so many thousand manipulations that repair had to be superimposed on repair, and Kong in late reels is twice as beetle-browed as when he first snatched Fay from the jungle altar.

For the human actors, there were life-size sets, notably the Skull Island village wall ("built so long ago," says the script, "that the people who live there now have slipped back, forgotten the higher civilization that built it"). In plain fact, the wall had been built in 1926 by Cecil B. De Mille for *King of Kings*, and a few years after serving *Kong*'s purposes it was burned to ashes in about six minutes as part of *Gone with the Wind*'s Atlanta.

Its gates (who forgets the scene when Kong batters them open?) were typical Hollywood serendipity. On Skull Island they make no strategic sense (if your wall is to keep Kong out, why build into it a portal tall enough to admit him?) but De Mille had left a twenty-by-sixty-foot gap to be hung by huge curtains, and the Kong carpenters had to close it with something. So a sequence was born. Once a gate had been built, Cooper trusted his showman's instinct about gates. A gate is to smash.

And Willis O'Brien, who did all the special effects—in fact some two-thirds of the picture—had a deeper instinct still, manifested when he issued sets of Gustave Doré engravings to the painters of the exquisite glass plates that served, plane behind plane, for tabletop jungle scenery amid which his model saurians roared and thrashed. Scene after scene paraphrases effects of Doré's; that is why a hazy light as of early creation outlines the myriad treetops; why the source of light is always impenetrably deeper within the scene; why little humans move backlighted through Edenic glades that conceal (like Milton's Eden) nameless menace: darkness inexplicably menaced by brightness. O'Brien was inspired by Doré who was inspired by Milton, for whom the dispositions of light and dark were less schematic than his theology made them.

It was also O'Brien, plotting the intricate stop-motion choreography, timing the gestures, touching nuance into gigantic grimaces, who in effect created the character of Kong, filmdom's only interesting monster. The assignment he had received from Cooper was no more than to animate a gigantic gorilla who should menace the movie's lovers, scare citizenry, get killed. (Milton the poet received a similar assignment from Milton the ideologue.)

But in the footage O'Brien delivered the movie acquired its hero.

No one has ever cared a pin for the lovers, no one even remembers their screen names (Fay Wray's was Ann Darrow, and if you didn't know that, neither did the reviewer for the *Times*, who garbled it). But audiences still feel uncanny sympathy when Kong understands that he is mortally wounded, and lifts Fay's limp form for a farewell look.

Despite all Milton's pains, his Adam and Eve became in the same way stick figures; despite all Milton's fierce theology, his Satan became the hero of *Paradise Lost*, a poem that didn't set out to display a hero. And the huge dark Kong derives at several removes from the huge dark archangel whose very shield hung on his shoulder huge as a lunar world.

Which is not to make Willis O'Brien a student of Milton: only to note what came of his study of Gustave Doré. For the majesty of Satan is caught in the same engravings from which Kong's animator, imitating their decor of light and foliage, absorbed more than he knew. The authors of *The Making of King Kong* note how "the wonderful scene in which Kong observes his domain from the 'balcony' of his mountaintop home" resembles a Doré illustration to *Paradise Lost*, "Satan Overlooking Paradise." The resemblance is more than scenic; Kong has Satan's imperial stature, here as at many such points infused into the film.

The movie ends where *Paradise Lost* begins, with white-winged powers driving the black bulk into an abyss:

> Him the Almighty Power
> Hurl'd headlong flaming from th' Ethereal Sky
> With hideous ruin and combustion, down
> To bottomless perdition . . .

King Kong (1933) was the last of many remakes in many media of *Paradise Lost* (1667), and the most popular since Byron transfixed the imagination of Europe with a role he'd modeled on Satan. *King Kong* (1976) will be lucky if it's any more than a vulgar enlargement of *King Kong* (1933). What a big ape they're fabricating! But that wasn't the point.

The Folklore
of Kinetic Man

This review of a little paperback by Milt Gross appeared in National Review *(September 24, 1963) and lost me the book: so many people subsequently borrowed it, and I never heard again from the last of them . . .*

The Great American Novel (who coined that phrase?) is, thanks to Dell Publishing Company, the best current forty cents' worth at your nearest drugstore. Specifically: *He Done Her Wrong*: / The Great American Novel / told without words / by Milt Gross / introduction by Al Capp. The original copyright date is 1930; the goings-on smack of 1910; the presentation is timeless.

Not an audible word, not so much as a Bam or a Zowie, defaces these pages. Impact is measured by the deformation of the body impacted: a jaw, a chair, a lamp-post. Motivation is graphed by limning objects of desire. Character is not lingered on; in strict accord with Aristotle's canon, it is depicted not for its own sake but for the sake of the action, and its index, corresponding to Aristotle's masks, is the orientation of feet. The villain's toes turn out with urbane nonchalance;

the heroine tiptoes in perpendicular purity as though suspended from heaven by a string.

These limits enclose indefatigable comic energy. Gross lavished virtuosity on just two elements: the syntax of kinesis, the vocabulary of voiceless passion. Kinesis (Buster Keaton, Harold Lloyd) was the rhetoric of the 1920s, a decade that did in America with pure motion what the English did about 1600 with language, and the French about 1880 with color. For those few years, before American eyes, the Newtonian universe flowered like a languid rose, disclosing, before its petals dropped away, all its intricate repertory of action, reaction, equilibrium. Man and machine, in that enchanted truce, met nearly as equals. You could understand how a thing worked by looking at it: a locomotive, a steam shovel, Calvin Coolidge hid nothing from the mind; they did not need to be explained as all subsequent technology has required endlessly to be explained. Trajectories Everyman intuited with ease, and the parallelogram of forces irradiated his mind as Love does an angel's.

Milt Gross outdid his successor Disney in the authority with which he could link movement to movement. Our Hero must Stop the Wedding. Swinging from the hook of a handy crane, he crashes the church window feet first. As he hurtles, *deus ex machina*, upon the offenders, the crane's cable, paid out after him, hurtles too; the heavy hook pendulums upward as he thrusts loose; the momentum of the drum feeds in additional cable; and the system hangs poised an instant in ominous slack.

Then as the villain, in tripartite synchrony, (1) blasts a fusillade with his ever-handy Colt, (2) clutches his astonished bride by the necklace, and (3) propels her father skyward with a kick, the hook's potential energy is actualized. It swings down to clutch her precisely about the neck, and snatch her, bouquet still in hand, out of necklace and wedding-dress at once.

She is not the heroine but an ugly woman with a pekingese and so merits no sympathy: only the ritual fury of a frieze of frantic cops, as the crane, suddenly energized, whisks her off airborne toward an ideal vanishing point. This takes just four drawings out of some 350.

As for the way of articulating voiceless passion, Gross got it straight from vaudeville, which got it from melodrama, which got it from the rhetoricians' handbooks of the eighteenth century, which got it from (perhaps) the *commedia dell'arte*. The Method and the talkies killed it; Eisenstein's *Ivan the Terrible* was its ceremonious farewell. Knees bend, eyes roll up, heads slump, chests expand sixfold to register every nuance of rage, calm, lust, defeat, servility, purpose.

Two dozen postage-stamp vignettes run, by minuscule alterations of posture, the gamut from lordly expansiveness through annoyance, rage, violence, fanaticism, and madness as a fortune is squandered, clothes and belongings pawned, wife and bairns abandoned to eviction, by a man in combat with a recalcitrant gum machine. Monte Carlo has not seen the like. In the last drawing, torso thrown back, he tears his hair, eyes clamped into slits. The machine rests, battered, sated, a mute nemesis: for man is under Fortuna.

A still more intricate cadenza, forty-two pictures long, takes our heroine stage by stage into the very penetralia of pillared and mahoghanied Business, repeating over and over the four tearful gestures of Economic Despair, and teaching hierarchies of subordinates to relay these gestures to their hierarchies of superiors. She is Applying for Work; and receptionists, chairmen, vice-presidents carry her cause upward, writhing, imploring, evoking with a horizontal hand the stature of her starving children. For a whole day and into the night this Stanislavskyite Saint Vitus Dance infects the corporation; at last comes the written decision, in a sealed envelope, from the Very Top; it reads simply, "O.K." Joy is on every face; virtue and desert have triumphed. So we find her at the end of her long quest, in the light of dawn, fully employed, at the foot of pillars scrubbing a marble floor.

It has long been understood that the Great American Novel, could it exist, would have something to do with Horatio Alger. Nathanael West among others simply travestied Alger (in *A Cool Million*) with sulphuric wit. But Alger was himself a pale travesty; he was a hack, and no hack ever presides over the initial metamorphosis of myth into language. That is done either by the folk, who keep all myths, or by genius. The Alger myth (so miscalled) has stayed unverbalized; except in Scott Fitzgerald, the American literary tradition has never courted it.

Only the popular stage, the silent film, the comic strip, evolved the appropriate vocabulary and syntax; and only Milt Gross (1895–1953) got the whole ramshackle tradition of despair and triumph between covers. His invention never flags; he is unfailingly funny.

Yes, the ending is happy. Yes, the buzz-saw is stopped in the nick of time. And yes, the hero possesses that crucial birthmark. His pants are cut, by a tailcoated flunky, for the better examining of it, and his face at this moment is a study in coy complaisance. As for the villain, he is trapped into *six* simultaneous shotgun marriages, and shipped to Turkey, where harems are not inconceivable, and where the six wives still clutch each one her rolling-pin.

Ezra Pound
and Music

From Musical Quarterly, *July 1979, an austere journal I was surprised to find myself appearing in.*

EZRA POUND AND MUSIC: THE COMPLETE
CRITICISM, *edited with commentary by R. Murray Schafer.*
New York: New Directions, 1977. 530 pp.

The hideous cost of this book enforces one of its themes. Do not blame profiteering; no publisher in his senses would willingly ration his sales to the few hundred fanatics who can scrape together forty-two dollars for a volume of ordinary letterpress. No, the publisher is caught in a tightening vise of which one jaw is the immovable cost of production, and the other is the minuscule number of people whose interest in both Music and Ezra Pound can be counted on. Dividing the former figure by the latter yields a per-copy price, so high it restricts the size of the public still further. Allowing for this, further calculation yields a further price, forty-two dollars, no more absurd than any other amenity in the cost accountant's miasmus we inhabit.

When several years ago Robert Hughes conducted and recorded the sole known intact performance of Pound's chamber opera *Le Testament*, the brief trumpet part, what with rehearsal, performance, and recording fees, was computed at something like sixty dollars per note; it will surely be omitted from any future production. And a concert harpsichordist once told me why she could not use the Dolmetsch instrument of her predilection: it was not loud enough for the back rows, and her recitals of music that had been composed for small rooms required 500-plus paid admissions.

So "music in the great cities has been damned and crushed by the overhead," whereas "I have said for a number of years [as of 1936] that a group of 500 people can have *any* (I mean positively *any*) kind of civilization they want. With the afterthought: 'up to the capacity of their best artists.' I doubt if Pericles had more than 80 citizens who knew the worse art from the better" (page 377).

The eighty had Pericles, and four decades ago the citizens of Rapallo, on the Tigullian Gulf east of Genoa, had Ezra Pound, who had settled there in 1925. Acting on his principle that "civilization begins when people start preferring a little done right to a great deal done wrong" (page 322), Pound proceeded in 1933 to organize a series of concerts in which considerable artists—Gerhart Münch, piano; Olga Rudge, violin; others—offered things like twelve Mozart violin sonatas on three successive evenings, to the end that the auditors, who numbered at most eighty, could get Mozart's transactions with the violin firmly into their heads: a little done right, in a town hall the use of which was donated: maximum admission ten lire. You could not have heard the likes of that, or of Münch performing the entire *Well-Tempered Clavier*, or the Gertler Quartet doing Bartók, in London or New York. And in Rapallo, thanks to Pound's correspondence with the musicologist W. Gillies Whittaker, they heard the William Young violin sonatas Whittaker had edited before their British première at Oxford.

Such insight and enterprise remain exemplary.

If only [Mr. Schafer remarks] small towns throughout the world could show half the touch of inventiveness displayed in these concerts, in-

stead of aspiring to acculturation by the unanimous ambition of producing yet another civic orchestra or opera company. . . . For the same
amount of money expended annually on the average semiprofessional
orchestra a small city could have in residence one of the world's great
string quartets. This is Pound's argument. The small town is to form an
antipode to the mercantile system of metropolitan concert life. (page
324)

Pound had more than enthusiasm to contribute. Let us scotch gossip about his amateurishness: he could read a score, in fact himself
copied note by note about 1937 Vivaldi concertos obtained on micro-
film from Dresden, "and being pleased by the quality of Vivaldi's
mind therein apparent, became more enthusiastic over the possibilities of the unpublished Vivaldi than I wd. if I heard even the same con-
certi played (as I have) by a heavy and heavily led orchestra" (page
445). That was before more than a few musicologists had heard of Vivaldi; the thrust into unfamiliar territory was characteristic.

Pound was also a minor composer of genuine accomplishment.
Hughes's fine production of *Le Testament* has been available on Fantasy Records for some years, and the late Tibor Serly thought the
Ghuidonis Sonata of 1931 worth transcribing for string orchestra
(page 335); the sonata has since entered the repertory of the violinist
who recorded it last summer for National Public Radio. How much
other Pound music is extant I do not know: ten or a dozen pieces?
Murray Schafer has a second volume in preparation, for which we are
promised reproductions of the available scores.

Meanwhile the present volume documents Pound's twenty years'
active concern with the conditions of musical performance. It began
in London as a by-product of his interest in troubadour melodies, a
study germane to his self-education for poetry. Notebooks survive in
which he copied out texts and tunes from manuscript sources in European libraries, alert to the fact that "both in Greece and in Provence
the poetry attained its highest rhythmic and metrical brilliance at
times when the arts of verse and music were most closely knit together, when each thing done by the poet had some definite musical
urge or necessity bound up within it" (page 4). Ideally poet, musician, and performer were the same person, setting his own words

and singing them, and it was against this ideal that Pound measured the unsatisfactoriness of what he heard, as music critic for the *New Age*, in London concert halls from 1917 to 1921. A word man, he was drawn to singers, and what he heard seemed a frightful muddle: the composer typically uninterested in the specific movement and sense of the words, the singer typically unwilling to articulate them.

"Her voice sounded as though it were being strained through a bag," he would find himself writing. "She did not add to our pleasure by dragging 'can rain' into 'kerrain,' 'kiss' into 'kees,' 'queen' into 'kuh-ween,' 'my' into 'hmi'" (page 84). Or, "To sing [*sic*] 'O had I a HELL-met and doublet and hose'; to repeat this with increasing volume, such as cannot be rendered by any capital letters at our disposal, must be regarded as purely comic by any vigilant listener" (page 85).

The *New Age* reviews occupy nearly half the book, and, incapable as one is of pretending to an active interest in the sounds emitted by Miss Carrie Tubb on an unimportant occasion sixty years ago, one reads at first with an eye for the vivid asides and the comic exaggerations: the excoriation of a pianist who had "a touch like an Army boot" (page 166), or the spasm of impatience with Franz Liszt: "Liszt was stupid. . . . He would try to make a watch go by beating it with a potato-masher" (page 170). Gradually, though, one's better faculties grow engaged: one commences to detect the pattern underlying what the critic approves. Pound approved, for one thing, of performance that concentrated on exhibiting *the music*, "as if the performer were to bring out a painted picture and hang it before the audience. The music must have as much a separate existence as has the painting. It is a malversion of art for the performer to beseech the audience (*via* the instrument) to sympathise with his or her temperament, however delicate or plaintive or distinguished" (page 83). Analogously, he applauded, when he encountered it, signs of intelligence in the choice and arrangement of the program. One model was a violinist's all-Bach recital:

Concerto in E Major (Allegro, Adagio, Allegro assai)
Adagio and Fugue in G minor (unaccompanied)
Aria on G string

Chaconne in D minor (unaccompanied)
Gavotte in E
Andante in C (unaccompanied)
Prelude in E

Despite the fact that there were several points in the Chaconne at which the composer "might have stopped but didn't," and despite Miss Kennedy's lack of certitude in execution, this programme served fully to demonstrate that Bach is *not* monotonous; and that the people who find him monotonous do so on the same principle that a man finds a foreign restaurant monotonous having, in his ignorance of the language of the menu, attempted to dine off six soups. Here we had an hour-and-a-half of one composer, and I would gladly have sat through another hour. (page 830)

Enough of the composer's work for one instrument to exhibit his variety: here we have the principle of the Rapallo presentation, fifteen years later, of twelve Mozart sonatas in three evenings: contrast and variety introduced not by the programmer nor the performer but by Mozart, whose inventiveness was attested to by the very fact that such a block of sonatas could be scheduled.

The eye is caught, too, by remarks on rhythm, and the need for performers to sense it:

One can listen to a singer who possesses this sense; one can listen to her for an hour or so, without exhaustion even though she be unable to take a high note *forte* without an uncontrolled squall. . . . A drag, a lack of the wave force, deadens, tires, utterly wears out the audience. Rhythm-sense is not merely a *temps mesuré*, it is not merely a clockwork of the bar-lengths. Measured time is only one form of rhythm; but a true rhythm sense assimilates all sorts of uneven pieces of time, and keeps the music alive. (page 85)

That was written in 1918, at an early stage of Pound's thinking about the structure of his long poem *The Cantos*: how to organize a miscellany of materials, without a "story"? Rhythm, very broadly interpreted, was the key. Reexamining the Bach recital he commended, one can perceive in its progression of pieces a large-scale rhythm; and within any composition "all sorts of uneven pieces of time" are discernible, which thanks to rhythm-sense composer and performer may keep alive. By the mid-1920s, *The Cantos* well under way, rhythm had become for Pound a kind of metaphor for every manifestation of the alertly working mind. He was the most sophisticated thinker about large-scale forms in our century, and his one effort to articulate their doctrine occurred in the domain not of poetry but of music: the *Treatise on Harmony* of 1924. We find it just past the center of the book, pages 293–306: some of the most important pages in the vast Pound canon.

Music was the appointed domain for such an exposition. The time art par excellence, it contains events whose time scale is several thousand occurrences per second (the sounds of the notes); events whose time scale is measured in seconds (the notes in the measure); events whose time scale may occupy many seconds or minutes (the structural units of the composition); events gauged in fractions of an hour (the compositions on the program). It was Pound's contention that these time scales were micro- and macroversions of one another that might even prove to exhibit simple mathematical relations. Hence, his interest in the threshold—around sixteen c.p.s.—where the low notes of the pipe organ can be discerned "not as pitch but as a series of separate woof-woofs" (page 301), marking as it does a point of continuity between what the ear discerns as sound and what the mind discerns as time. "The percussion of the rhythm can enter the harmony exactly as another note would. It enters usually as a Bassus, a still-deeper bassus; giving the main form to the sound" (page 303); which is why we can sense that a passage is being played, or a speech being read, "too fast" or "too slowly." Pound formulated a law:

A SOUND OF ANY PITCH, OR ANY COMBINATION OF SUCH SOUNDS, MAY BE FOLLOWED BY A SOUND OF ANY OTHER PITCH, OR ANY OTHER COMBINATION OF SUCH SOUNDS, providing the time interval between them is properly gauged; and this is true for ANY SERIES OF SOUNDS, CHORDS OR ARPEGGIOS. (page 296)

As long ago as 1961, Murray Schafer, writing in *The Canadian Music Journal* (V/4), grouped Pound's brief *Treatise* with Schoenberg's *Harmonielehre* and Schenker's *Harmonielehre*, the three "contributions to the science of harmony in our century." It deserves mention along with Schoenberg and Schenker, he tells us now, because "a superior work of theory can alter our entire conception of music just as much as a masterpiece," and "no modern book on the subject so cogently forces us to see harmony as a study in movement" (page 294). It is little known because (1) it appeared in a book (*Antheil and the Treatise on Harmony* [Paris, 1924]) that has never been easy to obtain; (2) Pound was not a certified musician; (3) as so often with Pound, a side issue muddied things: the praise of Antheil, published just when Antheil was on the threshold of betraying his promise; (4) the central assertions of the *Treatise* are outrageously simple, and collide with two centuries of emphasis on harmony as a vertical, not a horizontal art, complete with tables of permitted consonances. Their fructive simplicity, moreover, was mixed with a more dubious simplification Pound had absorbed from Antheil, the notion that time notations in score are to be implicitly trusted; thus he cited his copy of *Le Nozze di Figaro*: "Presto, half note equals 84; Allegro, black equals 144," and risked having the whole argument dismissed by anyone who knew that *Le Nozze* predated the metronome by some years (page 303).

Reading through the *New Age* reviews, one glimpses the intuitions the *Treatise* was to formulate. Emerging as it does, firmly stated, in the middle of the book, it comes as clarification and climax. The second half of the book, like Pound's musical life, changes theme, as we attend to the chronicle of the Rapallo concerts, 1933–39. It is less attractive reading matter, partly because we are not reading Ezra Pound's inimitable English, but (for the most part) English translations of his Italian, or of Italian translations of his English. It chronicles, all the same, a remarkable deed, culminating in the Siena Accademia Musicale Chigiana's "Vivaldi Week" of September 1939 for which it had served as model: great blocks of one composer's work, and that composer virtually unknown.

"The dream of the music lover," he wrote in the last article here reprinted, "is to be able to choose the program." The music lover who entertained that dream, and in Rapallo for six years was able to indulge it, had survived—at what psychic cost!—years of immersion in metropolitan performer-worship; in London, he recalled, "posters

twelve-by-eighteen feet carry only the name of the performer and almost no details of the program. Naturally whoever goes to hear a cox-
comb whacking a piano, in the end becomes less sensitive to the
value-shadings of the music itself. This enlarges indifference to the
internal *meaning* of the music, as well as to the quality of the performance" (page 462; from *Meridiano di Roma*, June 15, 1941).

As well as discreet annotation throughout, Mr. Schafer has supplied a brief survey of Pound's statements on what he called *absolute
rhythm* and *Great Bass*, to the end that we may learn what was meant
by them, and a most useful Glossary of Important Musical Personalities. He has performed impeccably. So, in making the whole available, has the publisher. But that price! If ever he intuited that his casual articles might be packaged some day at such a figure, Pound
would have seen ample confirmation of his darkest views of the role
of money in contemporary history. At this rate we will soon not be
able to afford to be civilized.

Illuminations

Text solicited by Architectural Digest, *to go with some sumptuous color reproductions; December 1986.*

What people simply *did* with themselves—reaped and raked and bundled, played lutes and bagpipes, drifted in boats, trod grapes, baked loaves, fetched wood—not till Pieter Brueghel painted *The Months* in 1565 would serious art be gratified by the themes it could fetch from so mundane an order as that. And Brueghel's title links hands with a tradition: Books of Hours, Books of Days: books with texts for leisure to ponder, while the one sure thing took its course, the passage of time.

Time, in Christian Europe, weighed heavy on men and women. It elapsed in the interval between the two eternities, one before the womb, one subsequent to the grave. Time brought to your eyes the brilliant surfaces of things: the clouds, the blue of the sky (how gradations of blue were loved!), the bloom of grapes, the lazing fish. (But *two* fish did more than laze; they said "Pisces," February.) Time brought sounds and scents, too, all manner of transient delights.

All that, in which we're immersed, is a show and is passing, as time reminds us in bringing us, day by day, the saints' days, days that were birthdays although by inversion. The saint's day was the day the saint was born into a second and a glorified life. In worldly language, it was the day the saint had died: perhaps peaceably or perhaps horribly, but had anyway died, and into a serenity pigment couldn't venture to limn. That did turn normal experience upside down, death being something it's natural to fear.

So, cunningly, by a three-level hierarchy of images, the Books of Hours enforced some ultimate truths.

As you turned the pages, what they spread before you was a lovingly illuminated list of deaths. That was the foreground, caught by an alphabet that needed your trained intellect to decipher. Words to be read are not for unskilled eyes, anymore than the riddle of death was for unskilled minds.

But if those lists spoke solely to your literacy, they were bordered by two more orders of visual experience. One was the picture your ploughman could read as easily as you—"That's Master Jacques and Jeanne making ready the loaves." The other was the emblem his eye could identify though it took your knowledge to decipher it. "That's a scales." "Yes, but it's really Libra: September."

Alphabetic words then, to evoke the highest skills; next, icons, to be both seen and interpreted; finally, vignettes of the everyday, to be looked at merely. Everywhere in the Middle Ages, and lingering into the Renaissance, we find threefold hierarchies such as those.

They exemplified orders of diminishing difficulty, of lessening sophistication: from marks for arcane translation into speakable sounds, right down to the ephemera one merely *saw*. Oddly, we've come to invert their hierarchy. As creatures of print, we read words without thinking. Habituated to icons like highway signs and airline instruction cards, we interpret an enskied bull as Taurus with little more effort. It is over the easy pictures that we love to ponder.

We examine the crook of an elbow, the stance of a foot. Did people once carry themselves so differently? Or is that an artist's schema, not information? Did nuns indeed play lutes? Why do hills seem to carry towers? What is a windmill doing so high above water? And with what composure, with what sure juxtaposing of color, did the illuminator of this page or this one perform his office of gratifying the eye!

Though he gratified it, likely, to convey the transience of all such gratification. This month, cold February (Pisces), wood is carried in; the chatelaine, hatted, her shoulders wrapped in wool, sits indoors close to the fire. In our exiled estate, in a world from which the very sun rhythmically withdraws, merely keeping warm enough to survive entails work. Another month (any month) loaves get carried to the oven. By the sweat of many brows is bread now gotten, and a planting-month scene (Cancer: June) can be relied on to show us fields being readied, seed being sown.

Such is our annual round. Yet of such we derive our pleasure: in the first place, from the stillness of such pictures, which catch in their serene stasis of ultramarine and ochre moments we have all experienced, when the daily round, just because it was appointed, seemed briefly right. I am doing this; I seem to have always done this; this is the stuff of my life; yet on an earlier day I did something else, which I'll later be doing again. On such a cycle do I fondly build ideas of stability.

And design, the calm of design: the endless leaves unfolding in the borders, the flowers and the odd little nameless creatures whose names Adam knew, the exfoliation of floral forms into capital letters—the very alphabet, that supreme arbitrariness, gathered by courtesy into nature's order.

The scale, finally: the people suitably small, their work overshadowed and crowded toward the margins by a clerical magic, writing. They do seem snug in their margins. Even so, in quattrocento Italy, we glimpse mundane gardens and castles, and hounds and lawns of unexampled green, back over the shoulder of a Virgin or a magnifico. In the background, that's where simplicities belong. That is a lost Paradise, the brilliantly simple.

And when Pieter Brueghel moves simplicity into the foreground, what's arresting is its bustle, its busyness, its sweaty claim to negate the serene transcendental: its pretense to *be* the substance of whatever reality we can know. From Brueghel to Berenice Abbott and beyond runs a documentary tradition we come to terms with every time we open a newspaper: the clutter of the here and now, the claim of detail (this shoe, this jaunty arm) to co-opt all attention. So we prize for their sweetness these long-ago visions that were meant to show us what man is doomed to forsake.

Eye of
the Beholder

Harper's, *August 1983*.

From a long-ago time when locomotives attracted sermons ("If God had intended us to travel at twenty miles an hour . . .") machines have been roiling word-oriented psyches. Just the other week an editor called up to dislike some pages I'd elicited from a word processor. ("If only it hadn't been written by a machine . . .") "If" indeed, and if there's ever a next time remind me to send that bimbo handwritten copy.

The late Marshall McLuhan, media guru, personified an earlier array of biases. He fastidiously did not own a typewriter. A fountain pen, yes, because he liked the nib, but he wouldn't fill it, he *dipped* it. From the little pump on its glorified eyedropper, he shied as from the devil. Useless to cite the simplicity of the process. "That kind of knowledge," he would say, "has been so dearly bought it behooves you to have as little of it as possible."

And from still earlier: when a shutter goes *schnick*, does some devil not see to it that the ensuing photo can never be Art? Whether it can (also what Art may be if it can't) has racked worriers for more than a century. Susan Sontag still inclines to think it can't. Then there are people who equate Art with well-augured investment. When an Ansel Adams print went for $71,500, someone was voting that yes it was Art. "Don't they know I'm not dead yet?" was Adams's own comment.

So can photographs be art? Part of the problem here is making sure what "art" is. An operational definition would be this, that Art is whatever accredited Art Historians find they can talk about with sufficient involvement. Somehow, you see, the criterion moves back toward words, for the excellent reason that it's natural to talk about what interests us. And what, it has been wondered repeatedly, can there be to say about a medium that gives you so accurately the *look* of things, and that's that? Does it, moreover, not by hand but with optics and chemicals? Deep down, there's been all along a confused feeling that Art entails honest toil, not just a machine that goes *schnick*. "*C'est man graphique*," cries a polyglot voice in *Finnegans Wake*, and proceeds to rejoyce because "*ce n'est pas Daguerre*."

But there's been a still deeper, a less articulate confusion: a centuries-old prejudice against any art, manual or no, that seems not to go past the look of things. Is not the mere look perhaps *empty*? Where is Significance? Three centuries before Nikon, painters in Holland were setting forth the look of cows, clouds, towns, churches, food, drink, while bemused tourists could find little to say save that the pictures did indeed contain cows, clouds, etc. That's little for a connoisseur to be able to say, and don't think that the connoisseurs weren't exasperated.

One of these connoisseurs remarked, "Dead swans by Weeninx, as fine as possible. I suppose we did not see less than twenty pictures of dead swans by this painter." Or, "Cattle and a shepherd, by Albert Cuyp, the best I ever saw of him . . . but the employment which he has given the shepherd in his solitude is not very poetical: it must, however, be allowed to be truth and nature; he is catching fleas or something worse."

This tourist in Holland (1781) was Sir Joshua Reynolds, painter and

president of the Royal Academy. A friend of Dr. Johnson, Boswell's
Life of whom is dedicated to him, Sir Joshua breathed easily the air of
noble truths. His most congenial medium was the annual presidential address, of which he delivered fifteen. "The object and intention
of all the arts," he declaimed in 1784, "is to supply the natural imperfection of things, and often to gratify the mind by realising and em-
bodying what never existed but in the imagination." But these Dutch-
men reduced him to counting dead swans, or wincing at the thought
of something worse than fleas. Clearly, Dutch painters did not know
enough to know what they ought to have been about, which was rec-
tifying natural imperfection.

Though no one has ever been able to slight their technical accomplishment—"Two fine pictures of Terburg; the white sattin remarka-
bly well painted"—Reynolds was neither the first nor the last to hint
that it concealed a certain mindlessness: "He seldom omitted to introduce a piece of white sattin in his pictures." Why on earth paint such
trivialities at all? A century later the French artist and art historian Eu-
gène Fromentin would ask, "What motive had a Dutch painter in
painting a picture?" and answer himself with a triumphant thunder-
clap: "None." What Fromentin's rhetoric bespeaks is, alas, vacuity:
and, until recently, it was in vacuity that the matter more or less remained.

Svetlana Alpers opens her book on Dutch painting* with Reynolds's predicament—what on earth is there to be said?—and does
not close it till she has shown us how much there is to say if you'll not
require a picture's claim on your attention to be somehow theatrical;
also if you'll be open to the optical sciences that were new in the seventeenth century. (A Dutchman invented the microscope.) In the year
of the Stieglitz exhibition at the National Gallery, *The Art of Describing*
is a book luckily timed. So well did seventeenth-century Dutch painters anticipate the camera's absorbed *looking* that any ways we can find
to think and talk about them can give us ways to think and talk about
photography. When we ask if it's art, what we're asking is how to talk
about it.

The Art of Describing, by Svetlana Alpers. University of Chicago Press, 1983.

What art historians talk about with most confidence is Italian painting, partly because Italians were showing how the talk should go just
when painting itself was being invented. It was Leone Battista Alberti
(1404–72) who defined "a picture" the way we still imagine it, in Alpers's paraphrase: "a framed surface or pane situated at a certain distance from a viewer who looks through it at a second or substitute
world." Note that Alberti commences with the frame: the boundary
around our view of the second world. It is like a proscenium arch surrounding a stage on which, at least in the Renaissance, "human figures performed significant actions based on the texts of the poets. It is
a narrative art."

So Botticelli's Venus rides her great shell according to the text of
Angelo Poliziano, court poet to the Medicis, who gleaned hints from
earlier poets and learned from Ovid that one of her hands ought to
hold her wet tresses. He describes her hand so; Botticelli paints it so;
they show us a classical story, the Birth of Venus. Schoolchildren today are still taught to enter a picture by way of its story; in *Life* and in
your daily paper, captions guide you toward extracting a story from
each picture—were there no story in it, you well understand, it'd not
be granted space. So tight, still, is the grip of Renaissance Italy.

Though Cézanne has long since shown us that two men playing
cards, or fruit upon a table, things with no special literary credentials,
may be enough to see in the second world, even these have a latent
story content. (What fruits? What time of year? What country? What
sort of house? Or perhaps an inn?) Something we're not left free for is
unpestered gazing, especially since Cézanne, as he turns sleek surfaces into painterly blobs, urges us to witness his transaction with the
painted surface: his *performance* in this ineluctable theater. And Picasso does no less.

Man, went a Renaissance motto, is the measure of all, and you'll remember that Alberti specified his framed surface or pane as "situated
at a certain distance from a viewer." That clause controls the whole intricate science of a key Renaissance invention, perspective, since it
makes the viewer the key to what is viewed.

Perspective, as everyone knows, entails a Vanishing Point. This in turn is located with respect to a viewing point, a certain distance from the picture and generally opposite its center. You'd get a perspective drawing of the view from your window if you simply traced its outlines on the glass, always careful to keep your eye steadily located. Your drawing would then "look right" to anyone who placed an eye in just the same spot, but not otherwise. All explanations of perspective follow this scheme. A Dürer woodcut shows the draftsman and his model with the frame between them, and what he's going to draw is exactly what he can see of her through that frame when his eye is at a position he has marked with the end of an upright stick. The frame is squared and so is his drawing paper. He, she, and the frame exemplify a good orthodox Alberti situation.

Svetlana Alpers spells out a meaning for this: "Alberti's picture . . . begins not with the world seen, but with a viewer who is actively looking out at objects . . . whose appearance is a function of their distance from the viewer." The viewer, you see, is paramount. The viewer controls what is there (man is measure of all things). Alpers underlines another Italian bias when she adds that the objects are "preferably human figures" (i.e., not cows or clouds).

But Dutch paintings of the seventeenth century are bafflingly indifferent to a spectator. Landscapes (like views through a telephoto lens) are so remote no vanishing point can be ascertained. A church interior by Saenredam offers you *two* vanishing points: what you see when you turn your head left, then right.

Dutch painters might create views without reference to any viewer, by placing people, in effect, inside a large model of the eye. This was the famous camera obscura, a room with a lens in the wall. In a 1664 drawing, two gentlemen inside such a room hold out a paper surface "on which is cast the image of the landscape beyond—people, trees, boats on the river, are all brought inside, represented for their delectation."

That is how sight gets into the eye, and it is also an "unframed image of the world compressed onto a bit of paper with no prior viewer to establish a position or a human scale from which, as we say, to take in the work. The gentlemen standing by, detached observers, also remind us that such an image, rather than being calculated to fit our space, provides its own."

Sir Joshua Reynolds was contemptuous of the camera obscura. If we suppose a view of nature represented with all the truth of such a gadget, "and the same scene represented by a great artist," the first by comparison will appear "little and mean." Sir Joshua thought that what was merely there to be seen required significance pumped in. The Dutch thought otherwise. They thought the visible world, the telescopic, too, and the microscopic, so wonderful no eye ever could exhaust it. A small viewer would even be placed within a picture, looking up, encouraging us to enter the space and look up with him, at an area perspective lines do not converge on: so little privilege has the "point of view" outside the frame, where Italian custom places the only spectator who matters.

Spurred by such sciences as optics and cartography, these Dutch painters created what Alpers calls a "descriptive mode" that the late twentieth century can find startlingly congenial, one reason it has had to wait till our century to get itself described. It comprises numerous effects we now take for granted. As Beckett's contemporaries, we can accept its self-possessed indifference to *effectiveness*. Long since at peace with Georgia O'Keeffe's painted bones, we accept the willingness of a Jacques de Gheyn to let a foregrounded hermit crab dominate a lurid human scene. Porers since childhood over encyclopedias, we share the fascination of descriptive painters with small things lovingly rendered to no particular scale, in images set in no essential arrangement.

In one astonishing color plate we are shown a *View of Amsterdam* so indifferent to Albertian perspective no human eye could ever have beheld it. The city is displayed from above as on a map, but obliquely, like an aerial photo, with the whitecaps on the waves, the ships in the harbor, each single building and its windows rendered, and mottling the whole the shadows of moving clouds that the picture omits because they are above the viewer. These shadows are the imprint of an instant, their transience in tension with cartographic stability. I once glimpsed Venice like that, from an Alitalia 727. Save in his own picture, Jan C. Micker three hundred years ago never saw any such thing. Yet he had a rationale behind every line.

No, photography is no art, if by "art" we mean the picture defined by Alberti: which, Alpers remarks, is the kind of picture every party to the old debate about photography has firmly fixed in mind. Such was the picture long-ago photo-artists aped when they'd hang white robes on at least three girls, who were then instructed to comport themselves like Graces, a thing they did by holding their arms aloft. That was thought Art, as were kittens out of focus.

Alfred Stieglitz discovered the virtue of sharp focus early; also of selective focus, a single plane clearly rendered, the way the eye pays selective attention. Stieglitz all his life entangled himself in rhetoric about "the *meaning* of the *idea* of photography," and was a long time pulling free of kitsch. But look, here's a girl with a paint box, sitting on a cushion (because her skirt is white) on the dirt next to unruly plants. Her brush, just being lifted from the waterglass, is held the professional way, not like a pencil but between thumb and forefinger. Her sketch pad is still blank. What does she mean to paint? Probably the sky, which has caught her eyes the way alarm catches a fawn's. The print is postcard size, dated 1918. Its downward glance is indifferent to canons of perspective. It could nearly be anyone's snapshot. In its mixture of nearly abstract tonal balance and unassuming human observation it is a masterwork. (The girl, by the way, is Georgia O'Keeffe.)

Such an image is worth a ream of theory. It is plate 43 in *Alfred Stieglitz: Photographs and Writings*.* Plate 45 is *Shadow on the Lake*, just that, two human shadows cast on unruly water where leaves float and clouds are reflected too. Dutch scientific curiosity would have prized it. And plate 57 is a modulation of pearly grays with, right at the bottom, a remote dark gray hill set off by close black treetops, and partway up the valiant disk of the sun showing small through an edge-lit cloud.

***Alfred Stieglitz: Photographs and Writings*, by Sarah Greenough and Juan Hamilton. National Gallery of Art, 1983.*

To look through this album with an eye sharpened by Svetlana Alpers's account of the Dutch "descriptive mode" is to empathize with Stieglitz's lifelong struggle to get free of the tacky Art he had in his blood. In the year that he photographed the pearly image of sun and cloud (1922), he was also capable of something as awful as plate 50, where a nude, contorted by feigned abdominal pain, seems to be demonstrating nature's remedy: press three oranges where it hurts. That attempts to be Art in the Albertian mode, and the thing to do with it is look away.

"The photographic image, the Dutch art of describing, . . . Impressionist painting": these, says Svetlana Alpers, "are all examples of a constant artistic option in the art of the West." By contrast, both Michelangelo and Picasso are in Alberti's line: theatrical. But just to let the eye guide the hand (not a facile notion), or to let the mind glimpse what light entering a camera may record . . . before long there'll be Zen accounts I don't want to read.

Meanwhile, Ansel Adams: "The external world has nothing but shapes, we see form, weight, balance, values. We also see and feel more esoteric and intangible things. I want to take photographs that have all that in them." And Stieglitz (to Sherwood Anderson) "I have been looking for years—50 upwards—at a particular sky line of simple hills . . . I'd love to get down what 'that' line has done for me— May be I have—somewhat—in those snapshots I've been doing the last few years." When he entered Paradise God had forgiven his art, out of liking for his snapshots.

Georgia O'Keeffe

My own favorite among my forty-odd Art & Antiques *columns; from Summer 1986.*

Had Manuel Francisco Ciriaco Fenollosa del Pino del Gil del Alvarez been unable to learn the French horn overnight, he'd not have sailed with a military band to the United States but instead have been drafted into the Carlist wars. Then his son Ernest Fenollosa would not have been born (1853) in Salem, Massachusetts, of all places, and the world we inhabit would be a bleaker one.

Ernest Fenollosa was to spend twenty years, off and on, in Japan, where they made him Imperial Commissioner of Fine Arts. In the notes he scribbled while scholars explained old poems from China, Ezra Pound would find (1914) the way to *Cathay* and to much of the rationale of the *Cantos*. And the Japanese theme of pictures as balanced masses of color would take possession of Fenollosa's pupil Arthur Wesley Dow, for imparting (also 1914, at Teacher's College, Columbia) to the fervent Miss Georgia Totto O'Keeffe from Sun Prairie, Wisconsin, whose pictures subsequently . . . (and everybody knows how to finish this sentence).

That much, certainly, of the American century's aesthetic heritage came bubbling out of Papa Manuel's serendipitous horn.

Georgia O'Keeffe's pictures never finick about a "likeness," the way God intended ladies' pictures in her day to finick. But neither did she splash colors about the way Wassily Kandinsky seemed to. When Kandinsky called color the keyboard, and the soul a piano with many strings, Georgia O'Keeffe could read with close attention while distrusting all Russian enthusiasm for the soul. She preferred her pictures rooted in something she'd seen.

Chicken in Sunrise (1917) a red world with yellow sky, inky flowers, a huge stylized black chicken. *Morning Glory with Black* (1926) a yardsquare eruption of pastel floral curves from the sinister shrouding blackness, lower left. *White Flower* (1929) again huge—the very scale says "picture," not "flower"—an assault of whiteness controlled by its central radiance of yellows, greens, oranges: homage to pistil and stamen that send forth petals the way nuclei radiate lines of cosmic force. *Red Canna* (1923) an unfolding conflagration: flowery flames with hard edges eternally consuming the rectangular universe.

Not "lady-pictures," no. Among the new things to be seen in the 1920s were photos of nebulae from Mount Wilson Observatory, where the one-hundred-inch mirror got installed in 1917, and drawings of proton-neutron compactions with electron systems attendant, those orderly quiet solitudes of pre-quark physics. Monochrome systems and contours, not heeded as "art": invested by Georgia O'Keeffe's theatrical colors, such revelations of forms stupendously large, inconceivably small, appear everywhere in the flower paintings she made for two decades.

The bones succeeded the flowers, and New Mexico, New York (after the hive, the desert). White, absolute, egg-clean, the huge pelvic forms of the 1940s won't leave off soliciting memory. They say, examine the stripped contours of fertility. They say, we outshine the moon. They say, we, firm and curvaceous, are earth's durable ghosts. The sky seen through a pelvic girdle resembles a huge robin's egg. Erect, end-on, the wings of a cow's pelvis become two forms dancing to the indifferent moon. White, a dead cottonwood tree seems intricate as a bone.

They take dominion over the New Mexico landscape, a part of America otherwise resistant to gentling imagination. As Wallace Stevens in his poem imagined he'd set a jar in Tennessee, whereupon Tennessee arranged itself around that jar, so the Georgia O'Keeffe bones, dinosaur-huge, collect and arrange mesa and pedernal, arroyo and gulch, air and light and austere uncanny silence. Foregrounded, they debar you from entering their space. Curved, contoured, they are not unfriendly. Too huge to be the relics of anything dead, they resemble fantasies by Frank Lloyd Wright realized in gritty porcelain. They are firm and stark and their geometry is inflexible. You'll not talk around them nor talk them away.

Just before Georgia O'Keeffe died in the spring of her ninety-ninth year, the space shuttle Challenger exploded into billowy plumes of vapor. It had been reaching for an orbit like a moon's. Toward the end of her life we'd achieved the capability for disaster on a scale unattainable by the train wrecks of her 1890s childhood, but achieved the freedom, too, of vaster dreams. She's an artist whose accomplishment seems unabashed by such accelerations. Those flowers penetrate space; those bones assert imagination's obduracy.

American Homer

From the December 1986 Art & Antiques, *and can you spot the one sentence I cherish this for?*

Short, lean, going egg-bald in his thirties: a dyspeptic accountant, seemingly. The brown eyes lurked above a handlebar moustache. When father threatened a visit, the son's misdirection was to paint *Coal Bin* on his workroom door. Born 150 years ago last February 24, he was Mark Twain's almost exact contemporary (Twain eighty-six days older, and they died, in 1910, nearly in synchrony, Halley's Comet seeing them in and out). Heavenly twins, Winslow Homer and Mark Twain defined nineteenth-century America. It would have gratified Twain to be twinned with someone named Homer.

One instance of a new era starting is that Andy Jackson was president in 1836. Pre-Jackson America had been eighteenth century. And 1910, that's the twentieth-century's dawn. The nineteenth century lasted about seventy-five years. Homer spanned it exactly: a stirring epoch.

In 1857 he drew for *Harper's Weekly* a picture with a football dead center. On the left are Harvard freshmen, slight, jejune. On the right, Harvard sophs, stern, enormous. Their stature comes partly from top hats, their sternness from the moustaches they've grown since the freshman year. Several even look like Poe. The trousers on both sides are tapered, the boots pointed. Watch-chains, too, are visible. In a space filled with menace, nobody moves. Football has a long way to come.

Winslow Homer liked the look of something impending or doing. No static pyramids, for him, of "composition," no frozen French theatrics, German luridities, above all no insipid complicity with the genteel. In Paris, 1867, he drew for *Harper's* some fifty folk including a gloomy Pasha who are watching a man whirl his dancing partner off the floor. You can see her ankles under the flare of her skirts, and *Harper's*, adducing the brink of the abyss, reproved "this too curious crowd of spectators" and called for a preacher or a moralist. As late as 1870 a large oil now in the Met was judged "not quite refined" because a girl is wringing sea water from her dress. (You can see her knees!)

Illustration work helped save him from studio tushery. Drawing on a wood block the engraver would cut, he was his time's Alfred Eisenstadt, its W. Eugene Smith. Something, now, real, was going on! Dancers, skaters, even climbers (1870) to the summit of Mount Washington, where they take the breezes of "the coolest spot in New England" and ladies' scarves stream in a welcome wind.

None of that is "important" Homer, but his early illustrator's discipline did underlie his greatness: always the moment of action. *Leaping Trout* (1892): yes, two of them, mid-air. *A Summer Night* (1890): the glistening sea, with silhouetted watchers, and, foregrounded, somehow in light, a couple waltzing. Most astonishing, *Right and Left* (1909): two ducks in the instant of death, dropping dead from air toward water. Remote, the hunter's blast erupts straight toward us onlookers.

So when he spent the summer of 1878 at Houghton Farm, near Cornwall, New York, among girls and sheep his eye sought, at the very least, a confrontation. He found it between girl and air. One sheep is indifferent, one is sheepishly alert, but the shepherdess's day is being made by the wind that sends her bonnet ribbons streaming and drives clouds through the sky.

How exactly she's posed, stolid, pleasured by the gale; how exactly

Homer refrains from allegorizing her. "Shepherd": the word has been laden with connotations since Thessaly. . . . Pastoral! But here's a sturdy American girl, not flinging arms wide but liking what she's feeling. Standing on that ridge, up amid that coarse grass, she clasps her hands quietly because this cool is nice.

Such accurate delicacy helps us understand how Homer's better-known pictures—fisherfolk, peril, great waves—escape the Little-Eva melodrama that surrounds them the way sentiment surrounded Mark Twain: whose Huck Finn escapes it too. Between them, Twain and Homer redeem the America that kept wanting to pretend till it came up with Norman Rockwell.

Tumult of
the Limbs

Harper's, *December 1983. Writing in the Maine woods, I was drawing on memory for everything not in Gay's book itself.*

Bourgeoisie: sons of parvenus. EMILE ZOLA

The bourgeois sees in his wife a mere instrument of production.
MARX AND ENGELS

[They] bore you . . . by endless floods of clichés and solemn asininities. THÉOPHILE GAUTIER

. . . large, fat bourgeois sofas . . . HENRY JAMES

. . . Watch and umbrella . . . insipid bourgeois implements . . .
MARCEL PROUST

Where they love they do not desire, and where they desire they cannot love. SIGMUND FREUD

When you said "bourgeois" in the nineteenth century, you were letting irritation show. It was the word for people you disliked, who were inferior to you but not inferior enough. So "bourgeois" came to mean all that Matthew Arnold meant by "philistine," and more. It became an all-purpose slur.

Like the tree toad and the swamp adder, the "bourgeois" is named for his habitat, the "bourg"; he's an urban irritant, like the traffic jam. Whether affluent or threadbare, hearty or pale, he institutionalizes mediocrity. The satisfactions he craves, erotic or aesthetic, will be above all undemanding, reassuring. He's inseparable from his high collar, and his life is the reverse of free and easy. Constipation clogs his mind; also his shoes pinch, and (Gustave Flaubert observed) his consummation is a hat so little distinct from ten thousand other hats* it might get swapped at the office had he not thought to write his name inside it. He prides himself on such foresight.

This is caricature? Yes, of course. The avant-garde blamed him for trivializing public taste, the liberated for denying untrammeled love. The liberated avant-garde were the time's art makers, Monsieur Bourgeois their quintessential comic preoccupation.

Flaubert, his most resourceful chronicler, bids us to imagine a race whose opinions and sayings are as standardized as canned beans. In the *Dictionary of Received Ideas* he toiled at for decades and left unfinished at his death in 1880, Flaubert arranged these alphabetically by key word. The slim book is both a field guide for bourgeois watchers and a handy manual for aspirants to bourgeois status. Thus:

Erection	Used only of monuments.
Hiatus	Not to be tolerated.
Homer	Never existed; famous for his laughter.
Pyramid	Useless labor.
Redheads	Hotter than blondes or brunettes.
Sea (The)	Makes you think of the infinite.

Himself a word-and-dictionary virtuoso, Flaubert created his bourgeois in his own image. That was standard procedure; thus in their *Diary of a Nobody* (1892), George and Weedon Grossmith, stage comedians, created Mr. Henry Pooter, who, though otherwise what

---

*Though not in American twenties cinema, where the hat—Chaplin's bowler, Lloyd's skimmer, Keaton's porkpie—is his individuating mark.

you'd expect from his name, is subject to fragile dreams of being the life of the party, could a Pooter conceive a party to be the life of. "I'm 'fraid they're frayed," he heard himself say one day of his shirt cuffs. He took pains to record this *trouvaille* in his diary and judged it the best joke he had ever made.

Pooter's diary was a knowing touch. Keeping a diary was one way the bourgeois could sustain a precious conviction of existence: of being a continuing "I." The diary was an indispensable bourgeois prop. Numerous nineteenth-century diaries have survived. At Yale they store boxes of them. For, yes, there was a bourgeoisie outside of comic literature, its behavior to be sure frequently comic (rioting at *The Playboy of the Western World*, Dublin, 1907, or at *Le Sacre du Printemps*, Paris, 1913)* but its anxieties, miseries (and raptures) were much in excess of comedy's brisk resources.

They were Freud's lifelong study, and if Freud, like Flaubert, was a simplifier, he was no comedian. The bourgeois of his imagination epitomized Civilization and its Discontents, and not all of Europe could accommodate the couches it would take to straighten them out. For are we not defined by our sexuality? And the thought of sexual contentment tied any bourgeois in pretzels, especially someone else's contentment: for instance that of the lusty girl-next-door, she of the flouncing skirts.

Fie on her, and there ought to be a law, and there often was. Bourgeois opinion saw to that . . .

So their legend has grown, embellished with no doubt apocryphal stories. The one about the Massachusetts headmistress who concealed the "limbs" of a grand piano in "frilled modest little trousers" comes to us from a British yarn-spinner who may have invented her (Capt. Frederick Marryat, *A Diary in America, with Remarks on Its Institutions*, 1839).

Likewise the girl whose wedding night advice from Mother was to lie still and think of England: that invites disbelief, does it not? But

---

*And again, I've been told, at *Le Sacre* in Australia in the fifties, by which time Stravinsky's Slavic barbarity had at last crept as far as Down Under. That's one indication that the bourgeois species is stable: also that it tends to be in part defined by the capacity for outrage Flaubert paraphrased finely: *"Ne pas le tolérer!"*

don't be too sure. For we hear of another bride-to-be saying, "I'm afraid, Mamma—I want to know what will happen to me!" and Mamma snapping, "You can't be as stupid as you pretend." And hers is a true story; she was Edith Wharton, the novelist, whose mother thought she should have learned all she needed from statues that showed men "made differently from women." There's real anguish behind those cartoons; and which are cartoons, which daguerreotypes?

All manner of people in that era led all manner of lives. Yet joke, legend, caricature, actuality seem inextricable. Is any truth about the bourgeoisie recoverable?

Peter Gay, Durfee Professor of History at Yale, thinks it's high time for their rendezvous with sober history. To launch his multivolume series on *The Bourgeois Experience: Victoria to Freud,* Gay has dedicated Volume 1: *Education of the Senses* (Oxford University Press, 1984) to the unfamiliar proposition that, pantaloons on pianos or no, bourgeois senses did indeed often get awakened.

Gay's opening sequence draws on the diary perky Mabel Loomis Todd kept in Amherst, Massachusetts, all about the "orgasmic intensity" she enjoyed with both her husband, David Todd, an astronomer directly descended from Jonathan Edwards, and her elderly lover, Austin Dickinson, treasurer of Amherst College, who gratifies connoisseurs of symmetry not only by having kept Mabel doubly satisfied but by having been the poet Emily Dickinson's saturnine-looking brother. Mabel was the first editor of Emily's poems, and Emily rather applauded the affair with red-wigged Austin, who deserved some fun.

Gay uses her diary to challenge a cliché: that postindustrial women sat around being repressed till psychoanalysis came along to unscrew them. Mabel might have been invented to test that hypothesis. Her birth year, 1856, was also Freud's. Her upbringing in Georgetown retraces the diagram of affluent bourgeois culture. One emblem of that culture was the piano; when she was in her twenties, 424 German factories were shipping 73,000 pianos a year. Unsurprisingly, Mabel Loomis "played the piano and sang, wrote poetry and painted."

True, before long she was casually putting on paper what could strain the norms of gentility. "At times she felt flooded by words burning 'with the intenseness of their birth,' by a 'power,' a 'terrible sacred flame' which 'throbs so through my whole being.' " Gay may not be wrong when he finds such phrasing "erotic." If Freud is your mentor, erotic is what it is. Still, Henry James has feckless heroines who gush like that out of sheer misjudged literariness. And Mabel, when she was abroad, could sound as though James were inventing her;* didn't she judge "average American travellers" "the vulgarest people" in Europe?

A lively American philistine? In a way. None of this is incompatible with the D.A.R. chapter regent she became. But now the stereotype begins to blur. I can't say what she'd have made of *Le Sacre du Printemps*: for that matter, what she actually may have made of it—she lived till 1932, when it was two decades old.

But we can have no doubt about how she esteemed what W. B. Yeats in the new century would be calling "the tumult of the limbs," something James avoided though his heroines didn't always. "It was a thrilling sort of breathlessness—but at last it came—the same beautiful climax of feeling I knew so well. . . ." That's one jotting of many. Even in pregnancy, "my nights were ofttimes radiant, & my days glorified by this heavenly proof of our deep love for each other—never, however, often enough to weaken nor tire me—& sometimes carried to their fullest consummation. . . ." Here the ministering angel is her husband, who also, as she soon found, not only liked it when she "flirted outrageously" with every man in the room but would cheerfully carry messages between her and the lover who entered her life when she was twenty-five and just two years wed.

Austin Dickinson was then fifty-three, his back turned on a "vulgar, moody and vindictive" wife who'd aborted four children before a son was born ("and she had tried to abort him, too"). Through Amherst he moved with authority, wielding "a voice like thunder." His affair with Mabel Todd was a secret everyone in Amherst shared: "a test case for middle-class gentility." David Todd was especially sharing. He'd warn the lovers when he was coming home by whistling a

*See "A Bundle of Letters" and, of course, *Daisy Miller*.

tune from *Martha*,* and when she was away he would "join her lover that both might praise the woman they adored." "I think we three would have no trouble in a house together in living as you and I would wish," wrote Mr. Dickinson to Mrs. Todd, and we can't say he wasn't right. David philandered ad lib., without quenching his passion for Mabel. His extracurricular passions were "incestuous, polygamous, probably homosexual." As for Dickinson, he persuaded Mabel that "conventionalism is for those not strong enough to be laws for themselves," and she agreed that this was "dangerous doctrine for the masses, but one in a thousand can understand it." Thus they rose above castigation in a way that reminds Mr. Gay of Nietzsche. And that was all going on in the 1880s, in New England, not so far from where they'd once hung witches.

Madame Bovary without the unhappy ending? No, if the bliss was polymorphous while it lasted, the ending was less than idyllic. Austin Dickinson died in 1895, to the devastation of David as well as Mabel. David spent his last years in an insane asylum, sobbing, slavering, pawing, in a way that could nauseate his daughter when she visited ("he tried to kiss me on the mouth, and thrust his tongue into my mouth with all the accompaniments"). Daughter Millicent was oppressed lifelong by her family's past and by "a sensitiveness to injustice with a determination to do something to set things right." A brooder, a fixer, a meddler, what a destiny. And Mabel spent years as a remorseless clubwoman-organizer; one thing she organized was the Amherst chapter of the Daughters of the American Revolution, of which she was first regent.

When they opened up Charles Bovary after his death, they found, Flaubert tells us with grim accuracy, "nothing."

What was there to be found in the Mabel Todd of the last years? A relentless motor, probably. She lived to be seventy-five, and was remembered for her energy.

Her papers, in boxes numbered into the hundreds, are at Yale. They include the journals in which she'd commence each January to

---

*Readers of *Ulysses* will remember Mr. Bloom's discreet connivance in his wife's affair, and the catalyzing effect of a song from *Martha*. How accurate is art.

number the year's orgasms. What is to be learned from this archive is a question Mr. Gay, though on the whole an orthodox Freudian, is too sensible to wave aside. Respondents to *Playboy* surveys are doubly disqualified as an all-American sample—they (1) all read *Playboy* and (2) have all elected to respond—and likewise Mabel Loomis Todd, by the very fact that she kept the journals she did, has less to tell us about the Bourgeois Experience than about her tireless frenetic self. So what do they signify? That's a problem throughout the book. When our evidence must be the explicit document, a myth of normal hush-hush is hard to challenge, since the myth predeclares all explicitness as non-normal.

Here's a less spicy diary. A thirty-three-year-old Connecticut housewife kept it in 1880. We don't even know her name. Beckett might have invented her.

May 5: "A day of days. I believe I shall be insane if there is not a change some day." June 15: "Unable to work. An iron horse *can* wear out." June 18: "A home day. The figure-head looked on while the slaves labored." June 20: "Went to Baptist church in the evening. Mr. Knapp ranted." Sept. 6: "Aunt Sophia came up and assisted me at the wash-tub. Very romantic life." Sept. 10: "Shall I ever forget these dreary days?" Oct. 8: "An invalid today, but if I am sick I only have to work the harder so it does not pay." Nov. 13: "A day of hard work, but I am accustomed to that."

What that's all about is the housework she's doing single-handed. In achieving what Mr. Gay calls "a kind of mordant poetry," it documents, too, he thinks, a "war between the sexes" that smoldered in those years. Readers less preoccupied with sexology may choose to dwell on its chilling glimpses of a technology still not far from medieval, and the middle-class poverty that went with that. What would one day lift from such wives the dawn-to-dark burden of washboard and scrubbing brush, the interminable despair of work undoable and never done, wasn't psychosocial reform but electricity. Mabel Todd's time for rapture was earned by her servants, whose own journals, if they'd kept any, might make bleak reading.

Though Freud has much to tell us about the century in which he and Mabel Todd shared forty-four years, if you squint and peer with only a Freudian flashlight you bang against much inexplicable clutter. It's when Peter Gay stops to interpret that we learn least; then he Freudianizes by reflex. He's solemn in reciting the hoariest Viennese one-liners (e.g., "The erotic desires and fears stimulated by the rhythmic experience of the train ride"; so where's Amtrak when we need it?). What makes the book absorbing is the sheer range of his researches. He's at his best simply transcribing and paraphrasing the elements of a fascinating collage. For instance:

Here's Dr. Edward H. Clarke (*Sex in Education*, 1873) explaining why Vassar had turned a Miss D—— from a cheerful freshman to a "pale, hysterical" graduate who "almost constantly complained of headaches": life at Vassar was "out of harmony with the rhythmical periodicity of the female organization." Thus the "vital and constructive" force in Miss D—— had gone to her brain instead of to "the ovaries and their accessories" where it belonged, and so much for places like Vassar. Clarke "was neither a quack nor a crank, and his Harvard connections were impeccable." He seems to have been misled by a hysteric's fantasies. His book was reprinted eleven times in a year, and one of several refutations was undertaken by Julia Ward ("Battle Hymn") Howe.

Or here's Anthony Comstock, he of Comstockery, conceding, contrary to all expectation, that "the nude in art is not necessarily obscene, lewd or indecent": unless, that is, it was French. So he had Herman Knoedler arrested for displaying, in his Fifth Avenue gallery, photographs of "lewd French art—a foreign foe." No indeed, not even fanatics always failed to discriminate.

Yet "the whole country of the senses was befogged by delicacy." Here's "how Natalie Barney, celebrated international beauty . . . learned about her forthcoming menses around 1886: her mother pointed to fish in an aquarium who were 'giving off red fibers: "You will have them too when you are older. You must not be too surprised."' At twelve, when Natalie Barney began to menstruate, she was not surprised so much as appalled: she fainted."

But do not suppose that everything was concealed. "Nudes were . . . on display everywhere throughout the nineteenth century. They decorated parks and fountains. . . . They stood in niches, covered walls, spread across ceilings. They could represent, allegorize, celebrate, or symbolize almost anyone or anything: lying supine . . . — the dead Abel; playful and pneumatic—electricity; exuberant, youthful, dressed only in seductive long stockings—the bicycle." If symbolic distance was exactly calculated, as when Hiram Powers in mid-century sculpted the *Greek Slave*—young, female, totally naked, standing on display for prospective Turkish purchasers—whole families could feel religious awe. Wrote a witness, "Men take off their hats, ladies seat themselves silently, and almost unconsciously; and usually it is minutes before a word is uttered. All conversation is carried on in a hushed tone, and everybody looks serious on departing."

For she wasn't flaunting a seductive or a suspiciously innocent nudity; she was on sale, as much so as the innumerable copies of the statue. So she was pure, and invited (Gay says shrewdly) "the saving comment that she was really fully dressed." That's as central a bourgeois parable as you'll find, and not one to condescend to before you've understood it. As Stewart Brand, the anarchic aphorist, wrote in recommendation of the *Wall Street Journal*, "The money keeps them honest."

Darlington

Back in the sixties the old Life *began running book reviews up front among the ads, chiefly to confer more freedom on the reshuffling of ads among the regional editions they'd invented in vain hope of fending off disaster. Needing a science book reviewed, Dave Scherman for some reason turned to me, and during several years* Life *had me type-cast as a science specialist. Darlington's remains the most involving of the books I reviewed in that capacity. I'd have welcomed more room, but for* Life *you counted not just words but* lines. *They were using each (dispensable) review to reserve exactly the space for a half-page ad. From July 4, 1970.*

THE EVOLUTION OF MAN AND SOCIETY, *by C. D. Darlington. Simon and Schuster, 1969.*

Hitler put such a curse on the word "race" that even orthodontists have to talk evasively. All the same, Susie's dentition went expensively wrong because the size of her teeth came through one ancestral group and the structure of her jaw through another. Discrepancies perhaps generations latent collided in her oral cavity. The snaggle-toothed result, but for bands and forceps, would diminish her marriageability, in the race's way of making it less likely that things will go wronger and wronger. Even a half-blind swain would cool; odd teeth make for odd speech, and a man likes an agreeable voice on the pillow.

When the orthodontist eases Susie's lot he is imponderably altering the twenty-second century, as well as making jobs for future orthodontists. Also he is more likely than Joe the Bookie to beget future orthodontists; good eyes breed good eyes, deft hands deft hands, "People marry within the trade," crafts tend to be tribalized (hence the Professional Classes).

On which principles, having shut your mind to thoughts of "inferior" and "superior" races, you could almost write a racial history of mankind. Professor Darlington has: not a book to learn history from, but a book to correct other histories, historians not having hitherto thought of genetic knowledge as one of their sources.

Such knowledge is all rather recent. What happens when kin breed (the royal houses of Europe), what happens when races cross (Norsemen—"Normans"—with Celts) was profoundly mysterious until 1900, when Mendel's mislaid work with sweet peas was rediscovered. In a mere seventy years geneticists have grown learned and subtle enough to define breeding groups whose characteristics stabilize, and guess that every religion, language, caste, even trade tends to make such a group. And Professor Darlington tries out how this will work as a key to the whole history of mankind.

Breezily confident that official historical motives are probably fraudulent, he often rises to majestic crankery. Thus Christianity was "permanently spread away from southern countries by its neglect of cleanliness, its opposition to nudity and washing," because in warm countries with dense populations only hygiene will check disease, and Christians trusted rather to baptism than to bathing.

Whereas Mohammed impaired the northward spread of his cult by a different scientific mistake. He used a lunar calendar, and his fasts and feasts crept round the year; and "the day-long feast of Ramadhan could have been kept in high latitudes only if it had always fallen in winter." One fancies, in latitudes of the midnight sun, devout Lapps honoring Allah, fasting and fasting while the midnight sun refuses to drop out of the sky.

Like French farce, relying on one order of causation only, that which sweeps bankers to the doors of undulant blondes, such Swiftian reasonableness need not be wholly credited to be tonic. And often it yields revelations. If Christian monogamy "created a formal distinction between legitimate offspring from mating within classes and illegitimate offspring from mating between classes," we may see in a new light all those illegitimates of conspicuous endowment (Michelangelo, Sophia Loren), genetic potential having long accumulated behind barriers marriage refused till passion crossed them.

And if trades make races, races can make trades. The flood of religious immigrants who transformed Geneva from a town to a great city had in common the fact that Calvin attracted them. Hence, they were skillful folk, and diligent and grave; hence (yes, hence), the Swiss watch industry. But metal-workers of less exacting disciplines tend to wander. Post-Neolithic bronzesmiths carried their craft all over the early world, and even today gypsies mend kettles.

Such insights converge on a fascinating critique of Marx, who had his theory backward. "Class differences ultimately all derive from genetic, and, usually, racial differences. . . . It is the inequalities that create advances in society rather than advances in society that create the inequalities."

One last vignette: the paleolithic hunter, skilled in animals, impatient of regular work, incapable of long-term prudence; "no training or persuasion will ever cause him to change his opinion." Genes never die; even today "his fecklessness, his interest in killing game, his yearning for movement are found at the top and the bottom of society." Now turn your eye on Edwardian England's governing class, and ask whether World War I was not dawdled into by a clan of elegant Paleolithic throwbacks.

How the Cruiser Was Grounded and Finn MacCool Returned

Distilled for National Review (August 5, 1977), from press clippings harvested on a visit to Ireland. Surly rejoinders from IRA sympathizers all seemed boiler-plate from the same basement.

I had some business in Ireland with a man named Bloom, and by an implacability of scheduling arrived there toward the climax of the summer's excitement. With the Republic papered with posters and wired for sound sea to sea, 375 assorted patriots, competing for 148 seats in the Dáil Eireann, were abroad addressing rallies, ringing doorbells, asserting that the other lot was not fit to be washed, arranging for mass resurrections from Glasnevin Cemetery, and in other ways as well affirming the health of parliamentary democracy among a people whose talents in that line have been exported as far afield as Cook County, Illinois.

An election anywhere is a communal madness, fittest to be described by the conventions of science fiction. An entire harassed people shouts and dances its way through a space-warp into a domain where words and doings come unhitched from all normal significance and, after wild ritual gyrations there, emerges again into Newtonian space, having somehow agreed to submit for several years to a minimally altered pattern of harassments. No one afterward can quite agree on how it all happened, though The People are conceded to have Spoken, amid such intoxication it is true as attended the speech of oracles in Greece. What did they say? Wild stammering words, which only the new government is authorized to interpret.

The new government in Ireland as of this summer is Jack Lynch's Fianna Fáil, generally translated "soldiers of destiny." Here Dinneen's Irish Dictionary is of more help than the phrase books. The Fianna, in a tongue few Irishmen speak and fewer still really know, were the troops of Finn MacCool, under whom in a legendary time they were all defeated like most good Irish things. Finn was fifteen cubits tall and is thought to be sleeping underground, ready to return at his country's need. Fáil (rhyme it with foil) is still more romantic, the possessive form of Fál, the stone at Tara that was supposed to shriek on the inauguration of the rightful monarch of all Ireland: "destiny" indeed.

So Jack Lynch in this claptrap theater would be playing MacCool *redivivus*, though what was chiefly to be heard shrieking the day after his election was the English press, in whose soothsayers' judgment he boded no good at all, being allegedly soft on Northern terror. The English press, like the good gray *Irish Times*, which ran a Dewey-defeats-Truman kind of headline before the counting of votes had even started, would have preferred to see Liam Cosgrave's Coalition continue to bumble as it has since 1973.*

Part of the Coalition was Labor, in no sense an Irish word. The rest was Cosgrave's Fine Gael (Fine, two syllables, family, tribe; Gael, come on, you know that one). The Coalition's great virtue was its freedom from IRA influence, its great defect a talent for milling confusion

*And God help the Irish people if a government did anything but bumble. One remembers James Joyce's quipping fellow with the fleas: "By the hoky fiddle, thanks be to Jesus these funny little chaps are not unanimous. If they were they'd walk me off the face of the bloody globe."

that seemed inordinate even by Irish standards. Last year the Dáil even heard a speech in praise of the earthworm, which seemed at the time as pertinent as most other exchanges. In doing nothing as in doing most things there are styles, and the Coalition's style was never masterly.

Doing nothing may not in itself have been the worst of courses. It is hard to know what they ought to have done about anything. Not only was all Europe in a slump, Britain, to whose currency Ireland's is linked, exported its inflation Eireward week by week, and the rate by election day had reached something like 16 percent, while parts of western Ireland went on being poorer than the Italian Mezzogiorno. More than half the population must rely on the Department of Social Welfare at some time in their lives, and much of what passes for a work force is on disguised welfare.

While I was staying there a year ago, four cheery men in the pay of the Dublin Corporation spent eleven days just outside our front gate watching a large hole in the pavement, for fear no doubt someone might steal it and cut it up into little pieces for sale to a golf course. The hole had been dug by workers making an electrical repair. It was eventually filled by another gang, for paving over by yet another; in the interim the Fearless Four stood guard one by one in rotation, while three mates stayed in their little tent out of the cold playing non-stop cribbage, cooking bacon, brewing tea. It made better sense, friends explained, to keep the four on the "job" than shift them frankly to the welfare rolls. It's not that they were lazy; real jobs just didn't exist.

Despite savage rates of taxation, it is hard to know where the money comes from to support all this idleness even minimally. The self-employed in particular run revenuers a stiff race, on the sensible principle that cash is too scarce to be just handed over to a bureaucrat. Physicians collect their fees in untraceable currency; small businesses keep wondrous casual books. A year ago, tax dodgers were being offered amnesty with only two conditions. There would be no prosecutions and no penalties if by a set deadline (beyond which, unthinkable terrors) the feckless would do just two things: 1) arrange to pay their back taxes, 2) explain how they had stayed uncaught for so long, a thing the Ministry really needed to know.

Meanwhile, efforts to create non-hole-watching jobs have been turning Ireland into Europe's Taiwan, where a deft and low-priced labor force will assemble anything at all—slot machines, shoes, computer memories—in plants foreign corporations can close when a market shifts as fast as they opened them when the tax incentives glowed shamrock green.

Such expedients, however unsatisfactory, do help meet hand-to-mouth problems in a country half of whose three million people are under twenty-six, and whose schools disgorge another thirty thousand unemployed youths each summer. What on earth there may be to do with oneself after school is the massively unanswerable question for most of the country's adolescents.

The Coalition's line was, You Have a Good Government, Keep It. Fianna Fáil pledged to Get the Country Moving Again. (On the boat to Holyhead? one wag asked.) Its proposals dissolved, under hostile analysis, into big bold schemes for borrowing the land out of debt. A majority judged, according to one poll, that the country couldn't afford them, which didn't stop another majority, or the same one, from voting Fianna Fáil in.

As for the voters' mood, a sampling just before the day of decision told pollsters how much it mattered who won:

A great deal	30%
Quite a lot	26%
Not very much	30%
Not at all	13%

That makes 43 percent for little or no difference, not the mood of which landslides are normally made. Also 42 percent thought the Coalition possessed the best cabinet talent, though 54 percent preferred Mr. Lynch for Taoiseach. (This is pronounced T-shock and means something like "chief"; though cynics remark a semantic analogy with Duce and Führer, not even the most caustic foes of mild Jack Lynch detect in him any aptitude for one-man rule. His peculiar skill, says one political enemy, is for reassuring equally any two groups whose simultaneous contentment would be impossible had they access to the same set of facts.)

How all this contradiction and apathy issued in a Fianna Fáil triumph no one quite knows. Was Northern Ireland—important to only 14 percent of those polled—secretly weightier than it seemed? Did the old romantic fantasies of the Isle united surge in impatience with the Coalition's slow, unspectacular efforts to discourage support for the IRA?

Color is lent such a supposition by the single election result that most riveted foreign attention, the booting of Dr. Conor Cruise O'Brien: in a good deal of outside judgment, mine included, the one prominent man in Eire who talks any sense at all about the North. Bernard Levin, the London *Times* columnist, once had a joke: a measure for the Northern situation's madness was the fact that Conor Cruise O'Brien of all people was the best guide to it. Later he realized that he wasn't joking. For myself, I have only to hear the analyses of my most intelligent and well-informed Irish friends to appreciate the sanity, in this sector at any rate, of the Cruiser.

The fact is, says my friend C, that the IRA, however wrongheaded their methods, have hold of the right end of the stick. Get the British out, that's all. Then . . . then what? A bloodbath? No, says C, consciousness has evolved past bloodbaths. The two factions would come to recognize their common interest. (I should add that C is also a romantic Marxist, and finds a common interest for any oppressed in their opposition to capital.)

My friend N believes in a united Ireland under the tricolor and the Pope. In 95 percent Catholic Eire he can easily find a model for Protestant assimilation, can easily discount the obdurate fact that assimilation by an island-wide majority is exactly what the 65 percent Protestant majority in the North most dreads.

Another friend asks if the martyrs of 1916 shall have died, after all these years, for a miserable partition.

Romance, romance, exclaims Conor Cruise O'Brien, whose wisdom on this topic consists in having no rapid solution. What he has to say can't be summarized in fewer than the 315 pages of his admirably readable *States of Ireland* (paperback revision, 1974). What he stands for is well summarized (the *Times*, June 21) by Bernard Levin, who, while noting that on other fronts the Cruiser "has too often, by his words and actions, given comfort to the vile," asserts his lucidity on the Northern Question.

"For Conor Cruise O'Brien to suggest that the one million Irish Protestants in the North also have a right to self-determination not only caused stupefaction and horror among his compatriots but endangered his life, not to mention his seat in the Dáil. But he did not stop there; he went on to attack the upas-tree of Irish folly at its very root by attacking . . . the myth of 1916 itself": the myth modern Ireland is founded on, the myth of the 16 martyrs, a myth which he saw was not only engulfing the Republic in fantasy, but was "encouraging the belief that the IRA is in some way engaged on the 'liberation' of Northern Ireland."

The seat in the Dáil was not merely endangered but lost. Meanwhile Fianna Fáil's Charlie Haughey, the center seven years ago of an arms-running scandal in which he was romantically if somewhat technically* acquitted, rode to glory by a thumping majority. Was this symbolism designed by the electorate? Was their repudiation of the Cruiser, their opting for a Fianna Fáil government that will surely feature Charlie Haughey, part of a defiant message to the civilized world? Is romantic Ireland not only dismayingly alive but suicide-bound?

The answer, Not necessarily, commences from the fact that Haughey was enthroned and O'Brien repudiated by two different sets of voters. Haughey stood in Dublin-Artane. Conor Cruise O'Brien failed—narrowly—in Dublin-Clontarf, a working-class district on the upper shore of the Bay where he had won twice previously.

This time he campaigned under several disadvantages. His stand on Northern Ireland was not intelligible if you bought the myth of 1916 on which the mystique of the Republic is founded. (How many of his constituents buy that myth I don't know.) He was minister in a

---

*He was acquitted on exactly the charge that was brought, namely bringing guns *into* the Republic. What guns may have found their way out of the Republic into the North, and how, was a question on which the court didn't rule.

government of which the electorate had grown more tired than most polls indicated. And as Minister of Posts and Telegraphs he was apt to be saddled with responsibility for any TV program any voter disliked, as well as for the vagaries of a phone system that would give Ma Bell's hottest detractors pause.

Should you want one of the instruments for some reason—e.g., a wife with a bad heart—you might be three years getting it. Should you have one, you might find its habits unamusing. Hang up, for instance, and the chances are you are not disconnected from your party, on whose later calls you are often listening in when you next pick up the receiver.

For some months in 1976 the *Irish Times* kept a "Calling Dr. O'Brien" box on its letters page, affirming the tacit point that one didn't communicate with the Minister by post because the post— another of his responsibilities—wasn't reliable either. "Calling Dr. O'Brien" registered its finest hour when someone hand-delivered a letter to the *Irish Times* to report that the number you called to report telephones out of order was out of order.

Whether any of this lies within the Minister's power is less germane than the fact that the Minister seemed always to be engaged on something else: helping make Northern policy for instance, or instructing the Bishop of Limerick on faith and morals.

Still, into his district, bruised but unbowed by bad jokes about the phone and the telly, Dr. O'Brien sallied forth to campaign, one day with the *Irish Times*'s inimitable Maeve Binchy in tow. "He's not one to dawdle on doorsteps," she reports, "and he doesn't seem unduly grateful when he hears people are supporting him. He gives the impression they are doing the only sensible thing, and nods approval."

Miss Binchy also reports: "Don't bother going in there, the woman is dead now," to which Conor, "It wouldn't stop her voting for Fianna Fáil"; also this wonderment:

" 'I'm only concerned about prices, nothing else,' said a woman.

" 'We're very concerned about prices,' said Conor.

" 'Well, wouldn't you do something about them then?' she suggested.

" 'We have, we took VAT off food.'

" 'You took what off food?'

" 'VAT, it's a tax that Fianna Fáil had put onto it.'

" 'Well, maybe you should put it back on again—food was cheaper under them,' she said."

(Nobody, Miss Binchy reports, asked him about the North.)

After all that and much else, the Cruiser was forced, like every other candidate, to run the gantlet of Ireland's voting system, which takes time to explain. It was designed to prevent sweeping majorities, on the principle that in a 5 percent Protestant country simple majorities would ensure a 148-seat Dáil with not even a few token Protestants in it. But the system has evolved into an instrument of such subtlety as only the life-long Irish voter has mastered. New nuances are discoverable at every turn, and lore is divulged to the young on long winter nights quite as if a new sexual rapture was in question.

The usual result of all this electoral cunning is to keep anybody from getting a clear majority at all, which is why the last time around Fine Gael had to govern with the support of Labor.

The theme is this, that you more cunningly employ your vote the more closely you figure what other people are likely to do with theirs. (And they are thinking similarly.) For you have one vote (not a dozen as foreigners may suppose), but it does not just drop into the box and stay there. No, in the process of counting, it ricochets about like a ping-pong ball in a room full of mousetraps.

In any constituency there are three or four or even five seats to be filled from a slate of perhaps eight or nine candidates. Now here is Mr. Big, who has easily swept the poll with thousands of superfluous votes. Is it not a pity those votes should be used in driving an already driven nail? Might their owners not want to transfer them to a second choice? Indeed they might, and may. And as for the supporters of Mr. Small, who drew far too few votes to be visible, they, too, need not have wasted their franchise but may have a second chance likewise, even a third, a fourth. . . . Everything counts, all kinds of ways.

The mechanics are simple. You are given a list of candidates, and number as many as you choose in order of preference. The names are alphabetically listed, and numb-skull voters will number them in order, which makes it desirable for candidates to be near the head of the alphabet and explains why an O'Byrne some years ago had his name changed to Byrne. (The Cruiser got himself listed as Cruise O'Brien, fourth on a slate of twelve.)

The names are also tagged by party affiliation, but only if the party is a properly constituted one, which explains why a man named Sean Loftus, running on the slogan Save Dublin Bay, got his name legally changed this year to Sean Dublin Bay Loftus after the authorities declined to list Save Dublin Bay among the authorized parties. The words on the ballot stirred many memories, and Sean Dublin Bay Loftus, running in Clontarf, though not elected still helped interfere with Conor Cruise O'Brien's electability.

For there are endless nuances. You may number only two or three names, which means that after their fortunes are settled your vote will do no one else any good at all (so there). You may decide that the herd will elect your favorite anyway, so give him your Number Two or Three, throwing your first weight toward your second choice. You may . . .

Well, such mad combinations may occur as caused the counting in Mullingar, a while back, to take three weeks. All the population of the local madhouse had voted, in combinations so intricate as not to be believed. Why were mad folk permitted to vote? I asked my informant. Why not? he rejoined. (I was silent, thinking of Dick and Jimmy.) And indeed there was a minor Irish scandal this year when one girl was refused her ballot on the trivial ground that she could neither read nor speak nor in any way make known her choice of candidates. Indignation was rife at this denial of the franchise. Whoever is of age and can be carried to the polls has normally the franchise, and party workers are quite glad to help bewildered old women, not to mention electors who have merely died.

Then the counting. In Clontarf, with three of twelve to be elected, the count of first-preferences put a man named Colley easily on top, a Mr. M. J. Cosgrave second, Conor Cruise O'Brien third. O'Brien in? Not yet. Colley's surplus over what was needed to elect him was then distributed among the rest, and this distribution did O'Brien no good at all (not one Colley supporter named the Cruiser as second choice), while heavily advantaging a man named Woods who had polled fourth.

At this stage the low man was eliminated, a certain Malone, who had polled just 40 votes out of 30,963, and Malone's second choices were next distributed (O'Brien up one, Woods up three, etc.). Again the bottom man was dropped, and *his* second choices distributed. And again, and again. . . . And on the ninth count—which is why results are apt to take all day—the valiant Sean Dublin Bay Loftus was finally excluded, and it was his second-preference votes that decided the election. Cosgrave got some, and Woods some, and Cruise O'Brien some but not enough; and Cosgrave (originally Number Two) and Woods (originally Number Four) were elected, and O'Brien was out, and Bernard Levin saw the cue to pull all his apocalyptic stops.

With every detail of the nationwide count particularized on four pages of newsprint, there exist data aplenty to fill the pubs till next winter with arguments about just how it all came about. One sure thing, O'Brien's running-mate (Duffy, T.) did him no good at all, pulling so few votes (917) that his weight after he'd been eliminated weighed on O'Brien's scales like an anemic mouse.

And nationwide, how came the polls and the bookies (both of whom predicted a narrow Coalition victory) turned out to be so wrong, as Fianna Fáil swept to the largest majority in history?

By one theory, the Coalition lost because it failed to publicize the sort of poll parties normally hush up, a poll of its own that showed it was in trouble. So the idea that it was safely ahead went unchallenged, and voters erroneously thinking other voters were pushing it in thought they would accept its return but punish its presumption just a little. And they overdid it, like slapping your dog and having him drop dead.

So it's over for now, and, according to one old lady, even the defeated have this compensation, that, as former members of the Dáil, they are entitled to free cat food for life. Yes, free cat food, and she knew it for a fact; it was one of the perquisites of office, everybody knows that, and the gel from the *Irish Times* was an ignorant gel indeed not to know it.

If (as let us hope) she was correctly informed, the Cruiser has at least free cat food for life, assuming (as let us hope) he keeps a cat. And elections everywhere go on being communal madness, but the best we can do. And the guns go on sounding in the North.

Please Welcome
My Next Idea

Harper's, December 1982. The Baltimore PBS station courteously pre-screened for me as much of the "Great Ideas" series as anyone could sit still for on one afternoon. My review, alas, is rumored to have made a sensitive associate of Dr. Adler's throw up, the last result I'd have set out to achieve.

["Six Great Ideas," a six-part television series currently on PBS stations, features Professor Mortimer J. Adler presiding over seminars at the Aspen Institute and in conversation with Bill Moyers, executive producer.]

"I have, of course," writes Mortimer J. Adler, "read most of the great books on the subject, and some of the nearly great." The "subject" is God, and of the books about God that our man has not read, you will observe that he knows already which ones are great, which ones no more than *nearly* great. And how does he know that, not having read them? Does he trust the anonymous pasters of labels on packages? Does it take one to know one?

We take you now to the Next World. At his desk in a cubicle just past the receptionist's station, the Recording Angel fingers his Rolodex. Whether ablaze in some random shaft of transfulgence or occulted by floating wisps, his face does not lose its disorienting resemblance to Howard Cosell's. It has been a long day in Eternity. On the hatstand to his left he has hung his halo. Unbuckled, furled, his Dacron wings, all six, gleam from a species of umbrella stand. His tie is loose about an unbuttoned collar. The client of the moment, in yellow Lacoste shirt and slate blue slacks, hands clasped between his knees, hunches forward.

ANGEL: Adler, Mortimer Jerome. Born (*he consults the card*) N.Y.C., 28 Dec. '02; s. Ignatz and Clarissa (Manheim) A.; Ph.D. Columbia U., 1928 . . . Associate editor *Great Books of the Western World*, 1945–; dir. editorial planning, 15th ed. *Enc. Brit.*, 1966–; Columbia in the '20s . . . John Erskine's time, I suppose; and John Dewey's?

ADLER (*quick to ignore the mention of Dewey*): Marvelous teacher, John Erskine. I read the Great Books under his guidance. We read about sixty books in two years, and discussed them once a week on Wednesday nights. I learned, I think, how to discuss the Great Books and how to lead discussions of the Great Books from him. And the more I read them, the more I studied them, the more I led discussions of them, the more I discovered that the heart of the Great Books was the Great Ideas—the Great Ideas they discuss—there in those books is the Western discussion, the Western consideration. . . . ["Truth"*]

ANGEL: Wait, wait, we are not at Columbia. We are sticklers for syntax here. And "Western," what is "Western"?

ADLER: Western . . . why, Western. As in Western Man.

ANGEL (*producing a globe*): Man west of what? The Timor Sea? The Urals? Cincinnati?

ADLER: Bill Moyers never asked me such things.

ANGEL: True, I have the transcript. (*He opens a file.*) Bill Moyers asked you—that was at Aspen, in front of a TV camera—"But are you looking at the world from a peculiarly Western center?" He assumed you knew what he meant.

ADLER: He did know what I meant. And I told him . . .

ANGEL: I have in front of me what you told him. You said: "I have found that the ideas that—the great ideas that I've been concerned with are Western ideas. I think it is—I think I'm talking not about the great ideas of world culture, which doesn't exist yet, but the great

*Television transcript.

ideas of Western culture. I have to admit that this is parochial."
["Truth"] You were not at your most coherent. Perhaps at your most
impassioned?

ADLER: Perhaps.

ANGEL: Maybe most defensively impassioned?

ADLER: . . . Perhaps.

That exchange between Professor Mortimer J. Adler and Bill Moyers
occurred at Aspen, where the 1981 Executive Seminar on "Truth" (a
Great Idea, one of six finalists) had come to flash point, Adler having
incautiously put on notice an Indonesian academic named Soedjatmoko. Viewers of this fall's PBS series "Six Great Ideas," in which a
vociferous group of diplomats, academic administrators, and other
thinkers thrashed about in a sea of speculations, will remember the
exchange. Mr. S. had tried to deflect "the search for truth" toward
"the search for meaning," and Adler, aware that Mr. S. was hinting at
Eastern vs. *Western* meaning, laid down with staccato emphasis a
stern agenda:

"I'm going to hold you to the question of whether or not when we
talk about human rights, there are statements that are true or false
about human rights, transculturally." ["Truth"]

That was too much for Jamake Highwater, an engaging American
Indian half Adler's age with a *Who's Who* entry, for what that's worth,
already two lines longer. (". . . to dispel long-standing stereotypes of
Indians," it states as part of his mission.) "You are using truth as a
weapon," said Highwater. "Fourteen people are having very little input because your concept of truth limits what we are able to say."

Highwater next cited a racial slur from the 1928 *Encyclopaedia Britannica*, which Adler (since 1974 chairman of the *Britannica*'s board of
editors) was quick to disavow; whereupon Highwater ("That isn't my
point") said what his point was: that the concept of truth as Western-
ers have perpetuated it—"ultimate, fixed, singular"—"has upheld
all of the most negative aspects of the Western relationship with other
cultures": missionaries, for instance; coerced salvation. "And we're
doing it again here today." Adler mentioned the conquest of Mexico
as something available for objective discussion. Highwater bridled at

the very phrasing: "conquest," indeed: *"invasion."* And when the British historian Lord Alan Bullock thought they could at least agree on its date, 1519, Highwater denied even that. It didn't happen in 1519 at all. "It happened in the year One Reed": a different concept of time, a different concept of space. So what is Truth, unless the weapon of the victor?

Before long Adler was "having a great difficulty in agreeing with all of you, because I really do agree with almost everything that's been said, and yet you will not allow me to do it." It was from his quandary that PBS mercifully cut away to the Mort and Bill Show: Mort A. and Bill M. seated on a log in front of the timeless Rockies, chatting about something low-key: whether there can be true and false knowledge. (No, there can't; when it's not true it's opinion.)

ANGEL: Truth. It was Pilate who asked, "What is truth?" Could you have enlightened him?

ADLER: If only I had been there. "Truth," I would have told him, "is an agreement or correspondence between the mind and reality." I would have had him study page 37 of my book *Six Great Ideas*.

ANGEL: Should Pilate, I wonder, have attended an Aspen Executive Seminar? And would his attendance have forestalled the crucifixion? He asked "What is truth?" on hearing Jesus say, "Everyone who is of the truth hears my voice." Try to plug your definition into that puzzlement. "Everyone who is of the agreement between the mind and reality . . ." Jesus seems not to have heeded your definitions. He even said, "*I* am the truth."

ADLER: Meaningless.

ANGEL: Do not bang the desk.

ADLER: I always bang the desk. It is my emphasis.

ANGEL: True. We have on file much PBS footage of you banging the desk. Behind you, as you bang, in shot after shot, an Op-art tapestry afflicts the eye like a polychrome test pattern. It helps you at your most intense look benignly placid. The angel who invented Op-art is no longer with us, but centuries ago I had one of his creations in this office. Higher Authority removed it after it had so upset a client named

Rembrandt he commenced to gibber and was compassionately translated to Heaven when I had hardly begun my interrogation.

ADLER: That seems precipitate.

ANGEL: You must imagine him gibbering in Dutch. The fountains of the great deep were astir with the reverberations.

ADLER: In Dutch. But Dutch is Western. There are Great Ideas in Dutch.

ANGEL: Are you at home in Dutch?

ADLER: No, but it stands to reason . . .

ANGEL: Pah, reason. (*He consults the Rolodex.*) I see that you commenced (1943) to codify the 102 Great Ideas in the 443 Great Works by the 74 Great Authors. By 1952 the set was on sale, equipped with your General Index, the *Syntopicon*. It has sold mightily, notwithstanding that Kung Fu-tse (Confucius to you) was among the missing. Not Western; even though it was from his China, via reports of French Jesuits, that Western nations received an idea they have come to cherish more than they cherish Truth: a bureaucracy literate enough (alas) to read its own regulations. But let that pass. You did list Homer as one of your authors. Did you offer your customers Homer?

ADLER: In Volume Four . . .

ANGEL: In Volume Four, *Great Books of the Western World*, I find only pages of execrable translatorese. You offered that as Homer? This goes badly, Dr. Adler. (*There are two telephones on the desk, a red and a blue. His hand is moving toward the red.*)

ADLER (*quickly*): Ah, the Problem of Translation. I gave a whole page (Volume Three, page 1291) to that problem. Another lifetime I might well devote to the 102 Great Problems. (*He brightens.*) Might we make a deal?

ANGEL: No, no plea bargains here. A second lifetime is out of the question. Though I am aware that Reincarnation, if not a Great Idea, was great enough to sponsor eight *Syntopicon* references to Plato, not to mention one to *Moby-Dick*. Do not look surprised. Your *Syntopicon*, all 2,428 pages, is much thumbed in this office.

ADLER: That is very flattering . . .

ANGEL: Not at all, not at all. Our junior clerks amuse themselves with its naïvetés. Here, for instance, under Wealth 10a ("The nature of wealth as a good: its place in the order of goods and its relation to happiness") we are referred to *Othello* I.iii, where the villainous Iago keeps saying, "Put money in thy purse." Is the customer to take that for a great mind's pronouncement on a great idea?

ADLER (*humbly*): Debatable, I concede. But consider the scale. The *Syntopicon* contains 163,000 references. Our staff of 175 went through all 443 books four times. I assigned six ideas a week. We made 900,000 decisions. We included as well the seventy-seven books of the Bible, and Additional Readings to the extent of 2,603 titles by 1,181 authors. It all cost . . .

ANGEL: I know, a million dollars. Numbers do not impress us here. Any of us—my office boy, in fact—can call up the infinite digits of transcendental *pi* in the interval between shelling a peanut and ingesting it.

ADLER (*sternly*): Aha, I am no longer sure you are even an angel. Angels do not ingest peanuts. Behold in me the twentieth century's authority on angels. In *The Angels and Us* (1982, $11.95) . . .

ANGEL: No commercials, please.

ADLER: . . . I point out that angelic bodies, on the occasions when angels assume them, "cannot perform any of the vital functions that properly belong to living organisms."

ANGEL: Please do not bang the desk. And do not suppose that uniting one's essence to the essence of a peanut need be a bodily act. Here, where there is no marrying or giving in marriage, here we ingest—the word is metaphor—the Essential Peanut, miraculously multiplied.

This year's *The Angels and Us* lists eighteen other Adler titles since 1927. It's an incomplete list; the *Syntopicon* itself is missing. They are none of them books for specialists. He has been a resolute educator; *Aristotle for Everyone* (1978) is subtitled "Difficult Thought Made Easy," and ways of making thought easy entail not just cutting corners but assuring your reader that "philosophy is everybody's business." This means: if we are going to talk about Justice, as we do, day to day, we need to know how to talk about *Justice*, an unwobbling concept, not an elastic bag. The bullying some seminar participants have resented issues from Adler's insistence that for the duration of their talk the word under the spotlight shall not slither or mutate. "Justice" can never mean "fulfillment of my passions," however altruistic one's passions.

He does cut corners, as in a throwaway line about "Plato's wish to expel poets and painters from the ideal state because their portrayal of the gods so grievously misrepresents them." The amount of learned controversy that sentence cuts short has filled many books, notably Eric Havelock's *Preface to Plato*, which argues that what upset Plato about poets was that the poets he knew were prior to books. There were only Great Books after there were books, when much shaping of the Western mind had already happened. Plato, by Havelock's account, represented the new literacy, poets such as Homer, the old illiteracy, which you ingested by letting it possess you—memorizing the words, dancing out their tempo: swaying and chanting, in the grip of the god. The fastidious Plato thought that unphilosophical.

And no god grips you in the filing-card universe of Mortimer Adler's writings, where difficult thought is made easy, if sometimes tedious. There it suffices that Homer shall be tamed to a prose that stirs no pulses, while fine-tooth combs locate *ideas* in Hector's speeches. Here abstractions hold still the way marks do on a blackboard. What made the six PBS broadcasts lively was something absent from the books, the complex tug of particular passions in a room alive with spoken discourse.

Justice: would a *guarantee* that you could get away with it ease your problems about acting unjustly? Plato proposed an example: a ring that could make you invisible, that would let you get away with anything you wanted. So the question went round the seminar: if you saw that ring in Tiffany's window, price unstated but said to be "moderate," would you: a) go in and price it? b) buy it? c) use it?

Physicist, judge, lawyer, entrepreneur, one by one they temporized. Someone even spoke of buying the ring to destroy it. But Ruth Love, Chicago's superintendent of schools, saw no problem at all. She'd, by golly, *use* it. How? "To get rid of all the unjust laws . . . unjust by my definition." Adler: "You'd need to be invisible to do that?" Ms. Love: "No, but it might help sometimes." (*laughter*) ["Justice"]

In great good humor, Adler refrained from pronouncing her radically ineducable. TV showed an Adler readers would barely recognize. Alert, ingratiating, witty—was this the editor of the relentless *Syntopicon*? This the director of the Institute for Philosophical Research, where in thirty years they have only made a start on repackaging "the whole realm of the great ideas"—so far "two volumes on the idea of freedom; one volume each on the ideas of justice, happiness, love, progress, and religion; and a monograph on the idea of beauty"? That such books will help save mankind is a notion so high-minded it verges on self-parody. Ideas, ideas: no tang of the particular. Outside his books, away from the scriptoria where acute ears catch no sound save fifty pens scratching, Adler proved a master diplomat of particularity.

But at the Aspen of voices, persons, particularities, what becomes of ideas? Each participant wanted to describe the view from his window, and when Adler framed topics and held them to the framing, you could guess from their faces how at any moment some felt they were politely playing a game. "An intellectual game we are playing," said Mr. Soedjatmoko at one point, and Mr. Highwater spoke of "sticking with the rules." ["Beauty"] If people don't do that, they brawl, as Earl Weaver can testify, and seminar leaders, like umpires, can give high priority to a brawl-free two hours. The unwanted implication is apt to be that definitions have no other utility.

What utility, for that matter, have the prescriptions in Adler's other 1982 offering, *The Paideia Proposal*? One more high-minded committee job, it prescribes for the desperate state of American education, grades one through twelve, in terms as difficult to disagree with as they seem impossible to implement. Albert Shanker, president of the American Federation of Teachers, has supplied what must be the funniest blurb of the year: "If to some it seems to go overboard, it goes overboard in the right direction." Chicago's Ruth Love thinks it's a dandy book, too. So do Gus Tyler (assistant president of the ILGWU), Benjamin Mays (president emeritus, Atlanta Board of Education), and William Friday (president, University of North Carolina). Such a chorus of packaging experts is instructive.

Save for one gritty specific—all electives should be abolished, since "allowing them will always lead a certain number of students to voluntarily downgrade their education"—not a thing in the *Proposal*'s eighty-four earnest pages will disquiet any school administrator. Most will purr; isn't this what I've always said we were doing?

Adler's love of numbered lists seems tailor-made for glib reports to trustees. "Three different ways in which the mind can be improved" are "1) by the acquisition of organized knowledge; 2) by the development of intellectual skills; and 3) by the enlargement of understanding, insight, and aesthetic appreciation."

Reading that sympathetically in context, setting it beside classroom reality in, say, East Baltimore, you can just glimpse its revolutionary intent. It is even safe to pretend that it can help change a bad world ("truly a manifesto," coos Ms. Love), safe because its potential for igniting anything is slight, educators having co-opted its jargon long ago. That is a political fact, of a kind seemingly hidden from discussants of Great Idea Number Twenty (Education). In his eightieth year, still fighting a good fight, Mortimer Adler tempts the melancholy judgment that his chief effect, as he translates the lessons of 2,600 Western years into easy American, may be to make them seem finally irrelevant.

ANGEL: "Six Great Ideas"; six, or 102, no matter. And 900,000 decisions: I like that touch. The American obsession with numbers, the Western obsession with categories, engender in their fatal marriage the remorseless *packager*. "Great Ideas of Western Man: one of a series": that was the caption on a long run of advertisements that I keep in my file of Awesome Vacuities. A series of unmemorable high-minded clichés, each illustrated by a prominent unheard-of artist, it was sponsored for years and years by the Container Corporation of America, to the end (a cynic would say) that Americans might stand reverently holding their hats, all facing one way for the pickpocket's greater convenience. I perceived less difference than I should like between their enterprise and yours.

No, Dr. Adler, no, for all your fervor, what have you not trivialized? And yet for no trivial end. There is much to be said for you. You will not permit thought to be reduced to the firing of neurons. You will not suffer auto repair to be called education. In an age of the categorical denial of meaning, in the age of Roland Barthes and Jacques Derrida, you have insisted that there can be meaning—stable, immutable, as hard as this desk. And the day you talked to him of Goodness, you wrung whole minutes of consecutive sense from Bill Moyers. . . . I am getting old at this work. Back when the morning stars were singing together, I made my thousands of decisions with élan. Now I scarcely ever know which telephone to pick up.

ADLER (*quickly*): The blue one.

ANGEL: Hush, you do not know what you are saying. (*A long pause.*) I have decided. Your eternity shall be unique.

ADLER: Not . . . (*he gropes for the worst*) an eternity of culling the Great Thoughts of John Dewey?

ANGEL: No. An eternity at this very desk. You are a packager. So am I a packager. Heaven, Hell, those are packages. Our appearance, even, is not unlike. I shall change my pace for an aeon. I shall descend and run the Aspen seminars. You shall sit here and catechize the clients.

ADLER: With the files? The Rolodex? The video archive?

ANGEL: With all of it. You will find it comes naturally. I must tell you, though, the secret of the telephones. Red, blue, it does not matter: mere decor. Both go to the one Dispatcher. What matters is not which you pick up but the word you say: you say merely "Los Angeles," or "Kalamazoo."

ADLER: Los Angeles. Ah, of course: Heaven.

ANGEL: Your blind trust in categories! For once consider reality. No, for the deserving, seasons and Michigan air. But for the rest of men, in their infinitely greater number, an eternity of smog and issueless freeways.

ADLER (*speechless*): . . .

ANGEL (*donning halo and reaching for wings*): I am off. Do not bang the desk, it is rickety. Be assured, by the way, that time is of no moment here. Reconstructing the next client may take an eternity. I have left the Rolodex open at his card. (*In a blue flash he is gone.*)

ADLER (*rubs his eyes, seats himself on catechist's side of desk. Moving his astonished lips, he commences to bone up on the next client*): Derrida, Jacques. b. Algiers, 1930 . . .

McLuhan Redux

Marshall McLuhan was my first mentor. I met him in 1946, saw him for the last time in 1972, and in 1984 was grateful to Harper's *for an invitation to resurrect his memory. This appeared in November 1984.*

"Computer literacy," we keep repeating, meaning doubtless something or other. We surely forget to mean the most obvious thing about time spent at a computer terminal, that it is used in two supremely literate activities, typing and reading. Marshall McLuhan noticed long ago that the "content" of a medium is always a previous medium. He also remarked that we don't see a medium itself, save as packaging for its content. That helps ease new media into acceptability. Genteel folk once learned to tolerate movies by thinking of them as packaged plays or packaged books. Likewise, we sidle up to the computer, saying over and over that it's nothing but an electrified filing system. "Word processing" is another incantation. Souls are safe in proximity to *words*.

Yet something is altering. Here is *Byte*, a fat and glossy computer journal put out by no bunch of hackers but by staid McGraw-Hill. The July 1984 issue contains a long software review, tied to intricate fact in a way manifestly more responsible than anything likely to turn up in the *New York Review of Books*. Reviewers for *Byte* are not at liberty to be cranky or erratically informed. This piece undertakes an overview of the difficult language LISP before comparing two "implementa-tions," as they are called, in detail. For a rough analogy, imagine a point-for-point evaluation of two Sanskrit grammars, such as the *American Journal of Philology* might entrust to a senior professor. Imag-ine it, further, prefaced by a guide to Sanskrit for novices, the whole kept clear and readable throughout, and you get an idea of the *Byte* piece. So who wrote this paradigm? A computer-engineering major at Case Western Reserve, in collaboration with "a recent graduate of Sycamore High School" who designs relational database systems for a living.

In blunt archaic language: *Byte*'s authorities turn out to be an un-dergraduate and a system dropout who has traded his place in the ed-ucational queue for something more challenging. Computerist, dropout: a not unfamiliar linking. No reader of newsmagazines will fail to remember how Bill Gates (Harvard dropout) founded Micro-soft, how Steven Jobs (Reed dropout) and Stephen Wozniak (Berke-ley dropout) founded Apple. No, the filing-system model lacks ex-planatory power. Passion for filing systems, even electrified ones, does not bring about such a transformation of hierarchies. Yes, some-thing has altered. Marshall McLuhan again:

> The drop-out situation in our schools at present has only begun to de-velop. The young student today grows up in an electrically configured world . . . not of wheels but of circuits, not of fragments but of integral patterns. . . . At school, however, he encounters a situation organized by means of classified information. The subjects are unrelated. They are visually conceived in terms of a blueprint. The student can find no possible means of involvement for himself, nor can he discover how the educational scene relates to the "mythical" world of electronically pro-cessed data and experience that he takes for granted.

In 1964 that seemed one of McLuhan's wilder remarks. No longer. Today we find it pertinent that even when computers were far from ubiquitous he was observing the medium instead of its content, "files." He was foreseeing, moreover, a dramatic *effect* of the medium. And instances of his prescience multiply. Once brushed off by *The*

New Yorker as a "pop philosopher," the author of *Understanding Media* is starting to look like a prophet.

That is all the more remarkable since "the oracle of the electric age" (a phrase coined by *Life*) wouldn't drive a car, never turned on a radio, barely glanced at television, and checked out movies by popping in on them for twenty minutes. Apart from the Olivier *Henry V*, at which he'd been trapped on a social occasion, I don't know of a movie he saw from beginning to end. "Marshall McLuhan Reads Books," said a bumper sticker, graffito of the scandalous truth. He did indeed read books, and, other than talk and scribble, he did little else.

Such disdain for inconvenient fact could erode your confidence. "The horse that's headed for a can of Gro-Pup"—climax of one of his merry perorations—lost force if you knew that Gro-Pup was not processed meat and did not come in cans. Useless to tell him. He had picked up the name from an ad, and if Gro-Pup wasn't canned horse, as his metaphor required, its purveyors simply didn't know their business. His world was full of people who didn't know their business, such as nearly all of his fellow English professors. But though he was often wrong himself, as when he discerned "the abrupt decline of baseball," he never had the patience to sit through a ball game.

In those days he countered niggling by sheer assertion. It was after my time that he discovered a generic answer. People who raised objections were detailists, specialists, locked into local patterns: instances of what had happened to the Western psyche after Gutenberg gave his *coup de grâce* to the old oral culture by persuading everybody that one thing must follow another the way each printed word follows, on its line, the word that precedes it. Nigglers were confined to "the neutral visual world of lineal organization," and the specialist was one who "never makes small mistakes while moving toward the grand fallacy."

I have sometimes wondered if Marshall didn't evolve his whole theory of media as a way to explain why there seemed to be people who tried to interrupt his monologues. What cataclysm of history had spawned *them*? Why, literacy, with its first-things-first-let's-keep-it-all-straight syndrome. Were they not the very people who kept wincing at somebody's grammar? The word "grammar" itself derives from the Greek word for a written remark. That would have been enough to get him started. Much as Saul found a kingdom while out hunting for his father's asses, Marshall McLuhan found his skeleton key to the social psyche. Thereafter, he kept it hanging on a hook labeled "Media" and never bothered to explain what Media were.

Media included not only magazines and television but also roads, wheels, railways, electricity, numbers, clocks, money—they all did things we had once tried to do with our senses and our bodies; that was why he called them "extensions of man." Adjusting to any new medium, since it strained what had been a bodily and sensual relationship (his word was "ratio"), meant anguish and anxiety. So "the mediaeval world grew up without uniform roads or cities or bureaucracies, and it fought the wheel, as later city forms fought the railways; and as we, today, fight the automobile."

Media came in two flavors, "hot" and "cool." The hot ones saturate you with information; paradoxically, you are then passive, uninvolved, as when you half-listen to the radio. The cool ones draw back and leave you filling in. TV, with its inferior picture detail, is cool; hence, its viewer's rapt involvement.

Though his pronouncements on the electronic age and its global village made him briefly famous, what he really knew was literacy, and what he developed most fully was his insight into its consequences. What literacy achieves is the "hot" storage and retrieval of *words only*, as though their choice and sequence constituted the whole of human communication. But in the heat of conversation, relatively little is communicated by words. Silences, intonations, advances and withdrawals, smiles, and the whole repertory of body language—these in their elaborate dance enact most of what is happening.

Screen them out, leave only the silent words on a page, and your first requirement is *more* words. The dialogue Henry James's people exchange is wordier by a factor of at least three than any speech human ears have ever heard. James was making up for the absence from printed pages of what normal grammar and diction do little to convey, the ballet of interaction. (He brought written prose to its extreme of articulation just before radio took over.)

The next thing you need is a fairly strict one-two-three order, because written words exist only in space, and can presuppose only the words that came before them. Things on a line of print cannot overlap. This is the "linearity" on which McLuhan harped. Talkers allude to what they've not said, or have said on another occasion, or will say later, or needn't say save by gesture or dawdle or pause; but once discourse is controlled by writing, as even the spoken discourse of literates tends to be, its syntax (think of James again) grows fairly elaborate, out of need for strict systems of subordination among items that can be produced only one after another. Examine the sentence you've just read.

Finally, literates come to believe that controlled linearity is order, all else disorder: that the cosmos itself is structured like a Jamesian utterance, with primary, secondary, tertiary clauses. If any sentence of *Understanding Media* might have turned up without irrelevance anywhere in any chapter, that was because McLuhan thought that prose should work like the mind, not the other way round. Whatever he was thinking of grew in iconic power the more rapidly he could relate it to a dozen other things, if possible in the same breath. So he got called "the professor of communications who can't communicate," an academic Harpo unable to stick to a point. His point was that there is never a "point." Points are Euclidean junctures in such sentences as come to life only in diagrams.

There are aspects of his plight Beckett might have invented. What language may *say* in a literate society McLuhan deemed of little importance compared with what literacy had done to the literate. I once heard him deny that anything Plato wrote could match in importance the fact that in a given classroom all copies of *The Republic* have the same word at the same place on the same numbered page. Hence "The Medium Is the Message," his most quoted and most suicidal oversimplification. For it was precisely *what* he said that he wanted understood; moreover, what he said *in writing*. Using writing to expound the effects of writing was like explaining water to a school of fish. Fish understand nothing of water, but they judge you by the way you move your flippers. He got snubbed by print-swimmers who deemed measured prose a measure of character.

So obsessed was his readership by "content" that detractor and disciple alike tended to think he was talking about the effect of the medium on the message it carries: TV is highly visual, for instance, hence its fondness for crowds and confrontations. But that barely concerned him. (He said TV was "tactile.") What obsessed him is clearer after twenty years: the effect of the mere *availability* of new media on people's sense of who and what they are.

The medium called "money" presents a ready example. True, once money had been invented it changed bread and butter into commodities keyed to prices, a message that affected shopper and speculator alike. But in making subsistence by barter nearly impossible, money could also deform the life of a man who never touched it. Even so print, yes, structures its message; but McLuhan deemed it of far more moment that life in a print-oriented culture restructures the soul of even a total illiterate. Not only does he know that other people know things he doesn't, but he also picks up ambient assumptions about first-things-first. In not being felt at all, the latter effect reaches deeper than any felt deprivation.

Likewise, said McLuhan, all of us have been reconstituted by TV, whether we choose to watch the tube or not: "The utmost purity of mind is no defense against bacteria." If TV has a propensity for street happenings (which get staged for its benefit); if its pundits earn their welcome into our living rooms by coming on populist, hence chummily "liberal"; if TV is so "cool" that Bill Buckley—a man whose meaning even devotees have to construct—has been on it longer than almost anyone else; if it's Paul Harvey (strident, rightist, "hot") who is left to fulminate in the Hot Ghetto of Radio Gulch while George Will ("cool," puckish, bow-tied) gets welcomed as ABC's ticket-balancing House Conservative, still it's not because of someone's adroitness at packaging that Ronald Reagan sits in the Oval Office but Richard Nixon in itchy exile, Jimmy Carter in limbo. Articulate *opinion* of Nixon and of Carter got formed in print, still our only medium of articulate opinion. And yet, it was the omnipresence of television that determined what kind of opinions the older medium—print—could form and seem credible.

This means that in the television age even non-watchers gravitate toward "cool" personalities. Nixon was too jowly and affirmative to pass muster, Carter too morally opinionated. (Mondale? He's an Identi-Kit. Only TV could have made him a viable candidate.) The prevalent perception of "wake-me-when-it's-over" Reagan is that he falls asleep: a caricature that affirms his ultimate "cool." When you have to tell the President what's happening, that is your ultimate participation.

Reagan's successor might be Kermit the Frog. The night Kermit filled in for Johnny Carson, no one noticed.

Yes, we're governed by caricatures, because we perceive by them. There's no better instance than the regnant caricature of McLuhan, shared by print-folk who thought they were attending to his text and bypassing the electronic media, the wrong thing to do. For he was presupposing TV's cool collaboration, not print's hot "specialist," "fragmented" reading. Like another guide to the future, Bucky Fuller, McLuhan was discarded as unintelligible. Willy-nilly, trapped in hot print in an age of cool TV, he was taken at his (printed) word, just as if in his outrageous one-liners he hadn't intended audience participation, or hadn't counted on his audience to fill out and correct all those comicbook formulations. The apostle of "cool" came on "hot," a blunderbuss Nixon of the Media Era, and coolness made a joke of him and discarded him.

The Media Culture's Counterfeit World

Washington Times Magazine, *mid-1987*.

As the oldest living ex-McLuhanite (disciple in 1946, defected circa 1951), I approached Gary Gumpert's *Talking Tombstones and Other Tales of the Media Age* (Oxford University Press, 1987) with special anxieties: "Mushall McGloom," a mutual friend used to say in those years. Was Gary Gumpert going to tell us what Marshall McLuhan took to saying some time after I lost faith, that the "medium is the message"? Or—Mushall's next reckless extension—the "massage"?

As it turns out, no. A quick scan of Mr. Gumpert's notes turns up but one McLuhan reference, citing his observation that North Americans "may well be the only people who go outside to be alone and inside to be social," and it's cited to bear out an observation of Mr. Gumpert's, that "the Italian piazza, the French café, the English pub, the Spanish plaza, and the Greek taverna are still central to the dynamics and structure of those societies."

That's the kind of thing McLuhan could perceive by near inadvertence, amid his phrase-coining. Less a showman, Mr. Gumpert achieves it by dogged attention. Yes, the people who show up at American bars are the *lonely* people, the isolates. The formula joke casts the bartender as their analyst, and all *New Yorker* cartoons are about isolation.

But in England the pub folk are the *social* people, and the focus of *Punch* cartoons is their solidarity. Their most withering word, for seventy-five years, has been "highbrow," meaning someone non-consensual. (In an Irish town forty years back, no one thought it strange when a politician threw "highbrow" at a scheme for sexually segregated public toilets. For there'd always been just the one kind and that was that.)

Highbrow, Mr. Gumpert most assuredly is. In wanting to know what's going on, he defies a social consensus that nothing much goes on save exchange of chat. But how is it exchanged, he asks. On the telephone? Very well, what does that entail?

It entails an alteration of dynamics so profound that (as I never tire of reporting) Alexander Graham Bell wouldn't have a telephone in his home, no more than he'd have admitted a cash register. The impersonal data of business were what Bell meant those copper wires for, and in James Joyce's steely-eyed *Ulysses* no one in 1904 uses them for anything else. But by T. S. Eliot's 1925 *Sweeney Agonistes*, a phone in a floozie's flat seems unremarkable; and an Eliot character remarks in a later play, "You can't tell the truth on the telephone."

Today, Mr. Gumpert accurately remarks, "a house without a telephone isn't a home," and "puberty means having your own telephone." Bell's "Mr. Watson, come here; I want you" ended civilization as it had been known since they called to the man painting bison on a cave wall to announce impending mastodons. The painter was within earshot of the people who called. But Mr. Watson heard Bell's voice and *Bell was not there*.

In England, within living memory, people used to answer the phone with "Are you there?" They had a point. And Mr. Gumpert's point is that when the voice you're hearing isn't there, it's a quick transition to:

Horny?

Phone Sex.

Six calls for the price of one!

We accept Master Card and VISA . . .

—which is part of what AT&T calls "reaching out and touching."

What you reach out and touch may even be a synthesized voice. (Imagine *that* at the other end of "Phone Sex"!) It means a set of binary digits keyed to tones, and it's what the human operator switches you to after most directory calls. Yet you pretend (you must!) that *someone* is telling you! And Mr. Gumpert adds that both participants in a phone call imagine a spatial and a visual context.

For there's nothing they can do but imagine it. "The voice issues from a body; there is a visual component to the primarily aural dimension. But there is *nothing* intrinsic in the medium of the telephone that indicates location. Without that information being willingly disclosed or getting clues from background noise, location has to be assumed or asked. (Have you ever asked 'Where are you?' but doubted the response?)"

And an 800 call "takes place in a spatial limbo." *Where is* that chirpy operator for Widgets International? Part of Mr. Gumpert's theme is that we don't think to ask. So little is she real, she has no "there." Or: So little does thereness by now reflect reality, we can sense her as "she" but also as disembodied. And if she-ness pertains to nothing save the pitches on a sequence of phonemes, she may well be synthetic. (Are we sure she isn't?)

From end to end, Mr. Gumpert's book raises questions of that order, needling us to perceive how radically alien other persons become when media intervene. For our contact is solely with the medium— TV screen, PA sound—out of which we have learned to *construct* a person. Mike Wallace, Peter Jennings are people we invent out of audiovisual cues. We've learned to do that so well we don't realize we do it; hence the need for a book to jerk us back into awareness. For we have abdicated, Mr. Gumpert tells us, "sensory responsibility": we feel absolved from "processing the accuracy of sensory impressions."

Informed that chunks of "60 Minutes" were taped last week but other chunks months ago, that the tapes have been cunningly edited, that the "hosts" aren't in that room *now* where we seem to be seeing them, that their chitty-chat, even, was scripted; accorded such information we're unlikely to aspire past asking, "What difference does it make?" A response, says Mr. Gumpert, that "goes far beyond narcotization."

He quotes an eyewitness to a "60 Minutes" taping, when Mike Wallace "smiled and encouraged the subject to continue talking, only to insert cutaways in which Mr. Wallace has a stern, doubting expression." "Cutaways" are random shots of the reporter, filmed separately, nodding perhaps or frowning or making notes. (What a charming fiction, that TV reporters need written notes!)

Cutaways have other uses besides altering the mood. "When an interview subject begins a sentence, then in the middle of that sentence a cutaway is inserted of the reporter's reaction, followed by what seems to be the remainder of the subject's sentence, chances are it was never one complete sentence in the first place."

You can see the possibilities. "I sympathize with those who would punish severely monsters who beat their wives." Edited version: "I sympathize with those who" (cutaway to the reporter, nodding) "beat their wives." Yes, that's likely too drastic to get past any network's legal department. Still, you see the fatuity of "what difference does it make?" It makes the difference between a transcribed reality and the ideal one we reconstruct from cues.

Mr. Gumpert's entertaining book is in that way all about media. He's concerned to show us that, whether "the message" or not, they're always in there, fragmenting and displacing experience, yet—this is the central point—so familiar to us we don't notice them, don't recognize our own skill at constructing a "reality" from the fragments. The phone puts a "voice" in your head: you synthesize a person you may never have met. The TV puts sight and sound before you; you comply in inventing a real world from hints.

And could Aristotle himself have hoped to be a finalist on "Jeopardy"? Certainly not. But take a half-hour off to reason out explicitly why not, and you'll be within hailing distance of a doctorate in philosophy.

Gary Gumpert, unlike Marshall McLuhan, hasn't transcended moral judgments. About some things, he avers, we just should not be so bland. McLuhan used to think likewise, back when his first book was still called "Guide to Chaos." Rewritten and published as *The Me-chanical Bride*, though, it said, "Let 'er rip." He was coming to believe in the "global village," perhaps because he liked the way the phrase sounded.

Mr. Gumpert's theme doesn't rise free into slogans. Page by page, never turgidly, he confronts the essential unreality of what we've learned to take for real, and shows us, painstakingly, how its "reality" is constructed by us. (The reality, even, of an instant replay is some-thing we connive at; should it really overrule the referee?) "Mirror on mirror mirroring all the show," media create a many-faceted counter-feit. Tombstones may one day "talk." But the dead will stay as they are.

The Wherefores
of How-To

This Harper's *(March 1984) piece is what's left of an idea I once had for a book to be called "The Poetics of How-To."*

The first how-to Almighty God dictated, giving Noah both the ark's dimensions and its materials. He specified cabins, and a lower and an upper deck, and the size of the windows, and the need for a door; and he stressed that the boat should be waterproofed within and without with pitch. That was a little less than two thousand years after he'd created Adam, having earlier warmed up his skills by fabricating a universe. So Noah's instructions came from a credentialed artisan. Sure enough, the ark floated.

Among the books discussed in this essay: *The New Oxford Annotated Bible with the Apocrypha, Expanded Edition*. Oxford University Press. *BASIC and the Personal Computer*, by Thomas Dwyer and Margot Critchfield. Addison Wesley, 1978. *Oh! Pascal!*, by Doug Cooper and Michael Clancy. Norton, 1985. *Pascal*, by David Heiserman. Tab Books, 1980. *Word Processing on the KayPro*, by Peter McWilliams. Prelude Press, 1983. *Moby-Dick*, by Herman Melville. Modern Library, 1981. *Life on the Mississippi*, by Mark Twain. Bantam, 1981. *The Waste Land and Other Poems*, by T. S. Eliot. Harcourt Brace Jovanovich, 1955.

The Fabulous Artificer did not let up; among his creations was a literary genre. By Chapters 25 to 30 of Exodus, he's prescribing that Israelite craftsmen make such items as a table of acacia wood, two cubits by one, gilded with pure gold and with a gold-rimmed edge. He even specifies the number and placement of the rings through which to pass the poles they'll use to carry it. And the scale of his dictations grows ever larger. By the end of the Bible, Chapter 21 of Revelation, he is all the way to city planning, still strong on numbers: 12 gates, an enclosure 12,000 furlongs square, a 144-cubit wall . . .

And lo, millennia later, Jerry Pournelle, whose ear seems nailed to the ground, passing on (in *Byte* magazine, December 1983, p. 526*) what his publisher friends are saying: that "computer books"—the latest subspecies of how-to—"are the most popular nonfiction line in the industry."

As I'm sure they are. The bookstores I walk into are adding extra tables for computer how-tos, moreover moving them up toward the entrance. The books are mostly paperback, and costly: $15.95, $19.95. Some are about the machine you've bought or are thinking of buying: Apple, Atari, Commodore, Sinclair, Zenith. Some deal with systems and languages: UNIX, BASIC, Pascal, C, COBOL, even the dinosaur FORTRAN. Some are just hand-holders. What will computers do to you? What might one do for you? And there's so much overlap, so much duplication, that most of them are, by any strict standard, unnecessary.

Some are splendid, some miserably produced and proofread. An oldie but goodie (first printing, 1978) is Thomas Dwyer and Margot Critchfield's *BASIC and the Personal Computer*; for fun with BASIC I don't know of a better place to start. For a Pascal equivalent try Doug Cooper and Michael Clancy's *Oh! Pascal!*, and be sure to check the index under "Hansen, Patti."

The kind of book to shun is one like David Heiserman's *Pascal*, which illustrates most of the ways a random purchase can frustrate.

---

*Yes, that's page 526 of a single issue, whose final page is numbered 656. Last year two computer journals, *Byte* and *PC World*, both surpassed what had been the fattest single issue of a consumer magazine in history, the 610-page September 1981 *Vogue*.

Its generic faults include (1) being for a specific machine—the TRS-80—but not saying so; (2) assuming Dark-Age hardware (cassette, not disk drive); (3) confining itself to a dialect—Tiny Pascal—that won't let you do much; (4) having been proofread by a purblind alligator, which matters when you painstakingly copy programs that won't run because of dropped semicolons.

Machine specificity can be especially insidious. Many books, for instance, presuppose an Apple, which is okay when they say so on the cover, but can infuriate the non-Apple owner when they don't. He's apt to part with his money before learning that half the examples won't quite work as written.

On the other hand, some books that flaunt a brand name are doing little more than beckoning to a market. Peter McWilliams's *Word Processing on the KayPro* has surprisingly little to say about the KayPro computer, and I've flipped through a self-styled guide for IBM users that turns out to be chiefly one more BASIC primer.

Chaos, muddled. A few obvious things I'll say quickly. Yes, there are computer books because people are afraid of computers. Yes, there are computer books because the manuals that come with computers are of famous impenetrability. There are even computer books because the proliferating courses in "computer literacy" are not infrequently taught by self-taught souls who need help as much as their pupils do. And yes, many books take care to define their aims and are literate and helpful. I'll not conceal that I've written one myself.

I could extend that list and so could you, and still we'd be talking about the surface of the phenomenon. We'd be explaining the sales of computer books as if they were bought just for their usefulness, like screwdrivers and hammers. What we'd not be explaining is what strikes the most casual eye: their near senseless proliferation. For they multiply like Harlequin Romances: not two or three guides to the BASIC language, for instance, but more like twenty, and a new one every few weeks. And no more than the writer of a Harlequin Romance does the writer of this week's BASIC primer feel required to say why yet one more is needed. Is there an insatiable appetite out there? A market for a new screwdriver every week, if it has a new-colored handle?

One publishing-house editor I've talked with thinks there is. Computer books, she told me, seem not to compete with one another in the normal way of the marketplace. If three books on the Pascal language are available, the clearest and most comprehensive doesn't drive away the other two. Thousands of people buy all three. That explains why publishers galore jump fearlessly into computer books. By the rules of prudence in the publishing jungle, entrenched competition is eyed with paranoid caution. But not so with computer how-to.

And here we are on to something. For what gets written and sold in the computer market may resemble the Harlequin Romance in yet another respect. Might the book of computer how-to be . . . escape reading? An aid to getting more varied pleasures from one's computer than simply using it affords? Like James Bond's blondes, escape books vary but slightly. Each is for tumbling once and discarding. Likewise, surely not all those buyers of three or five Pascal books are studying that austere language in depth. What many of them do is repeatedly caress the *idea* of Pascal, a language for which they have, likely, no practical use at all.*

None of this seems at all unlikely if you reflect on a parallel phenomenon, the cookbook. The number of cookbooks Americans buy defies computation. Many are inherently worthless, and the very best aren't necessarily bought to be used. A woman I know reads *Gourmet* magazine monthly, cover to cover; she'd never think, she says, of cooking anything from it. Too difficult.

How-to, therefore, as escape? Back now to Genesis. American history is largely the story of what Americans have done with the Bible, to which, as I've noted, the how-to genre is traceable. A how-to liter-

---

*People who use small computers to get a job done—word processing, bookkeeping—don't "program" them or use a programming language. They buy prewritten software, debugged by experts. At home, programming is primarily a recreation, more taxing than Scrabble and a tad more rewarding, since the results last. Books that make you think you *must* learn to program are relics of dark-ages technology, before the floppy disk made canned thinking transportable.

ature of ships and houses was a necessity on the new continent, where people were starting afresh without communal skills to draw on. Subsequently, American literature got entwined like no other in how-to, and it's unsurprising, once we perceive the pattern, that junk how-to should lately have become a genre sui generis, the indigenous American literature of escape.

I'll run that all by more slowly. In the British Isles, how-to books commenced to flourish in the eighteenth century, with the slow breakup of the apprentice system. Lore formerly passed on was now looked up by increasingly polymathic entrepreneurs. Joyce in *Ulysses* preserves a charming instance: an Irish carpenter in 1822 who bought a *Short yet Plain Elements of Geometry* (London, 1711), the better, we guess, to deduce the fit of stairways into stairwells, of gables onto frames. (That book was already 111 years old; books lasted then.)

I've a still older one at hand. My great-grandfather Peter Williams in Wales, and after him his son Hugh Williams in Canada, made a living with the aid of a book. "Pedr Gwilym," reads Peter's signature inside the cover, "1840"; and he has written his name in English as well: "Peter Williams." Other notations revert to his native Welsh. Was he uneasy with English? I don't know. The book demands little English of its user, its lore being almost wholly numerical. It is a presilicon artisan's calculator, sized three inches by eight to fit a long, deep overall pocket. The Williamses, father and son, were masons and carpenters; their crafts entailed much figuring.

In the 181 years since a London binder gathered its acid-free pages between calfskin boards, the book has weathered thousands of consultations. Today its condition is remarkable, considering. Its half-title reads "Mr. Hoppus's Measurer, Greatly Enlarged and IMPROVED." The title page has much more to say:

> Practical Measuring
> made easy
> to the MEANEST Capacity
> by a
> NEW SET of TABLES:
> Which shew at SIGHT,

The *Solid* or *Superficial* Content (and *consequently* the Value) of any *Piece* or *Quantity* of *squared* or *round* Timber, be it *Standing* or *Felled*, also of Stone, Board, Glass, &c. made Use of in the *Erecting* or *Repairing* of any Building, &c.

Contrived to answer all the Occasions of *Gentlemen* and *Artificers*, far beyond any Thing yet extant: The *Contents* being given in *Feet*, *Inches*, and *Twelfth Parts* of an Inch.

WITH A

PREFACE

Shewing the *Excellence* of this *New Method* of Measuring, and *Demonstrating*, that whoever ventures to rely upon those OBSOLETE Tables and Directions published by ISAAC KEAY, is liable to be deceived (*in common cases*) 10s. in the *Pound*. . . .

The date is 1803, the edition is the fourteenth, and the preface addresses itself briskly "to those who are unacquainted with the *intolerable Mistakes* and *numerous Imperfections*" of rival books, two in particular: Darling's *Carpenter's Rule made easy* and Keay's *Practical Measurer*. Darling is passed over quickly. Not so Keay, who was either "ignorant" (if he believed his own system) or "dishonest" (if he didn't), and eighteen pages of preface leave dimwitted or disingenuous Isaac Keay hardly fit to be washed. Keay was a menace. Any innocent who let Keay monitor his dealings always paid too much, by up to 50 percent.

Fourteen editions by 1803! And rivals to be fended off! Today Simon & Schuster would be saying, by golly a *market*. (A market of "Gentlemen and Artificers"? We could speculate about those categories.)

But back to my grandfather. When Hugh Williams crossed the Atlantic in the mid-nineteenth century, carrying a book of how-to, he joined a North American tradition: people doing things they'd never done before, guided by printed instructions. Cabins were no longer built by men whose lifework was building cabins. On the frontier *you* built a cabin, once. Likewise you did many other things just once. It was Herr Gutenberg's invention that made that possible: printed instructions, adapted to "The Meanest Capacity." And from being a New World necessity, how-to quickly became a New World art form.

Books to feed the imagination took for their models the books people had needed for survival.

What is *Moby-Dick*, stripped to its armature, but "Whales and How to Hunt Them"? And Mark Twain: what is his *Life on the Mississippi*? It is a how-to for neophyte river pilots: not all that they'll need to know, since the shifting river must teach them, but how to confront all that they'll need to know. And Hemingway: How to Catch Trout, How to Fight Bulls. (And Eliot's *Waste Land*: How to Read the Poets.)

But we shall never be riverboat pilots, most of us, nor bullfighters. No matter. Most of us aren't London pickpockets either, yet we'll happily read *Oliver Twist* (which has some fine how-to passages). Writing was invented to record things that couldn't easily be remembered: things like Mr. Hoppus's tables of figures. Later, when it had begun to record narratives (as in the *Iliad*), you could retrace with its aid how something was done, step by step: how a ship was beached, a boar slain. The greatest how-to book in history is *Robinson Crusoe*, but the English let the genre lapse. Or we might say that their novelists became preoccupied with the how-to of social maneuvering. It fell to American imaginations to maintain the great tradition of Jehovah and Homer.

Thoreau, in *Walden*, tells you in exquisite detail how he built his cabin, right down to the cost of the nails. He doesn't expect you'll go out and build a like cabin. You're to gain your satisfaction from following his narrative. The father of W. B. Yeats read *Walden* to him, and Yeats later generated a famous fantasy about how he'd retire to a lake isle,

> . . . and a small cabin build there, of clay and wattles made:
> Nine bean-rows will I have there, a hive for the honey-bee . . .

That dream, and not hammer-and-nail technology, is where Thoreau's instructions lead. Imagine Yeats of the pince-nez lifting a hammer, or a trowel!

And what of *The Whole Earth Catalogue*, whose founder, Stewart Brand, is now appropriately busy at a Whole Software Catalogue? It began as a floppy resource book for the 1960s counterculture, printed on newsprint and published out of a warehouse in Northern California. It told you about good saws and axes, about books on natural childbirth, about where to get the know-how to build wooden geodesic domes: all needful lore for a commune of dropouts.

And lo, a Major Publisher (Random House) took it over; and it grew to many hundreds of pages and went into colossal printings, and its four-color cover was visible on many thousand suburban coffee tables. And it won a National Book Award, from which one of the judges, the classicist Garry Wills, dissociated himself. In *The New York Times Book Review* I had called it, and I still think accurately, a space-age *Walden*, though Garry was unpersuaded.

In its late days that catalogue of catalogues, the how-toer's how-to, became escape literature and no mistake. Its half-million buyers sat in split-level comfort, reading entries about tools to split logs and oils to facilitate intimate massage.

Soon Stewart Brand will be the Stewart Brand of computers; meanwhile the place is held by Peter McWilliams, a generous, puckish fellow whom I'll honor here for always returning my phone calls. He won't mind my quoting the *Time* reviewer who attributed to him "a terminal case of the cutes," or my remarking on my own that his presentation of computers is superficial (he'll reject a $3,000 machine because he dislikes the sound of its key-clicks). His market—this is valuable to have had demonstrated—doesn't really depend on anyone's understanding anything. He grows rich (I hope) on *The Word Processing Book* and *The Personal Computer Book*, and has now done us the service of putting down the whole genre in *The McWilliams II Word Processor Instruction Manual*.

The McWilliams II Word Processor, I should explain, is a plain pencil with an eraser on the end. In 1982 Peter sent it to friends at Christmas, along with a leaflet listing its many virtues, as that it commanded all known character sets including Chinese (take *that*, IBM!), and that what it had processed it could as readily deprocess if you reversed it end for end.

Last Christmas an improved model arrived, accompanied by a McWilliams Word Deprocessor (a large eraser). The leaflet had grown to a full-fledged instruction manual, now on separate sale to a public unfortunate enough not to be on Peter McWilliams's mailing list. The manual is mostly pictures. You can see, for instance, the Discovery of the Microchip (by a lumberjack high in a tree) or a still from *The Peter McWilliams Story* that looks suspiciously like a frame from the Late Show.

Since the whole book devotes itself to extolling a lead pencil, its information content approaches zero. Its escape value, by contrast, is high. Daydreaming bookstore managers, misled by the title, will put it among the books on FORTRAN and IBM, where it will sell and sell. Its buyers will get what they didn't know they were really after, instant relief. It correctly includes scenes from several biblical epics.

Mazes

Brainstormers at Discover *decided they wanted something on mazes, and thanks to an ex-student on their staff I got asked to write it. Only later did they learn I was an English professor. Published in February 1986.*

In Umberto Eco's novel *The Name of the Rose*, the fourteenth-century Franciscan Brother William of Baskerville—a dead ringer for Sherlock Holmes, hawk nose, drug habit, and all—finds himself deep in a labyrinthine library where he has no business to be, looking for clues to a rash of murders. Rooms have up to five doors to other rooms, while some connect to nothing more at all. "Elementary," William says to his dear Watson, an easily scared young Benedictine named Adso, as they confidently plunge ahead. But elementary it is not. Soon the monks aren't even sure if they're in rooms they've been in before. Only one thing to do—leave, for a new try when they're fresher.

Leave? The sole way out is via the eastern tower, and after so much wandering, where's that? At this point Holmes might have cited a trifling monograph of his own invention—perhaps called *On the Solution of Mazes, with a Note on Multiple Connection*—but Brother William can only murmur a lengthy formula from "an ancient text I once read," perfectly useless at present because it requires you to put marks on walls, and the brothers have nothing to make marks with. After many hours, they stumble out by sheer chance, which is what's apt to happen to novices in labyrinths.

It happens daily to visitors at the Hampton Court maze, about thirty minutes outside London, where a garden maze has been enticing the curious since at least 1690. To explore it nowadays you pay thirty pence, enter between high yew hedges, and face a blank hedge you can't see over. No choice but to swing right or left. Right soon proves to be a mistake: dead end. About-face then, and redraw your mental map: that other option, on the left when you came in, now stretches straight ahead. After sundry zigs and zags, a fork and a new decision: Right? Left? Your mental map will take only so much redrawing. Before long, in blind retreat from a blind alley, you're unsure which mistake got you there. So, trial and error; if you've a train to catch, panic. Never mind finding the center, just get out. . . . If every tourist does get out eventually, it's thanks to the guard who leaves the exit gate open at closing time. (Years ago, guards used to shout directions through megaphones to those still trapped inside.)

Yet the Hampton Court maze is childishly simple. For all the turnings and redoublings, its half-mile of pathways really presents only eight forks. They can seem more like eighty because of two closed loops. If you've blundered into either, you could spend an afternoon making the same wrong decisions again and again. Better to rely on a rule they don't tell you on entering: always take the left fork.

That rule works for a large class of mazes, but not for the diabolical one a specialist named Greg Bright has designed at Longleat, a stately home in Wiltshire. Six cross-over bridges lift Bright's puzzle into the third dimension, frustrating all easy solutions.

The rule won't work, either, for a wonderful maze British sculptor Michael Ayrton designed in 1967 for New York financier Armand Erpf's estate in the Catskills. Erpf, who died in 1971, had read Ayrton's *The Maze Maker*, a fictional autobiography of Daedalus, who designed the most celebrated of all mazes, a prison for the monstrous Minotaur of Crete.

At the Hampton Court entrance, although you don't know it, you're so close to the center you could arrive there by breaking through just one hedge, but the polite way takes you sidewise. The maze Erpf commissioned from Ayrton encloses not one center but two, containing a bronze Minotaur and a bronze Daedalus. Its 1,680 feet of coil are enclosed by sturdy walls of brick and concrete, rather than by hedges, and so they may still be beckoning adventurers a thousand years from now. Unlike Daedalus, Ayrton wasn't building in earthquake country.

Whatever their material, labyrinths put forth a fascination that's hypnotic as well as intimate. To find one you need look no further than your thumbprint. Inside your body, too, are labyrinths, coil within coil, and Ayrton even thought that "the inextricable yards of intertwining intestine that man first revealed when he inserted his flint knife into his victim" gave humans their first obsession with the labyrinthine. Out of somewhere in the midst of all that, a child emerges, joined to its mother's innards by a cord. Was that, Ayrton wondered, what had prompted the story of Ariadne's thread?

For Ariadne's thread joins neophyte to source. In the myth, Ariadne gave the thread to Theseus, who was about to enter Daedalus's labyrinth and would have to get out when he'd coped with the Minotaur. Paying out thread behind him was the solution. Having in effect entered the earth mother, he could follow his cord back into daylight.

Getting to the center in the first place was a different story. Time and again, like any Hampton Court tourist, Theseus would have encountered a branching, a place to decide. Trial and error, trial and error, and try to remember what it was you tried last. It's reassuring to know you're a high form of life, equipped with almost unlimited memory banks—though in countless labs lower forms do well with mazes. Even earthworms can learn to manage, if there's no more than one place where they need to decide. Ants have been known to cope with as many as ten decision points. As for rats—once they've reached the center and returned, do they set up seminars for brother rat? Cartoonists like to think so.

What bewilders rats and people is the twisting and turning. Clear your head, take a deep breath, and one thing is obvious: if there's a route to the goal at all, we can imagine it stretched out into a straight line. If that were done, visitors could simply march along it like a parade down Main Street, ignoring all other options. Those are merely blind alleys to left and right, or else loops that leave the main path but come back to it. Likewise, you could think of your intestinal system as a straight tube thirty feet long (more or less) with just one blind alley, the vermiform appendix.

If you were so minded (and had the time), you could explore every blind alley in a maze. Just turn into it, and on reaching the end, turn back. On returning to the main line, resume your forward march. If blind alleys branch off blind alleys, keep doing the same. You'll get back on course, eventually.

Or, to be efficient, you could explore only the blind alleys on (let's say) your left. *Whenever there's a left turn, take it*. That left-turn rule is the only one you need at Hampton Court. At the end of a blind alley, two left turns will point you out again. A loop will return you automatically. In either case, once you're back at the main path, a left turn sends you on your way again.

Once you're convinced that the rule works with a straight main path, you can see how it would work quite as well if we folded the main path, accordion-style, to fit into a box, the challenge now being to enter the box on one side and leave on the other. It works just as well, too, if we coil our main path into the kind of maze Theseus explored, a spiral with the goal at the center. Only then the explorer will have to traverse the maze a second time, in reverse, to get back out. That was where Ariadne's thread came in handy, though Theseus might have coped without it. If the left-turn rule was what got him to the Minotaur, then the same rule would return him to daylight.

So, straight, folded, or coiled, a maze is essentially unchanged. That's a way of saying mazes are problems in topology, a branch of mathematics we may loosely describe as the science of connectedness. However the maze is deformed, its connections don't alter and the left-turn rule always works.

Or almost always, because the maze designer has one fiendish trick up his sleeve. He can put in a loop that leads you clear round your goal, and then make the one path to the goal branch off the loop on the right, so followers of the left-turn rule will be sure to miss it. And don't think that you can defeat his scheme by following a *right*-turn rule; if you do that, the crucial path will be on your left.

Are you condemned to march round such a loop forever? No, your fate will be even more humiliating. At the junction that seduces you into the loop you fork off to the left. Then you pass the path to your goal, but it's on your right, so you miss it. After a while you re-enter the seductive junction. Not knowing you were there before, you head left: and that's into the main road again, but you have turned clear around. Now you're marching back toward where you came in, and you may need to explain there to an anxious maiden how you never got as far as the monster you went in to slay. She'll feel let down.

The topologist who has designed a maze with loops may explain that it's "multiply connected," whereas the kind with only blind alleys is "simply connected." Multiply connected means there's more than one path joining at least one pair of decision points. That spells a loop, and we're ejected if some loop carries us around the goal. The loops at multiply connected Hampton Court do not, which is why the left-turn rule works there. The maze Ayrton designed for Erpf has an ejection loop surrounding nearly everything; there, the left-turn rule eases you out in about two minutes. And the maze that bemused Brother William of Baskerville was multiply connected in such complex ways that, lacking anything to make a mark with, William and Adso got free only by chance. For to be sure of solving a multiply connected maze we need a way to make marks. Luckily, we don't need foreknowledge of its connectedness, since the more advanced strategy works for simple mazes, too.

Let's suppose that wherever we must make a choice, we mark both our entry path and the one we'll choose. Can we state that as an unambiguous rule?

The "ancient text" recited by Brother William was one attempt at a statement, but it seems to have been translated from the Latin in a hurry. Here's a clearer version from my friend Joe O'Rourke, a professor of computer science:

Take a left turn at each juncture. More precisely, take the leftmost turn not already explored. This requires that you mark which turns you've taken. Keep on going until you arrive at a cul-de-sac, or the functional equivalent: a junction, all of whose exits have already been explored. In either case, retrace your last step, and decide what to do at that junction according to the same rules.

That says in effect, "Observe the left-hand rule; but a loop can fool you, so use marks and don't be fooled twice." Computer people call it a "depth-first" search, because it ignores all distractions until you've gone as deep as possible down the path you first elected. If "as deep as possible" brings you to the goal, well and good; if not, you work back out to a junction where you decide *according to the same rules*. That is, you check any marks you made at that junction and take the leftmost of the paths still unmarked. These may lead to other loops or blind alleys, but eventually you'll find a junction that opens on something interesting.

It isn't surprising that computer science has the wit to rectify Brother William's labyrinthine text. Computerists confront mazes every day. Their programs are perpetually searching through something: a mailing list, for a name; a chess position, for a sensible move. One of the hackers' all-time favorite games, Adventure, sends them searching a three-dimensional maze for treasures and trolls. On a grander scale, telephone-company computers route calls from town to town via switching-points, and whenever one is overloaded the computer seeks out an alternative route. Traversing mazes is a problem of the same order.

And the depth-first search they've evolved has a number of advantages, which are hidden in Joe's little phrase "according to the same rules." That means that the program can very efficiently repeat itself, by a strategy known as recursion. It isn't a good strategy for chess, where it could lead you on for fifty moves before it bottomed out with an absurd mate—one reason computers are still such duffers at chess. For chess you'd use "breadth first"—a rather quick survey of only the initial options before any is chosen. But for labyrinths depth-first is the way to go. Follow each option in turn to the bitter end; then work your way back out and again fare forward.

You'll have noticed that the normal option brings three paths to-gether, counting the path you came in by. If that tickles memories of the story of Oedipus, who killed his father at a place where three roads met, then memory, like a labyrinth, has brought you recur-sively to the domain of myth, one domain this all-encompassing sub-ject branches to. The devil, it used to be thought, could only move in straight lines; pious Christians could thwart him by moving in zig-zags. They did that on their knees, praying their way along labyrinths diagrammed on the floors of churches: there are still fine ones in Chartres cathedral and in the parish church of St. Quentin, in the Loire Valley. Meant to humble but not bewilder the faithful, such mazes have no branchings. They spiral haltingly inward, as if to Je-rusalem.

The pilgrims' Jerusalem is of another time; but (wrote Ayrton) "in a maze, time crosses and recrosses, and one time lives in another." To the Romans, the Sibyl spoke prophetic oracles out of a labyrinth of passages that honeycomb the great rock at Cumae. In our time James Joyce, who called his alter ego Stephen Dedalus, made a labyrinth he called *Ulysses* and another he called *Finnegans Wake*. The left-turn rule is useless in either. Daedalus emerged from his Cretan labyrinth on wings of his own design; later, as Ayrton reminds us, history's first air-borne invasion, in 1941, led to the capture of Crete. We seem un-able to emerge from labyrinthine myth. Even the Minotaur revives, as often as a few kids start a game of Dungeons & Dragons.

Hopscotch is another remnant of the cult of the maze: children hop it unaware of their pilgrim kin. Cranes, too, the Greeks noticed, hop while advancing and retreating in courtship, one link of maze with dancing floor and with Daedalus's wings. So Theseus danced at the entrance to the Labyrinth, and Shakespeare has words that connect dance with maze ("The nine men's morris is fill'd up with mud / And the quaint mazes in the wanton green / For lack of tread are undistin-guishable"). And a classical maze had seven decision points; was Joshua unwinding those when he marched his troops around Jericho seven times? For that matter, do other ancient tales of besieged cities reflect the cult of the maze? *Truia* on an Etruscan jug of the seventh century B.C. seems to mean "Troy," and it labels a maze from which warriors emerge. And the Welsh word *troi* means "a turn" or "to turn."

Mazes grew huge: Herodotus describes an Egyptian labyrinth of three thousand intercommunicating rooms on two levels. The Dallas–Fort Worth airport can remind you of that. They grow small, too; our microcircuitry puts an almost inconceivable labyrinth on a tiny silicon chip. It's with the aid of such chips, smaller than a thumbnail, that we switch long-distance calls round a network, the miniature maze frequently more intricate than the switched one that sprawls continent-wide. And the brain that devised both microcircuit and network? Its neurons trace, so far as we can conceive, an ultimate maze, the maze in which we try to conceive it.

Thought is a labyrinth; and topological thought, which sprang originally from the brain of Leonhard Euler (1707–83), gives us our best analytical approaches to the mazes of our recreation and our technology: the left-turn rule, the depth-first search. Such labels seem to announce little tinny formulas. Do not be misled, though. The formulas lift us, like the wings of Daedalus, out of everything labyrinthine, for an overview.

Ironies About Irony

Times Literary Supplement, *where they asked for a few thousand words on irony with some reference to Mr. Enright's book. I've since heard from Wayne Booth that he now gets students who take Swift's "Modest Proposal" straight, even speculate on its feasibility.*

THE ALLURING PROBLEM: AN ESSAY ON IRONY,
by D. J. Enright. Oxford University Press, 1987. 178 pp.

Irony, that catless grin, does hover these days. Wayne C. Booth, author in 1975 of *A Rhetoric of Irony* which Mr. Enright's book is quick to acknowledge, has more recently (in the winter 1983 *Georgia Review*) complained of an omnipresent mannerism, the use of "ironically" to say merely "What about that!"

"It is ironic that the employment we find for our students interferes with their academic work." (It's not ironic, merely unintended.) "Ironically, this year's nominee has just been convicted of embezzlement." (Not ironically, no; embarrassingly.) "The tornado struck out of an ironically blue sky." (Ironically? Just oddly.) Here Booth adduces addlepated Harriet Smith in *Emma*: "He was four-and-twenty the 8th of last June, and my birth-day is the 23rd—just a fortnight and a day's difference! Which is very odd!" Nowadays, he remarks, she would say not "odd" but "ironic."

So "ironic" and "ironically" have become "all-purpose, flexible slot-fillers," and the moment they spring to mind you'd best reconsider. You were about to say, "Ironically, she never did achieve her goal"? Either cut the word entirely, counsels Booth, or decide whether you mean "sadly" or "tragically" or "appropriately," or perhaps just "as all who knew her hoped." He even offers seventy-eight useful synonyms, thoughtfully grouped in four categories, and suggests that "but" or "yet" or "nevertheless" will frequently serve as well as any of them.

As to why "irony" has gotten so promiscuous, Booth sketches its present all-purpose definition: it pertains to "Every phenomenon in the universe that does not appear or behave exactly as I [the speaker] expected it to behave or wanted it to behave." Once, when we talked about the universe, we all meant an order with a ruling divinity whose designs transcended and often confounded ours: hence, the Sophoclean irony, which bespoke Zeus, and Thomas Hardy's Little (and Big) Ironies, ascribed to a dicing President of the Immortals. Though less theocentric, people now still assume a universe making promises it can neglect to keep. It observes "laws," does it not, cosmological laws? But these laws seem to claim a random right to exceptions. Hence, the tornado from the blue sky, called "ironic."

A tic, then, attending the Disappearance of God? More than that, apparently. We have to account for the way "irony" now bedevils discourse about literature, where we've come to sense a minefield. Most books on irony, Enright remarks, are recent; he might have added that the topic once seemed so slight as to be encapsulable in a few phrases. Johnson's definition (1755) was simply, "A mode of speech in which the meaning is contrary to the words." He offered two examples, one his own ("Bolingbroke was a holy man") and one Swift's: "So grave a body, upon so solemn an occasion, should not deal in irony, or explain their meaning by contraries." There "Irony" is no more complicated than "Poetess" ("A she poet") or "Poker" ("The iron bar with which men stir the fire").

For George Puttenham in 1588 "Ironia" (then still an unnaturalized word) was simply "the drye mocke": one example is the French king's retort to a man who claimed reward for facial cuts suffered in battle: "Ye may see what it is to runne away & looke backwards." It's a figure of aggression, drier than "Sarcasmus, or the Bitter taunt," and Puttenham groups it with other figures that alter the sense of whole clauses: these include Allegoria ("the Figure of false semblant"), Asteismus ("the civill jest"), Micterismus ("the Fleering frump"), Charientismus ("the privy nippe"), and Periphrasis, "as when we go about the bush, and will not in one or a few words expresse that thing which we desire to have knowen."

You can't miss Puttenham's implication that all such trifling with plain sense is dangerous; elsewhere he calls the figures "in a sorte abuses or rather trespasses in speach, because they passe the ordinary limits of common utterance, and be occupied of purpose to deceive the eare and also the minde, drawing it from plainnesse and simplicitie to a certaine doublenesse," which is not right. So "The grave judges *Areopagites*" forbade figurative speech in courtrooms according to Puttenham, and I have read somewhere that an Act of Parliament to prohibit metaphor was proposed in seventeenth-century England. I've also heard a literary critic loudly denounced for expressing some admiration of ironic modes: that was snobbish of him, seeing that irony amounts to deceiving plain folk who understand in a plain way. Too, it was naive of the denouncer, who seemed to believe with Puttenham that plainness is the norm you achieve without guile.

Puttenham resolved his moral dilemma by exempting the poet, who after all pleads "pleasant and lovely causes and nothing perillous" to "princely dames, yong ladies, gentlewoman and courtiers." Though even the poet had best be careful and keep measure, still by using Ironia and suchlike perversions sparingly, he can make "very vice goe for a formall vertue in the exercise of this Arte."

But from a local figure to be used with precaution, irony has now become a pervasive mode, inviting many biggish books (e.g., Muecke, *The Compass of Irony*; Booth, *A Rhetoric of Irony*; Japp, *Theorie der Ironie*), and now a smallish one like D. J. Enright's. Is Enright's yes-oh-dear-yes tentativeness itself a pervasive irony? One may suspect so. That has been his way as an ironic poet. "Irony," he says, "had always struck me as *alluring*: a way of making statements, not unlike that of poetry, which through the unexpectedness and the avoidance of head-on assertion had a stronger chance of discomposing, if not winning over, the person addressed."

"The person addressed": that's like Puttenham assuming that we set out to "express that thing which we desire to have knowen." But—Deconstruction admonishes—there is at the core no "we," no "thing," no surviving "desire": just Text, the plaything of a reader/interpreter who'll posit authors and intentions at his peril. The writer but lays an egg for each reader to scramble. The henroost, the kitchen, those are disparate spheres. So when Wayne Booth in his book (not the essay I drew on earlier) canvasses the question, How do we know it's ironic?, he's unblushingly pre-Derrida. For the very question posits auctorial intention, and the up-to-date line has it that, intention being without meaning, there's *always* irony, in infinite regress.

An author, Booth said, may cue us by a title; "The Love Song of J. Alfred Prufrock" isn't going to be the Love Song of T. S. Eliot. But, but, we hasten to point out, isn't Prufrock a decentered Eliot? (And it's true that his name appears only in the title. Homework: reread the poem, having changed its title to "October Thoughts.")

As for a plain style, we understand today (I don't say that ironically) how—as in *Dubliners*—it's an extreme form of artifice. So by its mere presence it invites us to detect the invisible quotation-marks irony confers. If a style may best be described as a system of limits, hence characterized by what it cannot say, then any style connotes irony and so does "absence" of style.

A perennially fascinating instance is *A Portrait of the Artist as a Young Man*. For decades it was read as James Joyce's autobiography: how he lived, erred, fought, and triumphed, to re-create life out of life. Forty years ago someone (myself: I imitate Enright's gesture of "sinking into my own anecdotage") suggested that the *Portrait*'s Stephen Dedalus was not perhaps wholly Joyce: was an *uncompleted* Joyce, indeed radically uncompletable, like Mr. James Duffy in "A Painful

Case" who'd done some Joycean things like translate Hauptmann but still was crippled in ways his creator had avoided. Stephen's one poem, I asserted, was jejune, his didactic manner a bluff.

Not to linger over the fortunes of that essay—someone instructively sneered that I took elaborate irony for truth—still it seems worth noting that by Wayne Booth's tests the *Portrait* discloses no marks of irony at all. Today adolescents read it as the naive book they'd like to have written. You can decide that "The Artist" in its title is ironic—not a portrait of Rembrandt by Rembrandt, but a look at the generic "artist" whom bright young folks may fancy themselves to be—but that is your decision. You may want to notice the book's very last lines,

Dublin 1904

Trieste 1914

and reflect that a portrait painted during ten years is very different from Rembrandt's afternoon before a mirror, subject and portraitist co-present *now*. But aren't you being a trifle ingenious? That depends on how seriously you weigh every cue from the text, including those dates.

That book is the *fons et origo* of modern fiction, not least in its eschewal of ironic markers. We're immersed from the start in Stephen's idiom of the moment; "When you wet the bed first it is warm then it gets cold" (plain sequence); "Her bosom was as a bird's soft and slight, slight and soft as the breast of some darkplumaged dove" (his chiasmic period); "John Alphonsus Mulrennan has just returned from the west of Ireland (European and Asiatic papers please copy)" (his ironic period, at an unstable moment of which we leave him). For it's noteworthy that Joyce brings Stephen all the way from "Once upon a time" to gestures of overt irony, and mixes those with efflations like "Welcome O, life!" and simply leaves us to observe what's going on. (If we stay content to empathize with Stephen, Joyce can shrug.) Now when Dickens wrote of Oliver asking for more, he didn't assume readers sensitive to an enormity. He poured a rich mix of Ironia and Sarcasmus and Asteismus and Charientismus and even Periphrasis, the better to denote that officialdom's sky was cracking:

"Mr. Limbkins, I beg your pardon, Sir! Oliver Twist has asked for more!"

There was a general start. Horror was depicted on every countenance.

"For *more!*" said Mr. Limbkins. "Compose yourself, Bumble, and answer me more distinctly. Do I understand that he asked for more, after he had eaten the supper allotted by the dietary?"

"He did, Sir," replied Bumble.

"That boy will be hung," said the gentleman in the white waistcoat. "I know that boy will be hung."

There's no mistaking the ironic intent of that. But Joyce thought it heavy-handed. He assumed readers who could pick up unprodded not only the enormity of the hellfire sermon but also things like a disparity between Stephen's theorizings and his solipsism. In the *Stephen Hero* draft he had cued response, sprinkling ironies like "this heaven-ascending essayist" on the paraphrase of Stephen's paper "Drama and Life," but in ten years' labor on the *Portrait* he achieved a detachment, which disdains such aids. So different readers are apt to read different *Portraits*, and is that fact a high irony or not? Is the work weaker or stronger in not declaring intentions? No one doubts the intention of Dickens. But we can deconstruct Dickens. In a getting-and-spending world he didn't radically question, did he know what his intentions signified?

Safer, an ironist might say, to leave intentions for readers to invent. As did Swift, or did he? For *A Modest Proposal* cannot be evaded. It is perhaps the sole example of English prose we can say no one-time reader has ever forgotten. And it works by soliciting a reader (you, me) who assents to its opening statements, what a deal of beggars, what a nuisance they are, trusting the lull of a reasonable voice, till in those same reasonable tones a sentence about cooking babies (you know the one) prompts a violent disjunction: this is monstrous! After that the modest proposer keeps on talking, confident that he is in sane company, from which, however, we have absented ourselves. And what keeps us reading, as horror climbs atop horror? Is it not partly that calm solicitation of *someone* who assents to every word? There's an awful fascination in postulating such a someone. But *we* assented, too, till the cooking came up. Is this what generations of usage have made of reason, of expressing in a few words "that thing which we desire to have knowen"? Is reason, is our trust in orderly prose, somehow entangled in our willingness to dismiss others' misery as a simple nuisance? That was one thing we assented to, as the pamphlet got started.

But don't we as readers normally comply with authors and by assenting help them get things started? Is not that the way we assure ourselves of something to read? For if our habit is to quarrel with opening words, we'll face empty evenings, alone with our own bad temper. So Swift (1729) deconstructed our very appetite for the printed page, for the reasonable voice. The force of irony has not further gone. Where were you, Derrida, in 1729?

Mr. Enright—but look, ironically, I've been scamping his book all this while. All right. It's a short book, a low-keyed book, a book without pretensions to system: an "essay," he calls it, in twenty-eight short parts with headings like "Definitions?" and "Chinese." It meditates with unspirited economy on all manner of examples, many of them transient. "It was announced in May 1985 that crocodile meat for human consumption was about to be available in Australian grocery stores since the reptile was no longer an endangered species." Thus, crocodiles might long to remain an endangered species, hence out of butchers' danger, though Enright (ironically?) calls that longing "not altogether logical."

Or a British rail poster, which lists cheques and credit cards, can end, "Cash is, of course, acceptable." Ironic or not? No, but "perhaps indicative of a faint sense that there are still old-world peasants who carry cash on them." Just so. And here's a report (TLS, 21 September 1984) that a New York State school board banned *A Modest Proposal* as being "in bad taste." Taste! Mr. Enright's palate for examples cannot be faulted. And he cherishes non-literary examples; devoid of ironic intention, they invite an ironic reading.

What he tends to do with an example is find something quietly ironic to say about it; I found the whole book running together like wallpaper, quiet (yes, I know I've said that), short-breathed (just two and a half pages on Pope), self-deprecating in an ironical way:

As for writing about irony, that too is risky since like enough you will emerge as either a smart alec or a dim-wit. Nevertheless, if you are an academic, publishing on even so equivocal a theme may help you to gain promotion. As we know, all teachers are good teachers, but in any structure involving seniority some need to be picked out as more good than others.

Mr. Enright doesn't conceal his erstwhile academic connections. But we needn't think them operative now. Thus, at whose expense is this irony? Or is it irony? Would Wayne Booth pass it as ironic? Would D. J. Enright? (Number your answers, and do not write on both sides of the paper.)

Some of the effects so produced can be labyrinthine. Sarcasm, Christopher Ricks is quoted as saying, is "inferior in its superiority"; irony means not knowing better but knowing otherwise. (Thus, *someone* can be imagined who'd credit the Modest Proposer, but for sarcasm two ways don't exist.) Ricks, it next turns out, was discussing a poem which Enright quotes in full "since it seems not to be in print." It's about the interchangeability, misery for misery under bombing, of Hanoi and Saigon. The gist of Ricks's analysis is quoted, too.

Enright then addresses the poem himself. He finds "a heaviness about it, a labour-intensiveness manifested in its repetitions, and a trace of preachiness. . . . The author's efforts to keep cool . . . evince themselves in a stolid, too deliberate hypothermia." (Fine word, that; I've not seen it in lit'ry discussion before.) Since "the author did not see fit to include the piece in his collected poems," we're to suppose that he felt misgivings such as those detailed.

The author? The notes don't name him. They simply send us to *New York Review of Books*, 13 August 1970, where, verifying a suspicion, we may ascertain that the poem "Streets" was written by—D. J. Enright. *Quelque chose là qui ne va pas.* Or else irony.

The trope expands like a gas: it's not only "the meaning contrary to the words" but saying (as above) less than is meant; also saying more than is meant; even (ironically) saying just what is meant and not being trusted. Who now, it's tempting to say, trusts anything said? There seem reasons not to wholly trust Mr. Enright. Mr. Enright, too, doesn't wholly trust Wayne Booth, who can crush his subject "under the weight of brilliance," or mislay it "under sudden decelerations and profusions." Booth is American. Have we here the English aversion to what gets called "cleverness"? Have we, in *The Alluring Problem* (coy title), a deliberately *English* book, pragmatic, unsystematic, chewing its cud while it chances on instances? Is that too ironic a reading?

Yes, it is; because our author seems without guile if not without reticence. What troubles him about books like Booth's and Muecke's is some disparity between the system implied by any book and the very elusiveness their subject has acquired. Hence, since the subject compels him, a kind of unbook, rich and modest and asserted by a simple pun, the one inherent in the keyword "Problem," which means both something you might solve and something that, in calling it a Problem, you concede is insoluble: is only for rotating, pondering.

No longer, as for Puttenham and Johnson, an isolate device, "irony" seems to have become the very condition of discourse. *The* Alluring Problem, indeed; the moment we're aware that it's discourse we attend to, we're aware of what theorists call its problematic. And it's to give that awareness a name that we've stretched the term "irony," to Mr. Booth's recent distress. Greek *eironeia* meant simulated ignorance; an *eiron* was a dissembler. If you dissembled or simulated you knew it. But those were simpler times. It's now routinely assumed that no one (save perhaps a crook) really *knows* what is conveyed by anything he's saying.

Language is just behavior; or it's just contrivance; or just self-deception, or just so many graphemes set down for pay. So we say. Yet its richness was the nineteenth century's great discovery, and inventorying those riches was the obsession of the century's most active minds. That human beings handled, every day, such unimagined treasures! A Skeat, a Murray, a Furnivall: they were men dazzled by linguistic vistas, drunk on linguistic lore. So, later, were Saussure and Bakhtin. So it may be again. What we live through today, having learned to drink so deep, is the hangover we miscall irony.

The Politics of
the Plain Style

For 1984, notorious year, Rosemont College in Pennsylvania scheduled massive Orwell Doings, including this lecture.

Monsieur Jourdain, the Molière bourgeois, was so misguided as to conclude he'd been talking prose all his life, his bogus instructor having defined prose as whatever is not verse. But as nobody talks in rhyme, so nobody talks in prose. Prose came late into every language, and very late into English. Chaucer, even, had few clues to its workings.

A special variety, "plain" prose, came especially late. Plain prose—the plain style—is the most disorienting form of discourse yet invented by man. Swift in the eighteenth century, George Orwell in the twentieth, are two of its very few masters. And both were "political" writers; and there's a connection.

The plain style has been hard to talk about, except in circles. Can plainness, for instance, even lay claims to a style? Swift seems to think so. "Proper words in proper places" is what he has to say about style;

not explaining, though, how to find the proper words or identify the proper places to put them into.

But Swift is teasing. His readers (1720) belong to the first generation to feel alarm at the norms of printed pages, the way fifties intelligentsia were alarmed by television. Swift confronts them with their own bewilderment about what "style" may mean on silent paper, where words have not cadences nor emphases but "places." He is nearly asking if "style" has become a branch of geometry.

Styles were long distinguished by degrees of ornateness, the more highly figured being the more esteemed. There was a high style in which Cicero delivered his orations, and a low style in which he would have addressed his cook. Rhetoricians gave their attention to the high style. The low style was beneath attention. It was scarcely, save by contrast, a style at all.

Evaluation like that has nothing to do with writing. It appeals to the way we judge oral performance. When Cicero spoke with his cook he was offstage; when he addressed the Senate he was in costume and in role and in command of a scene carefully pre-scripted. Of the five parts into which the Romans analyzed oratory, two pertained to the theatrics of performance; they were "memory" and "delivery." Here "memory" is a clue to something important. Cicero's intricate syntax, its systems of subordination, its bold rearrangements of the natural order of words, would have been impossible for an orator to improvise. So he worked them out on paper, then memorized them, then performed them in a way that made it seem he was giving voice to his passion of the moment. In fact, he was being careful not to let passion master him, lest it overwhelm memory.

A good public speech is something as contrived as a scene by Shakespeare. Even Lincoln, in what is represented as an address of exemplary plainness, launched it with diction he could only have premeditated: "Four score and seven years ago our fathers brought forth on this continent. . . ." The word "style" pertains to the art of contriving something like that. You contrive it by hand. A *stilus* was a pointed tool with which Romans wrote on wax tablets, and what you did with its aid was what came to be called your "style." It seems to follow that a "plain style" is a contradiction in terms. If it's plain, then surely it didn't need working out with a stylus?

But indeed it did. Something so lucid, so seemingly natural that we can only applaud its "proper words in proper places," is not the work of nature at all but of great contrivance. W. B. Yeats wrote, on a related theme,

> I said, 'A line will take us hours maybe;
> Yet if it does not seem a moment's thought,
> Our stitching and unstitching has been naught.'

Here's an intricate instance, writing that's saying it was *spoken* despite the fact that it rhymes, writing, therefore, that's inviting us to ponder its own degrees of artifice. Yeats has in mind poetry that has abandoned the high style and is managing to look not only improvised but conversational; yes, even while rhyming. That would be poetry contriving to be "at least as well written as prose." And it helps us perceive good prose as an art with a new set of norms: feigned casualness, hidden economy.

Since you're feigning those qualities, nothing stops you from feigning much more. George Orwell wrote *A Hanging*, the eyewitness account of something he almost certainly never witnessed; also *Shooting an Elephant*, his first-person recollection of a deed he may or may not ever have done.

We like to have such things plainly labeled "fiction," if fictions they be. Then we are willing to admire the artistry: so acutely invented a detail as the condemned man stepping round a puddle within yards of the rope, which prompts the narrator's reflection on "the unspeakable wrongness of cutting a life short when it is in full tide. This man was not dying, he was alive just as we were alive." That is like John Donne meditating on a sacred text, and we'd not welcome news that the text was nowhere in the Bible, that Donne had invented it for the sake of the sermon he could spin.

True, we can cite something Orwell wrote elsewhere: "I watched a man hanged once. . . ." Alas, that doesn't prove that he watched a man hanged once; it proves only that the author of *A Hanging* (1931) still had such an idea on his mind when he was writing something else six years later. An appeal to other writers may be more helpful; we soon find that Swift wrote a very similar sentence: "Last week I watched a woman *flay'd*. . . ." We could surely find more parallels, and in seeking them we'd be nudging *A Hanging* from reportage into literature, where questions of veracity can't reach it. For we'll half-accept the idea that printed words do no more than permute other printed words, in an economy bounded by the page. That gets called "the literary tradition," where statements aren't required to be true.

But if we'll half-accept the fictive quality of everything we read, don't we also tend to believe what it says here in black and white: what we read in the papers? Of course we do; perhaps because the printed word stays around to be checked, like a stranger with nothing to hide. (Though handwriting does that too, print has the advantage of looking impersonal.)

Plain prose was invented among consumers of print, to exploit this ambiguous response. It seems to peg its words to what is persistently *so* no matter how words drift about. Even incredibility, couched in printed plain prose, can hope for belief. It's the perfect medium for hoaxes. By publishing the word that a nuisance named Partridge was dead, Swift caused him vast trouble proving that he was alive, and H. L. Mencken's mischievous printed statement that the first American bathtub got installed as recently as 20 December 1842 is enshrined as history in the Congressional Record though Mencken himself tried to disavow it four times. Having grown famous for a baroque manner that advertised its own exaggerations, Mencken may have been surprised to find he could make people believe anything if he simply dropped to the plain style.

The science journalist Martin Gardner, whose style is plain to the point of naivety, had a similar experience when he sought to amuse *Scientific American* readers by extolling a bogus force located in pyramids; it could sharpen razor blades! The joke instantly got out of hand. Cultists of Pyramid Power made themselves heard, and Gardner has been trying in vain ever since to discredit them.

Like Gardner's pyramid and Mencken's bathtub, the novel, which we both believe and don't, has origins inextricable from fakery. Eighteenth-century readers could savor the Life and Strange Surprising Adventures of Robinson Crusoe, who'd been cast away on an island. That was an exotic thought if you lived in crowded London, and exoticism fostered the will to believe. The title page, moreover, said, "Written by Himself," so the account had the merit of first-hand truth. (Remember the trick? "I watched a man hanged once.") It was a while before "Himself" turned out to be a journalist named Defoe.

Today we handle the question of deception by saying that Defoe was writing a novel, a genre of which he would have had no inkling. Defoe had simply discovered what plain prose, this new and seemingly styleless medium, is good for. Nothing beats it as a vehicle for profitable lies, which can entertain people and may even do them good in other ways. Even now, knowing as we do that Defoe, not Crusoe, was the author, we contrive to read *Robinson Crusoe* as if it were true. The formula, "Willing suspension of disbelief," was invented to help us accept what we are doing.

The next step was journalism, meaning reports you could trust, statement by statement, fact by fact, because they appeared in newspapers. Gradually, newspapers gravitated toward the plain style, the style of all styles that was patently trustworthy: in fact, the style of *Robinson Crusoe*, with which Defoe had invented such a look of honest verisimilitude. A man who doesn't make his language ornate cannot be deceiving us: so runs the hidden premise. "A close, naked, natural way of speaking," Thomas Sprat called it in 1667: the speech, he went on to say, of merchants and artisans, not of wits and scholars. Merchants and artisans are men who handle *things*, and presumably handle words with a similar probity. Wits and scholars handle nothing more substantial than "ideas." Journalism seemed guaranteed by the plain style. Handbooks and copy editors now teach journalists how to write "plainly"; that means, in such a manner that they will be trusted. You get yourself trusted by appropriate artifice.

It's a populist style, and that suited writers like Swift and Mencken and Orwell. Homely diction is its hallmark, also 1-2-3 syntax, the show of candor, and the artifice of seeming to be grounded outside language, in what is called "fact," the domain where a condemned man can be observed as he silently avoids a puddle, and your prose will report the observation, and no one will doubt it. Such prose simulates the words anyone who was there and awake might later have spoken spontaneously. And on a written page, as we've seen, the spontaneous can only be a contrivance.

So a great deal of artifice is being piled on, beginning with the candid no-nonsense observer. What if there was a short circuit, no observation, simply the prose? Whenever that is suggested, straightforward folk get upset. But they were never meant to think about it, anymore than airplane passengers are meant to brood about what holds them aloft: thin air. *The Plain Style feigns a candid observer.* Such is its great advantage for persuading. From behind its mask of calm candor, the writer with political intentions can appeal, in seeming disinterest, to people whose pride is their no-nonsense connoisseurship of fact. And, such is the trickiness of language, he may find he needs to deceive them to enlighten them.

Thus George Orwell's masterful "plain style" emerged in full development with the 1938 *Homage to Catalonia*, an effort to supply a true account of a war while the Communists, his one-time allies, were fabricating a boilerplate account. Though their ostensible enemies were the so-called Fascists, much trouble, by Red reckoning, was being made when treasonable "Trotskyists" allied themselves with the Fascists, to undo the authentic modes of revolution. It was in Communist so-called "news" of the mid-1930s that Orwell first discerned Newspeak. It penetrated not only the *Daily Worker* but respectable London papers like the *News Chronicle*. It was "the news," and it was believed. How to counter what was believed?

Why, by the device of the first-hand observer—a device as old as Defoe, who used it in *Journal of the Plague Year* to simulate persuasive accounts of things he couldn't possibly have seen. When Newspeak is indulging in sentences like this:

> Barcelona, the first city in Spain, was plunged into bloodshed by *agents provocateurs* using this subversive organization . . .

then your way to credibility is via sentences like this:

Sometimes I was merely bored with the whole affair, paid no attention to the hellish noise, and spent hours reading a succession of Penguin Library books which, luckily, I had bought a few days earlier; sometimes I was very conscious of the armed men watching me fifty yards away.

After you've established your credentials like that, your next paragraphs can ignore the Newspeak utterance as mere academic mischief. And it literally doesn't matter whether you read Penguins in Spain or not.

Orwell was alert to all of English literature, from Chaucer to *Ulysses*. A source for the famous trope about some being more equal than others has been found in *Paradise Lost*. He had studied Latin and Greek, and once, when hard up, he advertised his readiness to translate from anything French so long as it was post 1400 A.D. Yet he is identified with an English prose that sounds monolingual: that seems a codifying of what you'd learn by ear in Wigan. Newspeak, as he defined it in *1984*, seems to reverse the honesty of all that; War is Peace, Freedom is Slavery, $2 + 2 = 5$. Political discourse being feverish with Newspeak, he'd concocted his plain style to reduce its temperature.

Observe, we are dealing now with no language human beings speak; rather with an implied ideal language the credentials of which are moral: a language that cleaves to things and that has univocal names for them. Cat is cat, dog is dog. That, in Swift's time, had been a philosophers' vision, and Swift had derided, in *Gulliver's Travels*, the philosophers who, since words were but tokens for things, saved breath and ear and wear and tear on the lungs by reducing their discourse to a holding-up of things.

Examine Orwell's famous examples, and you discover an absence of apposite *things*. War is not war the way cat is cat, nor is freedom freedom the way dog is dog. Such abstractions are defined by consensus. As for the sum of $2 + 2$, even that is subject to interpretation. I've read of Soviet posters that used "$2 + 2 = 5$" to help citizens make sense of an aborted 5-year plan.

Once we've left behind cat and dog and house and tree, there are seldom "things" to which words can correspond, but you can obtain considerable advantage by acting as if there were. The Plain Style, by which you gain that advantage, seems to be announcing, at every phrase, its subjection to the check of experienced and nameable *things*. Orwell, so the prose says, had shot an elephant; Orwell had witnessed a hanging; Orwell at school had been beaten with a riding crop for wetting his bed. The prose says these things so plainly that we believe whatever else it says. And none of these things seems to have been true.

We should next observe that Orwell's two climactic works are frank fictions: *Animal Farm* and *1984*. In a fiction you address yourself to the wholly unreal as if there were no doubt about it. In *Animal Farm* we're apprised of a convention when we're told of pigs talking to one another. But for the fact that we don't credit pigs with speech, we might be attending to a report of a County Council meeting. (And observe which way the allegory runs; we're not being told that Councillors are pigs.)

It is clarifying to reflect that the language of "fiction" cannot be told from that of "fact." Their grammar, syntax, and semantics are identical. So Orwell passed readily to and fro between his two modes, reportage and fiction, which both employ the plain style. The difference is that the fictionality of fiction offers itself for detection. If the fiction speaks political truths, then, it does so by allegory. That is tricky, because it transfers responsibility for what is being said from the writer to the reader. Orwell's wartime BBC acquaintance, William Empson, warned him in 1945 that *Animal Farm* was liable to misinterpretation, and years later provided an object lesson himself when he denied that *1984* was "about," some future communism. It was "about," Empson insisted, as though the fact should have been obvious, that pit of infamy, the Roman Catholic Church. One thing that would have driven Empson to such a length was his need to leave the left unbesmirched by Orwell, also Orwell untainted by any imputation that he'd besmirched the left. And it summoned Orwell's shade to Empson's side to abet the hysteria he was indulging at that moment. Empson was writing about *Paradise Lost*, contemplation of which appears to have unsettled his mind.

Now this is an odd place for the plain style to have taken us: a place where there can be radical disagreement about what is being said. "A close, naked, natural way of speaking," Sprat had written; "positive expressions, clear senses, . . . thus bringing all things as near to the mathematical plainness as they can." Close, naked, natural, that is terminology to depict a restored Eden, before both Babel and Cicero, when Adam's primal language could not be misunderstood: when words could not possibly say (as Swift mischievously put it) "the thing that was not." That was when Adam delved and Eve span, and they had, both of them, the virtues of merchants and artisans: as it were, Wigan virtues.

But the serpent misled them, no doubt employing the High Style, and what their descendants have been discovering is that not even the Plain Style can effect a return to any simulacrum of paradise. Any spokesman for political decencies desires the Peaceable Kingdom. Books like *Animal Farm* and *1984* show, speaking in parables, how readily its restoration can go awry. So does *Gulliver's Travels*, which ends with the hero-narrator longing vainly to be a horse. What the masters of the Plain Style demonstrate is how futile is anyone's hope to subdue humanity to an austere ideal. Straightness will prove reflexive if not crooked, gain will be short term, vision fabrication, simplicity an intricate contrivance. Likewise no probity, no sincerity can ever subdue the inner contradictions of speaking plainly. These inhere in the warp of reality, ineluctable as the fact that the root of two is irrational. Swift got himself called mad, Orwell was reviled for betraying the left, and divulging the secret of the root of two earned a Greek named Hippasos a watery grave.

Decoding Roland Barthes

From the August 1980 Harper's.

ROLAND BARTHES (1915–80), "PROLIFIC AND ECLECTIC WRITER WHO WAS ONE OF MOST CELEBRATED FRENCH INTELLECTUALS," was a semiotician (meaning meaning-specialist) and would not have missed the semiotic import of his own *New York Times* obituary, where, as in all obits, Life is reduced to Text: text, moreover, that *Times* regulars feel mysteriously compelled to read. That's a mystery for semiotics to unravel.

No matter if we've never before heard of the man; on page 11 of Section B (March 27) a headline rapidly creates him for us, so compellingly we feel a need to know more. What's entered our heads is a verbal construct called "Barthes," made up of clichés governed by what Barthes called the Five Codes.

The codes interweave with computerlike sureness. Play it over in slow motion. "Roland Barthes"—and who is he, taking all this newspaper space? Code 1, the Hermeneutic Code, has posed a question, and by the time the other codes have reinforced it we'll be deep in the smaller print seeking an answer.

"Writer"—that's a neutral designator (Code 2, the Semantic

Code). "French Intellectuals"—aha, we know about *them*, futile garrulous fellows: so works Code 4, the Cultural Code, which triggers received wisdom. But wait a moment, he was "Celebrated," hence all these column-inches. And we are in a familiar mental space, French Celebritydom, where inexplicable folk kiss one another on both cheeks, get chatted about in salons, write to *Le Monde*; what has installed us there is Code 5, the Symbolic Code, which designates zones where certain kinds of things happen.

What's more, "Barthes" was "Prolific and Eclectic": not a Will Durant grinding all his life at one project, but by his own choice a shifter of gears and directions. The domain of Choices is Code 3, the Proairetic Code. (Barthes named it, impishly one trusts, from something we'll not have encountered unless we're Greek scholars—Aristotle's proairesis, "choice" or "purpose"—and you can decide for yourself how to encode the information that Barthes often dropped that sort of grit into the clockwork.)

Enough clockwork is here already for the first page of a short story: a character with what will suffice to animate him, and a motive for reading on. The point is not that ingenuity can squeeze five codes from a headline; the point is that the codes work so effectively that *Times* readers every day find themselves scanning obituaries of people they've never heard of.

Barthes would next point out how much less his own obit tells us about Roland Barthes than about journalism: what the signals are that hold our interest, who we are that cooperate with them, how as well-drilled readers (and how did we get that way?) we create the fictional "Barthes" we're reading about.

The story we now anticipate is, like all stories, a familiar one. An obituary, most formulaic of fictions, routinely creates a character in the headline only to kill him off in the opening words of the text. It then reconstructs by flashback enough of a "life" to seem to merit the whole expensive operation.

The next event is the creation of a second character. This is what happens in a line that reads "By Tony Schwartz." Since we're even less likely to be acquainted with Tony Schwartz than with Roland Barthes, his fictional presence simply adds weight to the fictional "Barthes":

think of it, a by-lined obit! Observe that this would work even if no Tony Schwartz existed: if, for instance, the *Times* kept a stock of dummy by-lines, for dipping into when a page can use a little Star Quality.

You've surely begun to guess that the whole thing would work if there'd never been a "Roland Barthes" either. In a newspaper all is Text. The job of creating a "real" world beyond the text is performed not by the slovenly writers but by ourselves, responsive to codes and so little aware of our own contribution that we imagine we're being *told* something, called "the news."

Here we glimpse what has been Barthes's most scandalous claim: that there isn't a writer in charge, not even of *War and Peace*; his presence is merely something we project from our dealings with the Text he has assembled. Nor is there a "meaning" that the Text exists to deliver; nothing in fact but an unearthly ballet of Codes and Sememes and Reader Expectations. But back to the *Times*.

Now that Tony Schwartz is onstage to perform in the obituary genre, he had better do what we expect else we'll stop reading. His first act should be the ritual killing of "Roland Barthes." He obliges, and in the following way: "Barthes," his words say, died "of injuries following an automobile accident."

Symbolic Code again: a generic late-twentieth-century death; moreover, for cognoscenti a twentieth-century *Intellectual's* death: like Albert Camus or Jackson Pollock, smash. (Or poet Roy Campbell, pretender to twentieth-century status?) Had Schwartz instead mentioned tuberculosis, he would have tied Barthes nostalgically to La Belle Epoque, when intellectuals sported delicate lungs. In 1980 that would be a quaint plot complication. (Do not mutter about taste—we are in the domain of Text, where the dead are only dead the way words say.)

The domain of Text: that was the elected domain of Roland Barthes. Night and day he seems to have secreted Text, faster than several translators—notably the devoted Richard Howard—have been able to get it into English. This year's *New Critical Essays*, the twelfth

Barthes on the active list of just one of his American publishers, Hill & Wang, represents a French book already eight years old. Even the famous *Système de la Mode*, the 1967 book about the language of fashion, is still inaccessible to monolingual Americans. For some years yet the supply of Barthes will continue to seem inexhaustible.

Text, text. "To Write: An Intransitive Verb?" he asked fourteen years ago. Answer: yes. One does not write so-and-so, let alone write "about" so-and-so. One Writes. Someone else can read.

One's writing, moreover—this applies to any writer, even Gay Talese—simply retraces a gargantuan act of reading, for what is not yet explicitly verbal, the goings-on in massage parlors for instance, is nonetheless a set of codes to be read. All the world is text.

Barthes stated this claim in a 1957 book called *Mythologies*, much of which seems inconsequential till we catch on. On page 15 we're told that professional wrestling is text, one more thing we can learn to read. Wrestling—the big-time spectacle, not the pure college version—is unlike boxing in demanding "an immediate reading of the juxtaposed meanings, so that there is no need to connect them." This means that in moving through eloquent moments that might as well occur in any order—the grimace of pain, the sly kick, the grandiloquence of triumph—Grunt & Groan resembles a John Ashbery poem, whereas boxing "is a story constructed before the eyes of the spectator," like *Love Story*. Boxing goes monomaniacally somewhere. Its meaning is in its outcome: you remember who won in how many rounds, and very likely nothing more. (And you remember *Love Story* as the book in which the girl died.) But no one cares who wins at wrestling, and that is why no one resents knowing that the bouts are fixed.

So of wrestling you savor the moments, and if you are Barthes your excitement runs to pretty high-flown analogies:

Each moment in wrestling is therefore like an algebra that instantaneously unveils the relationship between a cause and its represented effect. Wrestling fans certainly experience a kind of intellectual pleasure in *seeing* the moral mechanism function so perfectly. Some wrestlers, who are great comedians, entertain as much as a Molière character . . . Armand Mazaud . . . always delights the audiences by the mathematical rigor of his transcriptions, carrying the form of his gestures to the furthest reaches of their meaning, and giving to his manner of fighting the kind of vehemence and precision found in a great scholastic disputation, in which what is at stake is at once the triumph of pride and the formal concern with truth.

"A man might write such stuff forever, if he would *abandon* his mind to it." In case you were thinking of that sentence of Dr. Johnson's, yes, much of Barthes does put one in mind of it—the doodles concerning the Eiffel Tower, plastics, detergents, and three-fourths even of his most celebrated book, *S/Z*, the marathon (271-page) reading of a 35-page Balzac novella, in the course of which the famous Codes emerge. "One obstacle to discussing these highfliers is their incapacity to think straight, so that it's essential to do some surreptitious tidying up before it's possible to say what or even whether they think." Barthes asked for that (and got it, from Marvin Mudrick) the way a terrier asks for a stallion's kick.

Still, the terrier is frequently barking at *something*; if only some sense of proportion governed his rhetoric! That is surely what disorients about Barthes on wrestling. Algebra . . . Molière . . . scholastic disputation . . . have we here the Professor surprised at the Hippodrome, protesting that he is, so, an Intellectual? Straining to dignify a tawdry spectacle? Being tipsily oblivious to differences of scale? Or have we just plain bubbleheadedness? Not quite any of the above, though it's true that Barthes's bubbling point seems to have been low.

What we have is one consequence of the structuralist enterprise, which has been afoot, chiefly in France, for two decades or so. It amounts to testing how far we can get by translating people's dealings with one another into the terminology of Ferdinand de Saussure (1857–1913), Swiss father of structural linguistics. (You begin to see why everything turns into Text.)

Language for Saussure was a special case of something larger, the theory of signs (semiotics): so general a claim that in the hands of a structuralist, especially a pop structuralist like Barthes, Molière and Mazaud and seemingly anything will seem interchangeable.

Saussure himself had no truck with dizzy interchangeabilities. He devoted his life to one project, which was to find out what there might be for a professor of linguistics to think about that couldn't be better tackled by someone else, historian or philosopher or Berlitz instructor. By 1907, he was trying out his findings on his students at the University of Geneva. He was to give his "Course on General Linguistics" twice more, and die without commencing the book it pointed to. What got published three years later was assembled from students' notes: an omen for the future of his ideas, which have been in the keeping of enthusiasts ever since.*

How might you study linguistics? Lots of people are out there speaking: you might tape-record them. What is more, they are understanding one another, never mind that a Brooklynite's "curl" is indistinguishable from a Vermonter's "coil." So how does one know what the other is talking about? What we record is *parole*, instances of individual performance, and reviewing our data we might be tempted to say that in different instances of *parole* the "same" word gets pronounced "differently." That doesn't take us far. What makes it the "same" word?

What we are after is what Saussure called *langue*, the system within which understanding takes place. Sounds never match exactly, and if they had to, understanding would be hopeless. What does match is a set of internal distinctions, observed by both speakers. That set is *la langue*.

Though my voice sounds quite different from yours, I say "cot" a little differently from "caught," and so do you. And we make the difference in the same way, shifting the vowel a little in the mouth. It's the *systematic difference* between "cot" and "caught" that permits distinct meanings, not the sounds themselves. Or consider "roof" and "hoof," and note that it doesn't matter whether one or both of us makes a vowel like the *oo* it "boot" or like the *u* in "bush." All we have to do is preserve the *r/h* difference. And the only thing that constrains the vowel in "roof" is the need for a systematic difference from whatever noises we make for "reef" and "rife."

So a language is not a collection of tape-recordable sounds, but *a set of systematic differences*, and the sounds are only there to encode the

*What comes next will have to be sketchy. For a good and short introduction try *Ferdinand de Saussure*, by Jonathan Culler, Penguin, 1976.

differences. And, Saussure hinted, anything human beings find "understandable"—a flirtatious gesture, the offer of a martini—they understand through a similar code of differences. An offer of coffee, or white wine, or lemonade would elicit other shades of understanding. We may think the point of the martini is the martini. It's not. It's that it's not coffee. This is surprising only because we've grasped the codes so thoroughly we don't realize we're applying them, unless we're engaged in something with an explicit code, such as chess.

One difference between language and chess is that chess players *know* where their interaction takes place: not on the board but in a domain of abstract patterns. Moving a piece does what uttering a sentence, or offering a drink, does: it translates a new twist of the pattern into a physical gesture. The move (not the piece) is a sign, observable by semiotics, the science of signs. And the mere shape of the piece is like the exact pronunciation of a word, unimportant so long as we can tell the pieces apart.

If you can follow the reasonableness of this, you can also sense that it's getting disembodied, since the elements the system differentiates simply don't matter. The great power of structuralism inheres in its ability to get rid of a clutter of elements, the way structural linguistics gets past a gaggle of pronunciations. The anthropologist Claude Lévi-Strauss, who pioneered applied structuralism, used it to reduce a bewilderment of folktales and kinship systems to a few lucid systems of difference. Likewise, when Roland Barthes examines wrestling as a spectacle, its elements seem interchangeable from those of other spectacles: a Molière play or an oral exam where the candidate takes on all comers.

This can amount to obtaining knowledge of the woods by vaporizing every tree, an extreme to which Barthes is driven by his impatience with people who may think the trees matter. We suppose, for example, that a wise and substantial man named Shakespeare wrote a play called *Hamlet*, a valuable possession from which we shall extract his wisdom when we get around to it, meanwhile placing an order for The 100 Greatest Books Ever Written (genuine leather, $31.50 each) and donning a velvet jacket to finger the bindings.

It takes no Barthes, not even an Irving Howe, to note that the bindings possess no literary significance save as they further the illusion that *Hamlet* is a precious object. Others might get as far as questioning whether "object" is a profitable metaphor for the way a work of verbal art exists. It takes Barthes to push the argument to a further extreme, where a work like *Hamlet* doesn't exist at all. A system of signs exists, and a cultural system that coaches us to interpret them, much as we interpreted the headline on Barthes's obituary in idle detachment from any nontextual Barthes.

And in having no intrinsic meaning, no more than has an isolated word in Saussure's system, *Hamlet* has no intrinsic value either. Value is conferred on it by a system of valuing. It is simply a text we inherit the custom of explicating (and *Titus Andronicus*, by the same author, isn't). And without stable meanings, won't we simply be obeying our teachers, who are paid to coerce us, when we talk about the meaning of *Hamlet*? And aren't we better off dismissing an old play that seems to funnel us toward a meaning, and opting instead for modern work, for a free play of signifiers in poring over which we can create what patterns we choose?

How about *Last Year at Marienbad*, by Barthes's friend Alain Robbe-Grillet? In the very fact that its options are all open, that we can never quite feel we have it right because the patterns have indeterminacy designed into them, isn't it richer than the deadwood of the past they worship at the *lycée*? Aren't Shakespeare, Racine, Molière mere middle-class gods?

You'll seldom read far in Barthes before you sense a clever schoolboy's harbored resentments. Or a schoolboy's facility: no one grasped quicker than Barthes the implications of Saussure's principle that we share the linguistic system without having knowledge of it, or the corollary that what applies to words will apply to any communicative system whatever. "I had just read Saussure," is his explanation of how he came to write *Mythologies*, a book that seems endlessly bright about social trivia.

But all the trivia have linguistic structure, because people (a) value them, and (b) use them to make statements ("Try some of mine"). So when Roland Barthes writes about wine and milk in France, he is explaining to his reader the system whereby they already order these matters. Wine is the French totem drink, like British tea. It is the "converting substance" that makes the weak man strong and the silent talkative. Milk, not water, is the French antiwine. . . . And so on.

The French know these things already, otherwise they would not be true; but they don't know they know them, hence the essay. Familiar with wine on the plane of *parole* (every instance of opening a bottle, and they've opened thousands), they are unconscious of the *langue*, which is what confers importance on drinking wine and not something else.

Barthes's *mythologie* is another word for *langue*. Myth is the domain in which you've made a gesture if you take your girl to the burlesque instead of the opera. Here the system of differences includes moneyed vs. vagrant classes, refinement vs. raunchiness, the cultivated vs. the visceral, treating her like a lady vs. showing her life (or immersing her in maleness).

Barthes will hasten to assert that these are not instinctual differences, preexisting a social difference that codifies them. No, acculturation has made them as it makes all meaning, and striptease, he tells us, has as rigorous an aesthetic as the Metropolitan Opera, quite as open to structural analysis.

In their "meticulous exorcism of sex" we observe how professional strippers "wrap themselves in the miraculous ease that constantly clothes them, makes them remote, gives them the icy indifference of skillful practitioners, haughtily taking refuge in the sureness of their technique: their science clothes them like a garment."

That is not to deny a difference between Gypsy Rose and Rosa Ponselle. What it denies—a denial that came the more easily to a man exempt from the cravings of heterosexuality—is that the appeal of Rose is "natural," that of Rosa "cultivated." Just as there are no intrinsic meanings, so there is no natural behavior: no priapic Original Savage aslumber down there, long ago subdued by culture. The codes alone are at work; all behavior articulates them. And the "natural" is a myth by which we bourgeoisie protect ourselves against people whose codes we don't read because we choose to call them uncultivated.

Just hereabouts the ground begins to shift, and wisps of smoke begin to be apparent. That our system of values may reflect a cultural conspiracy is an old Marxist theme, and when Barthes gets carried away he will let it surface in its naively Marxist form. Hence some of his sillier pages in *Mythologies*, for instance the strange assertion, in what set out to be a major piece on "Myth Today," that Left-wing Myth, even the Myth of Stalin, is of no consequence. "The bourgeoisie hides the fact that it is the bourgeoisie and thereby produces myth; revolution announces itself openly as revolution and thereby abolishes myth."

This says one intrinsic value does exist, revolution; and never mind the whirling of Saussure in his grave, Barthes will incautiously tell us that there is even a "real" language, that of the workman. "If I am a woodcutter and I am led to name the tree that I am felling . . . I 'speak the tree,' I do not speak about it. . . . Between the tree and myself there is nothing but my labor, that is to say, an action."

There speaks, by golly, all Saussurean pretense dropped, the authentic romantic revolutionary at play. He plays (in his imagination only) at chopping wood. For this stock figure, action is above speech, the very word *labor* exudes numinous value, and the whole cultural apparatus—thanks to which, rather expensively educated, Barthes was equipped to marshall words like *proairetic*—gets dismissed as mere bourgeois displacement of essential energies.

So that was what *Mythologies* was busy about, an exposé of the contortions of the bourgeoisie, whereby value is conferred on autos and fancy weddings, detergents and *la cuisine*. "The oppressed *makes* the world, he has only an active, transforming (political) language; the oppressor conserves it, his language is plenary, intransitive, gestural, theatrical: it is Myth. The language of the former aims at transforming, the latter at eternalizing."

We may now suspect whence came the energies that propelled so much Barthean assault on what passes in classrooms for the Literary Heritage. That heritage conserves, it stabilizes; it is—in the resistance it offers to whimsical revaluation—one emblem of a will to eternalize that the revolutionary finds intolerable. We need not be surprised that the first fashion for Barthes coincided with the decade of the French student riots.

And yet he got many things right, the quirky fellow. Words, sentences, works *are* meaningless in themselves. This means that they may not be left untended. Values are not intrinsic in anything producible. It is we who have conferred on them the forms of utterance that can receive them: on Homer, on *Hamlet*. And few are the utterances that can qualify.

Barthes has little to say about real literature. He flutters brightly around its edges: "Proust and Names," "Flaubert and the Sentence." Its coercive powers exceed what the codes account for. And decade by decade we keep remaking it in replenishing its power to remake us.

If we cannot read the Shakespeare Dr. Johnson read—something I heard T. S. Eliot say twenty-four years ago, over jugged hare—it is because we are perpetually changing Shakespeare into an author we can read. (We do not pay Jules Verne that compliment.) As for the author himself, it is meaningless to ask what he "meant." If he should come forward and try to tell us we should not understand.

It is superstitious—here Barthes is profoundly right—to ascribe to intrinsic nature the long working of culture. If it weren't, we'd be safe in leaving what we care about to look after itself. But instead of supposing that whatever rests on tacit agreement may therefore be bourgeois imposture, as inauthentic as The 100 Greatest Books Ever Written, we are free to decide that agreeing to sustain the agreement will be all that preserves whatever is worth going on with, including structuralism. This is not the same as agreeing to consume a product.

When an inability to stay interested in Sappho lasted longer than the parchment she was copied on, the poems of Sappho were lost. They are gone forever. Like the codes that say what the sense of the words doesn't seem to, that's a lesson Roland Barthes taught: we have it all in our hands. There's a lot that is easy to lose, and little to replace it with.

Frank Budgen, R.I.P.

This appeared in the Wake Newslitter, *February 1972, a journal for Joyceans, now alas itself defunct.*

Frank Budgen, the Man Joyce Trusted: that would be nearly enough for anyone's tombstone, unless The Man Who Put Up With Joyceans be still more of a tribute. It was no light burden he bore in his eighth and ninth decades, to command so much pertinent reminiscence and be subjected to the telephoned importunities of so many enthusiasts in transit through London. He was jaunty, patient, crisp. An index to the qualities that earned him Joyce's respect is that he made no career out of being a man who had known Joyce. It is common for intimates of a deceased genius to grow tiresomely egocentric, to make an elaborate show of withholding more than they tell, to grin distantly like Fafnir curled over riches the pleasure in which consists in restricting access. Not Frank Budgen. He was very much his own man, and the more time you spent with him the more vivid grew the impression of a man who depended not at all on anyone's interest in another man he had known.

Not that he enjoyed professional securities, for instance the certainty of being a great painter. He was a competent minor Impressionist, not even Post- so far as I could tell, and knew he had done modest things quite well. He was a competent minor writer, not ambitious in that direction either. In his whole lifetime he published just two books, and one of them was very nearly posthumous. He knew he had written them honestly. It is doubtful whether it occurred to him that both are irreplaceable. One—*James Joyce and the Making of Ulysses*—is a classic of literary reminiscence. The other—*Myselves When Young*—is a classic of post-Victorian autobiography.

There isn't a book in the world quite like his Joyce book. No contemporary left an *Alexander Pope and the Making of the Dunciad*, to invoke a surprisingly close analogy. Like *Ulysses*, the *Dunciad* is indecorous, ultra-modern, an ingenious structure modeled on classical parallels, a magnum opus into which went quantities of material touching on the author's raw nerves and his vehemences. If only some Budgen had recorded a variety of encounters with "Spitfire Alex," not merely the obiter dicta Spence preserved but remarks given contexts, illuminating a man in a milieu with a sure sense of what he was accomplishing, much more than the paying-off of scores on which annotators dwell: how different would be the accessibility of the *Dunciad* today! Many people have recalled encounters with Joyce, many people—occasionally the same ones—have helped us see how he fitted pieces of his artifacts together, but no one save Budgen has made the man and the Fabulous Artificer seem whole. His reminiscences do not debunk, nor his explications apotheosize. Consequently, it is intelligible both that a man wrote *Ulysses* and that *Ulysses* is not bounded by the limitations of the man.

In *Myselves When Young*, the work of a sprightly old age, he recalled in the third person and in a sequence of styles a sequence of discarded selves. That as times change men change with them is a perception as old as Vergil, whose resonant line on that theme Joyce quoted in the *Portrait*; that times might change so comprehensively, with an acceleration itself so accelerated that the corresponding human change amounts to a virtual series of personalities, that was an experience Frank Budgen's generation was the first to encounter. His book, with its multiple personae and its variety of narrative methods, is in keeping, plainly post-*Ulysses* though unobtrusively so. It does not say, how clever am I; in fact, the casual reader is so far from being distracted by technique that he is unlikely to give its presence a thought. Still, the world that surrounded each self is vividly there, a sequence of lost worlds: Victorian England ending amid crazy religiosities, the end of the Merchant Marine Conrad had known, the end of a world H. G. Wells never learned had ended, in which young men surfaced from the submerged classes, shaped by revivalist political orthodoxies they had ingested down below; the end of the century-old Parisian art-students' world; finally—how portentous it sounds!—the end of pre-war Europe.

That book was published amid little stir. Your reminiscences are nothing, out there where stirs are made, unless you are Somebody, and it was only to Joyceans, thus far, that Frank Budgen was indubitably Somebody. The Joyceans tend to concentrate on the thirty pages where the Joyce anecdotes are. But when history has discovered the times Budgen lived through, and there are students as much interested in those years of transition as there are now students interested in Joyce, *Myselves When Young* will have readers properly grateful for its existence.

Meanwhile anyone who ever watched Frank Budgen tug on his beret, to walk the visitor through London dampness to the more strategic of the two tube-stations between which he lived, will be grateful for the memory. How few men we really remember.

D. P. Remembered

From the Ezra Pound journal Paideuma *(Winter 1973)*.

MARCH 22, 1965

My day had commenced in Sirmione, and been shredded till 7 P.M. by busses and trains and the anxieties of catching them, in a country where the ticket sellers abound in misinformation.

It commenced with an emblem: a small sharp boat hung in the directionless gray-blue which constituted without seam or division Lake Garda and the infinite heavens. Every plank distinct, every spar, referable to no horizon, no wharves, no waves, it asserted nothing but its own crystalline presence, at no determinate distance (three-quarter mile? three hundred yards?)—a boat with the boat's world subtracted.

And the evening's emblem was Dorothy's stately descent, at 7:30 punctually, into the modest foyer of the Hotel Grande Italia e Lido. Her world, too, had been subtracted, though not by mists but by public history. This hotel in Rapallo was her winter address; she summered in England. Nietzsche began *Also Sprach Zarathustra* in Rapallo, and Ezra Pound wrote half his *Cantos* there. Today's Rapallo of Vespas and transistors was no more theirs and hers than today's England was King Edward's and Margot Asquith's. She remained aloof from such facts, and behaved as she would have behaved had nothing changed, without effort asserting simply her habitual presence. That habit had carried her through the St. Elizabeths years, and carried her still.

She had been, she said, "psychically haunted" by me all day; my unannounced turning up was thus no surprise. Psychic hauntings were a given of her world, like gravitation and digestion: her world had been Yeats's world, and her mother Olivia was the "D.V." of the diary in which Yeats in another century recorded their months of passion. She herself and Miss Georgie Hyde-Lees, being youngest members of two families interlocked by a remote marriage, found it natural to go off and paint together before Dorothy became Mrs. Ezra Pound and Georgie became Mrs. Yeats.

At dinner she spread out a clipping from the February 10 *Irish Times*: Ezra and Georgie Yeats, in Dublin just six weeks ago. Not he and Dorothy, but he and Olga Rudge, had flown there. Rumor had hinted at Dorothy's outrage, but no outrage was detectable. His visit was "appropriate" to the centenary of Yeats's birth, and as for herself making such a trip, well, of course she couldn't. She had now lived seventy-nine years. She was very white haired and deaf and growing frail. A year ago she'd walked me to the Municipio to visit the rooms where Ezra thirty years before had sponsored concerts (Gerhart Munch, piano; Olga Rudge, violin). Now she could no longer walk even that far, "but that's the way it is."

Where was Ezra now? In Venice? Why, no; nearby, as a matter of fact: up in Sant' Ambrogio, in the little house just below the church, with Olga. She imparted this information as one imparts the location of a planet.

She retired early, a black form ascending to a tiny room. In a dozen encounters since 1948, I never saw her in anything but black.

MARCH 23

Wind tossing palms, rain driving down the Lungomare. Through a picture window opposite my breakfast table I see two successive women, the first a nun, pause on the identical spot and turn to look at the Castello; whereupon the umbrella of each blows inside out. Dorothy by invariable custom spends the morning in her room. We meet for lunch by prearrangement.

"Ezra, I always said, was the most American thing going." And, "He was in reaction for twenty years against the English. They never called things by their proper names." She had American ties, the Virginia Tuckers, but American, nevertheless, she was *not*. "The moment I stepped off the boat in America, in '46, I felt the ground shifting beneath my feet; and it was that way for twelve years."

I took that shifting ground for metaphor, but now I think she was reporting an omen. She would not have thought that an omen merited narrative emphasis. Whatever happened was natural, and required no fitting to anyone else's expectations of the natural. Yeats, she said, once took his watch out of his pocket and set it on the table beside him so that he would remember to dress for dinner at six; and then spent two hours hunting all over the apartment for the watch. "To me that is quite understandable."

What was understandable was that a mind fixed on one set of realities should by consequence be dislocated from another. Realities on which it might fix had sharp corners; it did not fix on mists and shifty shapes. Lewis, not Kandinsky, described the contours of the real. Perhaps that underlay her distaste for most poetry. "I read poetry only with great difficulty. I never did much care for it. Of course at eighteen I read Keats, Shelley, what was around. When you are brought up among books you read what is around. And then I got all entangled with the *Cantos*. Ezra quite spoils anything else for me."

When Ezra tells you in his poem that they have set the lights in the water, you are to know that they have done so: at the three-day festival of Santa Maria dell' Allegre in July: "oil and a wick in a wax dish such as a child might make." They do it still. (Do they? I seem to remember her telling me a year ago that the war had ended it. Perhaps she meant only for the war's duration. It does not do to cross-question her, however tactfully. That would cancel the narrative circuits, a fist through memory's gossamer.)

From the good times, memory supplies bright isolated statements; from the times of privation, narrative. In the last year of the war, she and Ezra and Olga were evacuated to Sant' Ambrogio. Somewhere they found a cart with two horses to haul the books and heavy things up the hill. Food? A little bread every day, meat once a week, occasional fish brought home by Olga, who had a school-teaching job in Rapallo three days a week. And Dorothy had to cook (to Olga's disgust, since Olga could cook and Dorothy could not). "When Ezra and I were married we had an agreement that I should not be required to cook." And she quoted with amusement his reflection in the *Pisan Cantos* on those Sant' Ambrogio days:

> Some cook, some do not cook
> Some things cannot be altered.

She looks suddenly into my eyes. Her eyes always smile.

After Ezra's arrest she refused to stay in the mountains ("quite out of the question") and returned to Via Marsala 12, where a bomb in the street had brought down three huge chunks of ceiling and smashed five street-side windows. One of the ceiling chunks was where their bed had been, one where they had breakfasted, one in Dorothy's little dressing room. The water and the electricity were off. The South African troops who were managing the occupation of Rapallo helped get them turned back on, and the bed and one or two other heavy pieces of furniture came back from the German-Italian family who had stored them. Ezra's mother, who had been staying in a flat with Italian friends, was installed in the best room at Via Marsala 12 with friends to cook for her, and Dorothy moved to the rooms she had vacated. Not until Paige edited the *Letters* in the late 1940s did the books and papers come back down from the hills. . . .

Another narrative: St. Elizabeths. Ezra could never leave the ward without her; that "kept me close to the spot." On the lawn he could sit only at one designated place, not move around. Later Marcella Spann was allowed to drive him and Dorothy to a spot on the grounds overlooking the river, on the condition they stay all three in the car ("a very small car"). And he had refused psychiatric treatment: "only medical checkups. . . ."

MARCH 24

Bright sun, cool and clear.

She inspects a photo of one of my daughters. "That looks like a useful person."

This morning the narrative mode is investing the better times. At her marriage, an uncle gave Dorothy a five-guinea check—not for a wedding present, but for her next birthday and Christmas together. It was agreed that she look for a Chinese dictionary, Ezra having handed her two or three pamphlets—one of them "The 1,000 Most Useful Characters"—that came with the Fenollosa papers, and Dorothy having been exposed to the Oriental sensibility via Japanese prints of her father's, some of which she had copied with her careful brush. So in the Charing Cross Road, she found Morrison, seven volumes as she recalls, four volumes Chinese-English, three thinner ones of English-Chinese and primitive forms. "I learned to look up the characters but Ezra never quite did, though he learned many of the simpler radicals." In Via Marsala when he was working on Chinese he kept dictionary volumes lying open on three tables and chairs round about him. . . .

The Noh plays? He did several of them in Stone Cottage on their honeymoon. "I was not then preoccupied with plays and characters. I was trying to make out what sort of creature I was going to be living with." Did Yeats's presence at Stone Cottage then account for the infusion of Irish idiom into his *Noh*? No, by the time Yeats arrived he had finished. But he was also there with Yeats the previous winter; "that was when the infection occurred."

But he was soon off the Noh. "When Ezra got to Chinese he found it 'as hard as *that*'—remember?" She tapped the table with her room key; I was to remember a phrase from a late Canto. "'As hard as that'—that was said by one of those charming Italians I never met, whom he knew in Rome when broadcasting." The Italian had not been speaking of Chinese; his words were nonetheless applicable. "Japanese is all light, feather-light, wherever you touch it. Chinese is 'as hard as that.'"

And no, the ideogram for Ezra was less an element of language than a mystical virtuous emblem to contemplate and get ideas from, like Yeats's kabbalistic signs. . . .

That afternoon I ascend to Sant' Ambrogio, to be greeted by Olga Rudge at their cottage door. She understands, of course, that I have been talking with Dorothy, and we both understand that this fact shall not be remarked upon. Ezra, up from his nap, hears the narrative of my vain search, four days previously, for the signed column in San Zeno. Very faint voice: "I . . . think . . . it's . . . toward the . . . left." Is the signature near the base? He gestures at eye-level.*A promising beginning, but he lapses into the silence of those years, except to say, of some magazine's wish for a new Canto, "Some people think I'm a cocoon spinning out Cantos." We walk to Casa Sessanta, now Casa Due, the wartime refuge with the olive press in the basement. Olga recalls that she found its sound soporific, also that Dorothy never went down to see it, on the principle that irregular settlers in wartime should make as few conspicuous moves as possible.

Back at the cottage for tea, I am handed a copy of the new Faber 109 *Cantos*. For typographic uniformity they have reset *Rock Drill* and *Thrones*, reproducing with care all the old typos and adding some new ones. ("First Ezra proofread the *Cantos*," Dorothy had recalled two nights before, "and then I, and then a third party. It took three people. And *still* things crept in.") Olga Rudge's copy of *109 Cantos* contains an inscription in his still-strong handwriting; she is to save what is good in them: when epics were oral, skalds in their performances gradually eliminated the slag.

We walked halfway down the old *salita*, now paved. Vespas roar up; Miss Rudge abhors them. I gather a eucalyptus pip from beneath the sacred tree. Ezra is dissuaded from continuing down into Rapallo. We agree to meet there tomorrow in front of the church at one.

MARCH 25

Intermittent overcast. Since it is not clear whether Ezra and Olga will have eaten by one, Dorothy urges on me a precautionary lasagne. Talk is of food, of the Italian language, of the names of trees.

---

*I found it a year later. It stands to the left of the stairs going down to the crypt; from partway down you see the inscription at eye-level.

To his outfit, as yesterday, of gray slacks, gray sweater, green-and-white plaid sport shirt, black-and-white fine check jacket, Ezra has added a gray wool scarf, dark blue overcoat, and the gray fur hat he wore in Venice last year. Stout black boots, brown cane with transverse amber handle and leather wrist thong. Quantities of white hair spill backward left and right. White beard, not unkempt. Traces of reddish-yellow about the eyebrows. His flesh is pink, sagging noticeably in the cheeks. His hands are reddened, the joints rheumatic, which may help explain his preoccupation with them.

At a trattoria not far from the old Via Marsala, we have copious lunch of which Olga, from long habit of urging Ezra, requires me to eat the whole: this on top of that precautionary lasagne.

We taxied halfway up the hillside to a bend in the old *salita*, which we then followed on foot to the cottage at the top. Ezra stumped up aided by the cane, on which he leaned forward. Miss Rudge paused often, and once sat for breath. I need breath oftener than either of them. The tops of all the hills are visible under a high gray overcast. At the cottage he changes his boots for bedroom slippers, revealing a hole in the toe of his left maroon sock. Tea, and talk of Fordie and Fordie's father; Olga's recollection of being awakened in Venice at 5:30 A.M., to tape-record his reading of

> Winter is icumen in,
> Lhude sing GOD-DAMN!!!

—"with ferocious emphasis." Then a long taping session of other poems; he was in good voice, she says. He listens, silent.

A sudden rainstorm drives through yellow light; he cranes round in his chair to watch. Through the rain Rapallo bay glows amber. Then a dramatic clearing of the entire sky. Miss Rudge says the weather here comes from the south, up the bay from the sea and from Africa.

At 6:45 I decline pot-luck and leave, having an appointment to dine with Dorothy. I keep this fact tacit, though Miss Rudge surely penetrates the euphemisms employed. I descend the *salita* rapidly, aware that Ezra is standing in the door watching my retreating form. I never saw him at Sant' Ambrogio again.

Dorothy is punctual as always; she has brought a copy of the *Cantos* to the table. "I could tell you, " she says, "a lot about those *Cantos*." I demur a little; do we want to be so scholastic? She smiles. "Remember: this will be the last time."

So she turns the pages and comments. "Built like Ubaldo" catches her eye. "That means, tall but short-waisted. Ubaldo was built like his degli Uberti ancestors." And "Tommy Cochrane"—"an old school friend of Ezra's." And "in the arena": "that is always the arena at Verona"; and the time we sat there "considering Rochefoucauld" was when she and Ezra and Olivia Shakespear went there after the 1914 war. And "Astafieva" was "one of the Russian dancers in London." The reference is to her being glimpsed outside the theater by Ezra and Dorothy, thin, ghost-like, unlike her stage self. "Margot" was "Prime Minister Asquith's wife." Her death was "the end of an era" because she worked hard at maintaining the ceremonial and social meaning of her position.

Her hand turning pages pauses at the lynx-chorus in Canto 79.

> We have lain here amid kalicanthus and sword-flower
> The heliads are caught in wild rose-vine
> The smell of pine mingles with rose-leaves . . .
>> O lynx, be many
>> of spotted fur and sharp ears.
>> O lynx, have your eyes gone yellow,
>> with spotted fur and sharp ears?

"That chorus was for me." He had so inscribed it, having typed it in the evening in Pisa on the medic's typewriter. It had then been passed by the censor, and sent out ("small batches of transcript") to Dorothy in Rapallo, who passed them on for final typing to Olga. (I have heard Mary say she did the actual typing.) "He said the lynx-chorus was for me." All those sharp-eyed cats that prowl through the *Cantos*, do they commemorate Dorothy Shakespear Pound, who lived through her eyes, and kept her counsel, and understood, she said, this much about her husband, that "there was nothing for it but to give the creature his head"?

Her eye moves on to the name of "Old Bellotti." "He was the manager of an Italian restaurant we went to weekly in London for good

food at low prices. When the crowds were light he would tell Ezra copious yarns in Italian. One concerned his stint in a former job as door-
keeper at 'a big rich place.' Might it have been Claridge's? He got tips
for calling cabs, and the scale of the place suggested 10 s. or so. But
twice he got thruppeny bits: once from a Rothschild, once from De-
Lara, who lived in this hotel with a Princess of Monaco when she was
in London." More and more these are memories independent of the
text, merely prompted by some name. The text recalls her: "The point
about saffron is that Italians use it for cooking rissotto, and couldn't
import it during the war."

"Gold bars in Menelik's palace": Ted Press found them there under
Haile Selassie's bed. After Mussolini had removed Haile and abolished slavery, Ted Press went to Addis Ababa from his post at a Cairo
bank to try to account for a vast sum in missing gold, detected in the
government accounts. And "Sir Ronald," who thought the Negus
"not a bad fellowe," was someone "of ambassadorial level." He had
"translated Homer or something like that," which endeared him to
Ezra.

"Or from a fine old eye the unconquered flame": "No, in my opinion not Yeats, who had small, sunken and narrowly shifting eyes. It is
surely Blunt."

And "Talbot." "That was a cousin of mine, one of the Shakespear
names." He was Charles Talbot, and he inherited a magnificent old
abbey in Yorkshire with a courtyard and a double flight of steps to the
front door, a two-story main hall, rosette-carved beams. "My aunt
took me there a couple of times, and once Ezra and I crawled over the
roof to a turret to see a copy of the Magna Charta, kept there in a glass
case. Cousin Charles left the place to his niece, a Scotswoman named
Maud Gilchrist-Clark on condition she take the name Maud Talbot."
To pay the death duties Maud had to dispose of various treasures, including the Magna Charta, which she sold to the British Museum.
(They supplied her a photo-copy to go in the glass case.) The museum
sent the Magna Charta to Washington, for exhibition while the
Pounds were there; cousin Maud accompanied it by boat, and Dorothy last saw her in Washington. She died around 1960, and the estate
is now a home for the aged, in final fulfillment of an alleged curse that

it should never descend from father to son. Dorothy's father had and Omar now has a beautiful gold seal of the Talbots: their dog emblem both as handle and in imprint.

> When a dog is tall but
> not so tall as all that
> that dog is a Talbot
>   (a bit long in the pasterns?)

She suddenly rose and said a firm good night, and vanished up the hotel stairs, clutching the *Cantos*. That was to have been "the last time." When it was time for it to be over, she turned her back on it firmly.

It was not quite the last time; I saw her once again, in 1969. But by then she was having to rummage through memory painfully for simple elusive facts; so though her courtesy and her ceremony never faltered, 1965 *was* in a sense "the last time."

I do not know who the girl was that Ezra Pound married. What did a young woman from an "advanced" household—advanced enough to contemplate a union with the alarming "creature"—expect of life in those early years of the century? The war that swept her world away swept away also such young Englishmen as would have had the wit to ask. We have no social history of those years, no sense of the fine line they were demarking between matrimony and liberty. "She is very *Kensington*," said Agnes Bedford one day. "Do you type people? She is the Kensington type. I'm a St. John's Wood type myself." But I do not know the meaning of "Kensington": I knew only Dorothy, and only late.

Ezra Pound's story is inextricable from hers. "She can be alarmingly aloof," said a man who knew her well. He thought that perhaps the bond with that aloofness helped shape, for better or for worse, the way Ezra's psyche set during the First World War. On the other hand, would Gaudier, or would Lewis, have come to count for so much in Ezra's mind had Dorothy not lived through her eyes, and had her mother Olivia not purchased Lewises and Gaudiers? His alliance with Miss Rudge was with a musician, as though to redress some balance of the senses: an ear-world. For years he loved both women.

Eye-people seem to lose their eyes. Lewis did. By 1969, Dorothy had had cataract surgery. Ezra was developing cataracts, too.

She died in mid-December 1973, having outlived her husband six weeks more than a year. A time has gone with her. Will she have a biography? No more, possibly, than Homer's Helen. When an age goes, our way to understand it goes with it. The rest is reminiscent fragment, and fiction.

Marshall McLuhan, R.I.P.

From National Review, *January 23, 1981.*

The media sage of the sixties was created, he surely knew, by the media. The Marshall McLuhan I began to know in the mid-forties was a tall, trim pipe-smoker ("Cigarette smokers are not interested in tobacco") whose passion was aiding people such as me to knit up what he considered unexamined lives.

Our trouble—yours and mine—was insufficient attention to what we were doing. We smoked, but weren't interested in tobacco. We flipped through magazines, but didn't adequately ponder half their content, which was ads. We drove cars—he didn't—but failed to reflect that our cars were driving us. Twenty years later his famous slogan, "The Medium is the Message," simply generalized that order of preoccupation. What you're taking for granted, it says, is always more important than whatever you have your mind fixed on. On that principle, Marshall would undertake benign regulation of any life that came near.

Precisely because my mind was fixed on teaching, I had but to reflect that it was not what I was doing. Like it or not, I was embarked on a survival game, for which to begin with I needed a Ph.D. Most of my

Toronto instructors had been content with the Oxford M.A. For my part I had a Toronto M.A. Did that not suffice? I had been told it did. No, said Marshall, your mentors inhabit a backwater. The fields of force no longer emanate from Oxford. A Ph.D., and it had better be from Yale, where his friend Cleanth Brooks had just been installed as doyen of the New Criticism.

Twenty-four hours later we were headed south from Toronto in my car. In New York we paused to ascertain what anyone less rash would have checked before starting out, whether in that particular June week Cleanth Brooks was even to be found at Yale. He was not. We had five days to put in. Just time for a side trip to Washington, D.C., where (a passer-through had indicated) the allegedly mad Ezra Pound was accessible to visitors. (Half of my subsequent life was derived from *that* visit.) Then to New Haven where the bemused but unfailingly courteous Cleanth Brooks undertook to see what could be done about getting Marshall's new protégé admitted *now*. Three months later I was in New Haven again, a doctoral candidate.

Having since been a director of graduate admissions, I am in a better position than most to be awestruck at the prodigies Cleanth must have accomplished: one more gauge of Marshall's imperious persuasiveness.

And all those dozens of hours on the road—before freeways, remember, we puttered New York–Washington and return on U.S. 1, poking block by block through every obstacle, even Baltimore—he saw tirelessly to my education, which my profs had (of course) neglected shamefully. They had not even told me, for example, about T. S. Eliot, his sanity, his centrality.

Eliot was Marshall's talisman in those years. We started to collaborate on an Eliot book and read through the canon together, Marshall pontificating, I annotating. As to why that book never got written: its plan got lost, because as you can see (back to the principle) if you are thinking Eliot is important, why, he can't be.

That was a problem with the McLuhan system: its emphases were by definition self-destructive. Eliot, he came to think, was fencing insights stolen from Mallarmé. If you objected that Eliot barely mentioned Mallarmé, that merely proved what an old slyboots he was.

Later he had decided that Mallarmé in turn was retailing Buddhism, and later still everybody you can think of was feeding the world hidden Buddhism at the prompting of a fraternity of Freemasons. That was dangerous knowledge, and he even came to think the Freemasons had a contract out on him. By that time we were out of touch.

A few years later he discovered media, and became famous, rightly. I don't know of anyone else who has sucked himself down into a conspiracy theory and come triumphantly out of it. Conspiracy theories are normally terminal. But Marshall was unique.

What always saved him was his ability to get interested in something else. Nothing was too trivial. "Let us check on this," he would say, and steer the two of us into a movie house, where we stayed for twenty minutes. "Enough." Out in the light he extemporized an hour of analysis.

I think he did get a television, finally. I know he read books and books and books. (MARSHALL MCLUHAN READS BOOKS ran a bumper sticker in the sixties.) He read them especially on Sunday afternoons: long demanding books like Lancelot Andrewes's Sermons. He would nap at two, wake up at three, and start reading, pausing to pencil numerous tiny notes on the flyleaves.

A last glimpse: Marshall's unappeasable mother, in the back seat of the car, is sampling the *Pisan Cantos*. She is baffled, and means her bafflement to be a reproach. "What you have to understand, Mother," he improvises, "is that in the poetry you are used to things happen one after another. Whereas in that poetry everything happens at once." It served to quell her. As it stands it's not a good formula, but you can think how to go on from it, if you don't get flypapered. I've been going on from extemporizations of Marshall's for thirty years.

R. Buckminster Fuller, R.I.P.

National Review, *July 22, 1983.*

Two disciples once erected, in his honor, on his island, a geodesic dome like a silvery saucer. It was photographed nestling amid serene Maine pines, and a glimpse of the photo prompted someone to say, "They've come to take him back!" Yes, he did seem other-worldly.

Being around Bucky Fuller was never like being around anyone else; it was like fraternizing with a benign but unpredictable force. Though always active, the readiness, the generosity were also somehow aloof. Human impulse seemed to disorient him a little. "A self-balancing 28-jointed adaptor-base biped, an electro-chemical reduction plant integral with segregated stowages of special energy extracts": that was one of his descriptions of Man.

The aloofness probably commenced in the famous year during which he did not speak, lest he muddy discourse with some word he couldn't define. That was fifty-five years ago. In the ensuing years he uttered, at seven thousand words per hour (his estimate), many many millions of weightless cohesive words. That words weighed nothing was a thing he delighted to point out: our best products are our least weighty: simply mental patterns, like the invisible patterns of force by which the universe coheres. Ezra Pound, who met him in old age, called him "friend of the universe." It has had many denizens but few friends.

Young children were one manifestation of the universe with which he felt intuitively comfortable. So did they, with him. ("I feel so good around Bucky," said a six year old.) He was the only grown-up who would always answer their questions—"Why is the fire hot, Bucky?" "What are roses for?"—and in words they could understand. (The fire, he once explained, was the sunlight that the tree had once in-gathered; now it was "unwinding from the log.")

Unlike us, nature never hesitates; nor, generally, did Bucky. In a posh Philadelphia restaurant he spontaneously threw an olive over his shoulder, to demonstrate that it didn't have to make decisions about where to land. Two children followed the reasoning. Three waiters didn't. They mistook what he called "a scientific experiment" for a critique of the olive.

They'd have been more nonplussed still if they'd seen him approaching. The whole block from the parking lot, a child's hand in each of his, Bucky had come skipping, merry-faced. Yes, skipping, the three of them. He was barely taller than they. Behind, his wife, Anne, walked sedately.

He and Anne died, both eighty-seven, within forty-eight hours of each other, on the eve of their sixty-sixth anniversary. God is now hearing the universe explained, from first principles and with digressive excursions into a structural geometry for an evolving Heaven. God will not have heard any of it quite that way before, nor will Bucky ever before have enjoyed the bliss of such an encompassing attention.

Buster Keaton: In Memoriam

National Review *(February 22, 1966).*

He has left the world without ever being quite in it. Only saints and a few classic madmen have put forth a comparable power to suggest that this place where we all catch trains so deftly is yet not wholly the place for which we were made. He displayed no consternation, he uttered no protest (what does protest avail?): he gave his energies wholly to not being destroyed by a universe as implacable as an ice pack, as pervasive as Newton's three laws, as scrupulous as a grandfather clock. Denizens of that universe (and billions inhabit it expertly) would point out to one another that Keaton never smiled: as though it were not a serious business, to keep from being destroyed, really to triumph, never to know you have triumphed.

For it was against the nature of things that he was pitted, and you can never gloat over that adversary; you can only keep moving, only succeed in not being deprived of your mobility; that is your triumph, mobility. Chaplin's adversaries, by contrast, were great static beefy malevolence, pig-eyed and generally bewhiskered, blocking off the way between Chaplin and his simple desire: a meal, a girl. Knocked on the head innumerable times, they did not succumb, but when they fell, as they did eventually always fall, it was of their own weight. The law of gravity was Chaplin's principal ally. It was Keaton's nemesis.

Thus something could have been done about the world that so discommoded Chaplin, though he was not the man to do it. A Guaranteed Annual Income would have helped enormously; so would the extermination of greedy villains. (He did manage, from picture to picture, to pick off a few.) Meanwhile he had his pathos, and his dignity. Keaton's universe was irremediable, and he disdained pathos.

Keaton was the acrobat, engaging the nature of things in kinetic dialogue. Chaplin was the dancer, according to the nature of things with his little two-step a wryly lyrical comment. Bested (pending better times) he could shuffle off: toward the sunset, toward a lonely night, even in one film toward the guillotine. The rhythm of that walk, in *Monsieur Verdoux*, expressed Chaplin's opinion of a town that leaves men of feeling only the sunset for consolation. But Keaton had no opinion to express. Are opinions in order on the Precession of the Equinoxes? On the fact that one's eyes are not in the back of one's head?

For since his eyes were in the front of his head, he had no means of knowing that the motorcycle on whose handles he was riding had lost its driver; whereupon—let James Agee tell it: "Keaton whips through city traffic, breaks up a tug-of-war, gets a shovelful of dirt in the face from each of a long line of Rockette-timed ditch-diggers, approaches a log at high speed, which is hinged open by dynamite precisely soon enough to let him through and, hitting an obstruction, leaves the handlebars like an arrow leaving a bow, whams through the window of a shack in which the heroine is about to be violated, and hits the heavy feet-first, knocking him through the opposite wall. The whole sequence is as clean in motion as the trajectory of a bullet."

He had commenced the scene by doubling for the fallen driver, who was played by a man who did not know how to fall. He continued it without guy wires and process shots: "I simply trained myself to steer a motorcycle sitting on the handlebars. It was difficult to keep my balance, and I had a few good falls." In that disdain for doubles, we detect the continuum of his art: he had erected acrobatic skill into something more than a professional resource and higher than a philosophy of life: into a metaphysic. Man, that blank face implies, is not proper to this world, yet somehow manages. His center of gravity— which you could locate from instant to instant by producing to their point of intersection the flailing arms and yielding spine—was very nearly a metaphor for something—a gemlike flame, perhaps, like a pilot light—which it was unthinkable one could lose.

And brute intact survival, in acrobatic duet with forces there could be no question of besting, was the hidden theme of the screen art of the twenties, as remarkable an art, as nearly anonymous, and as nearly lost to reconstruction, as is the theater of the Jacobeans. Then, comedy was the realistic art, which went into the streets; the serious pictures of that era are today madly unreal, whereas Keaton, Langdon, Lloyd, and Chaplin engaged an actual world.

That world had commenced to organize itself, after the Renaissance, on the understanding that everyone would eventually receive back, from his consent to be organized, far more than he had surrendered. By 1850, it had at last become clear that the Renaissance was not going to pay off at all, though it had delivered as belated instalments a couple of revolutions. Whole populations, it was equally clear, were absorbed into systems, unreachable, so that sociology had to be invented to study them, and Newton's implacabilities had become the readiest metaphor of their behavior. Keaton's love for his cow, in one picture, or for his locomotive, in another, was a love transferred from girls diminished to abstraction by inexplicable rituals of courtship, through which alone they are accessible. The locomotive's rituals he could master. Everything human had receded into inviolable nature, rolled round by earth's diurnal force, a nature moreover likely to discharge itself, earthquake-like, in battalions of soldiers, maelstroms of traffic, cities-ful of cops.

It was never one cop, it was hundreds: the cop as Natural Force. Nor did popped buttons or jammed drawers, the small change of lesser comedians, inconvenience him: rather, stampeding buffalo, avalanches, shipwrecks, entire systems shattering round him. He was never shattered because he was never quite of their world: a visitor, not a native. (The very date of his birth is disputed.) More than one French critic has compared him to Poe, and one of them has quoted in his honor the line Mallarmé incised as though on Poe's tomb, *"Calme bloc ici-bas chu d'un désastre obscur,"* observing that it could have been written for him.

As though dropped to this earth from some obscure cataclysm, he coped with this earth's systems as he could. The ferocious requirements of his scripts could not hurt him; even departures from them could not hurt him. Running along the top of a freight train, he discovered a preference for a train moving in the opposite direction, and seized on a dangling cord to swing himself across. But the cord operated a waterspout, and not only did the water drench him as he swang, but its pressure hurled him onto the tracks, which was not according to script. Being an accomplished acrobat, he survived the fall, and remembered it years later over some X rays; that must have been, he reflected, the time he broke his neck.

Charlie Chaplin, R.I.P.

National Review, *January 20, 1978. And I hereby vouch for the cine-matic accuracy of the last paragraph.*

His death, unlike Garrick's, eclipsed no gaiety; the gaiety had long gone out of him, and yet it is there as long as scratchy celluloid can jerk through projectors. He was the first immortal of a medium he never cared much about. He had none of Keaton's fascination with the pos-sibilities, the sheer mechanics of film, nor Keaton's double awareness of how it was to be and to watch yourself be in a screening room. He was a dancer, a mime, and film was the way at hand to disseminate his art.

A dancer. No one can forget his *pas seul* with the globe of the world, miming an exuberant Hitler (who may have imitated his moustache), nor the shy smile and the little kick that registered his encounter with a rose. Nor—transcendently—the dancing buns on the forks.

When he talked—I once watched him talk, for two hours—expres-sions flowed over his face in lap dissolve, any type he mentioned in-stantly mimed, spontaneous as the movement of a Frenchman's hands. "Cover-girl," he chanced to say, and for half a second arms were framing a face crossed with a simper. He was talking dreary talk about John Kennedy's assassination—I've no idea how a cover-girl got into that harangue.

Eventually he got onto a richer topic: what had killed the art in which he flourished. Talk, it seems, had killed it. No, not the actors' voices, those were all right, but the need to pre-script, in a medium where a Mack Sennett story conference had once consisted of: "There's a flood in town—there's a flood in town—there's a flood in town"—followed by an opening of hydrants and everyone improvising; and the need to rehearse, rehearse, for the benefit of the huge crew that had to place mikes and monitor sound levels.

The great scene in *Limelight* was an instance, the one joint appearance ever of Chaplin and Keaton, as it were Shakespeare and Jonson. "We rehearsed it all day," he said; "we rehearsed it to death." It is a bravura sequence, a high sustained comic achievement: Keaton impassive at the piano, sheet music unendingly cascading into his lap, Chaplin distracted from his violin by the fact that one leg has grown inexplicably longer than the other. It grows clear, James Agee wrote, that no universe is conceivable in which these two could give a concert. As that warp in the fabric of reality is patiently demonstrated, audiences everywhere grow helpless with laughter. Yet the scene displeased him by comparison with some platonic idea of itself, which had danced before idle cameras while sound men fussed with their amplifiers, and had been dissipated in the endless rehearsals that technology exacted. *Modern Times*, it may be, sprang less from his social conscience (always rudimentary, naïve) than from his displeasure with the studio machinery of the sound men.

His recall of scene after scene was absolute: of the detail, for instance, in *The Great Dictator* when a man with a flying gadget leaps through the high window, and Chaplin, having scrutinized his catastrophic exit, turns to the Goering-figure with "Why do you waste my time with things like this?" Yes, he remembered it, he was pleased by my pleasure in remembering it; but "I craned forward"—he did so; a hold; "forward again; then out. Three movements. I held that second pause a shade too long."

It's on film; you can check. What you can't check is this. He came in out of the cold, in black coat and fedora, to the hotel where postprandial drinks were scheduled. The coat came off; then, suddenly, "Did you ever see the old man looking at pictures in the art gallery?" No one had. "Watch."

A tiny septuagenarian, perhaps five-feet-six, he got tinier as he turned toward the French doors. The coat was flung capewise over his back, the hat clutched above it. He was nothing but the back of the coat, and the hat: shrunken: a four-foot dwarf. The back grew eloquent; the hat began to quiver. Left to right, he scanned the door-panes from myopic distance; plainly they were lascivious pictures; the hat shook, moved on, jerked back magnetized. As he scanned, he grew. Invisible arms pushed the hat and coat higher and higher: he was a six-footer, a seven-footer. In the upper-right-hand corner of the French doors an especially luscious detail held his gaze. The hat shook, trembled, left, returned, left, returned, paused, sank, rose, mimed an orgasm. *Consummatum*. And Charlie Chaplin, smiling, sprung around, dropped his props, took a bow. None of that's on film. I'll remember it till I die.

George Oppen:
In Memoriam

From St. Mark's Church Poetry Project Newsletter *(October 1984).*

George Oppen, gentlest of men; Mary Oppen, shrewdest of wives; memory keeps them inseparable. His gentleness masked sinews of steel; her shrewdness, the encompassing care that could accept his sad last years (Alzheimer's). He knew me, that last time, because she'd told him; and yet he didn't. His decayed memory stranded him in the obviousness of each moment, the menu, the bread, the way to open a door, the simple thereness of whoever was there. Liking corn-cob pipes, he insisted I take away one of his. Later he was pressing another on me, the previous hour having slipped clear through his mind.

Yet when his faculties were intact, it was out of the transparent obviousness of the moment that he'd made poetry. Then, intermittently, in such moments as a poet lives for, the obvious had been a revelation.

PSALM

In the small beauty of the forest
The wild deer bedding down—
That they are there!

    Their eyes
Effortless, the soft lips
Nuzzle, and the alien small teeth
Tear at the grass

    The roots of it
Dangle from their mouths
Scattering earth in the strange woods.

    Their paths
Nibbled thru the fields, the leaves that shade them
Hang in the distances
Of sun

    The small nouns
Crying faith
In this in which the wild deer
Startle, and stare out.   [1965]

"The small nouns crying faith": such nouns as "deer," "grass," "sun," "earth," "fields," "leaves." He took a phrase from that poem to title a collection: "In This In Which." No noun there, just two prepositions and two pronouns, plotting points seemingly abstract as on a graph. But one of the pronouns jabs its finger toward the undeniable: "This."

That finger has been jabbed in America before.

            Make it of this,
            This, this, this, this

wrote Bill Williams. Bill's emphasis, though, was on "make," while George Oppen preferred an emphasis on "this": what is here, without you, unmade by you, autonomous. "A reply to Greek and Latin with the bare hands"—another Williams phrase—would not have stirred him. The urge to make gestures of reply didn't lead to poems.

In 1966, he was telling a French correspondent how a poet is weakest when he "attempts to drive his mind in *pursuit* of emotion for its own sake, in pursuit of excitement in the conviction that all that is not excitement is insincere." But people, as Charles Tomlinson has noted, "prefer Berryman's self-parade." In the forties they preferred Tate and Ransom, the rhetoricians (dare one say, the Southerners?). And even Yeatsian rhetoric can have a spieler's ring. Oppen again:

> . . . How does one hold something
> In the mind which he intends
>
> To grasp and how does the salesman
> Hold a bauble he intends
>
> To sell? The question is
> When will there not be a hundred
>
> Poets who mistake that gesture
> For a style.
> THE GESTURE, 1965

"It is possible," he also wrote, "to be carried away little by little, to find oneself, quite simply, trying to deceive people, to be 'making a poem.'" Williams, in the same vein, once remarked how fatally compromised would be Villon did we ever suspect him of trying to be "effective." And though Williams stressed (correctly) that poems were made of words, Oppen insisted (also correctly) that "one cannot make a poem by sticking words into it; it is the poem which makes the words and contains their meaning." Lord of language? Bah. Treat language with awe. "When the man writing is frightened by a word," that's when he's getting started. Close enough to an elephant, you might take sudden fright from the word "elephant." Then there'd be hope for you, no thanks to the dictionary.

Such remarks, however pithy, cannot communicate as the poems do. We've simply too brief a scale of terminology to keep every needful distinction clear at once, and the central truths are so simple as nearly to defy formulation. "Sincerity," "naturalness," those are American absolutes. Yet how to know them? Lately it's been easy to run mad after language, turning "problematic" into a noun for fondling. "Words, words, words," answered worrywort Hamlet, when Polonius asked what he read.

Hamlet's was a narrow sincerity. For blessed Oppen, sincerity lies *not* in acknowledging that we have only words; no, in acknowledging that there is non-linguistic experience; that a man can confront the small deer and find the words afterward. "The things he sees," wrote Carl Rakosi of Oppen, "feel like the gnarled bark of an oak tree. The tree is there, too. You can put your weight against it. It won't give."

> Children waking in the beds of the defeated
> As the day breaks on the million
> Windows and the grimed sills
> Of a ruined ethic
>
>   PHILAI TE KOU PHILAI

That was one fact that wouldn't give, and drove him to twenty-eight years' silence, before he could get it, or anything else that mattered, into new verses. As the same poem says,

>   and the myths
>   Have been murderous.

Myths plague you only after you've surrendered to language, to its glibness; after you've come to think you can talk your way out of anything. (English, said Eliot, needs writing "with a certain animosity.")

In his long life (seventy-six years) Oppen wrote little prose and fewer than 300 pages of verse. If we have more of him than we have of Catullus, it's not by much. He prized what took time, found the grain of materials, exacted accuracy. He'd been a tool-and-die maker and a cabinet worker. He once interrupted some blather about Biblical translation by remarking that what they needed for that job was a carpenter: no, better: "a *Jewish* carpenter."

WORKMAN

> Leaving the house each dawn I see the hawk
> Flagrant over the driveway. In his claws
> That dot, that comma
> Is the broken animal: the dangling small beast knows
> The burden that he is: he has touched
> The hawk's drab feathers. But the carpenter's is a culture
> Of fitting, of firm dimensions,

Of post and lintel. Quietly the roof lies
That the carpenter has finished. The sea birds circle
The beaches and cry in their own way,
The innumerable sea birds, their beaks and their wings,
Over the beaches and the sea's glitter.

It's after the bird of prey, and before the birds that circle and cry, that we hear of the carpenter's "fitting" and "firm dimensions."

> . . . Quietly the roof lies
> That the carpenter has finished. . . .

George Oppen's debility came on him slowly. So there may have been—anyone who knew him hopes so—the day of equilibrium when, incapable of further work, he could still admire how quietly the book lay that the Jewish carpenter-visionary had finished.

Louis Zukofsky:
All the Words

Harvey Shapiro, the poet who then edited the New York Times Book
Review, *June 18, 1978, commissioned this on hearing that Louis had
died. How dependent is our mental ecology on what a well-placed editor
judges important!*

"Eyes," he wrote, is pronounced "I's"; language blinks, his eye was
unblinking:

> Not the branches
> half in shadow
>
> But the length
> of each branch
>
> Half in shadow
>
> As if it had snowed
> on each upper half

Louis Zukofsky took pleasure in a language whose traffic signals—
"not" and "but"—sound (Knott & Butt) like stand-up comedians; a
language—he could remember learning it, didn't grow up with it—

where detailing two ways for branches to be half in shadow entailed saying words, "length" and "each," that you pronounce like kin-words to "branch." Moreover "shadow" and "had snowed" seem trying to be anagrams: just one letter left over. He pared shavings away to leave such impacted curiosities noticeable.

Not crossword curiosities he thought, something profound here. Not anything people do, not even lovemaking, is more intimately physical than speech. Hence "something must have led the Greeks to say *hudor* and us to say *water*": Some remote mystery of the body that sways to music and is chilled by fright (and eats tiny cookies on airplanes).

Louis Zukofsky's own body—"pulled forward," someone said, "by the weight of his eyebrows"—seemed a weed to gauge verbal winds. Our dog Thomas, we used to suppose, could nudge him over without thinking, though in fact Thomas never did. It was Louis rather who altered Thomas forever, by grouping him with Thomas Aquinas as a manifest contemplative. Furrows of anxious thought have been evident on Thomas's brow ever since.

The tiny cookies—any number of them, as though in foresight of a skyjacking and a long siege—were baked and carefully wrapped in aluminum foil by Celia before the hazardous flight from Port Jefferson, New York, all the way to Baltimore. Celia was Louis's collaborator, his virtual alter ego. Even their handwriting looked alike, and the notebooks in which they worked out their strange "Catullus" resist casual decisions as to which hand (hers) wrote the Latin and the glosses, which (his) the endlessly punning equivalents—*Irascibly iterating my iambics* for *Irascere iterum meis iambis*. "I want to breathe," he said, "as Catullus did." Symbiosis could scarcely farther go, he with Celia, both with Catullus.

If one obligation of language was to breath, another was to the world you scan with your eyes. And eye and music and lithe bodies meet in the woods where "Gentlemen cats / With paws like spats" prowl round in their nightly dance.

Ezra Pound's wife, Dorothy, could smile after forty years about the lines on the cats. A lifelong painter, she'd responded to the very young man who also lived through his eyes by drawing Egyptian cats on his typescript. That was in Rapallo in 1928; Pound had sent Zukofsky a check (never cashed) to help with the boat fare. There followed decades of mutual respect; in 1957 Zukofsky was reporting Pound's tolerant exasperation with the visitors he was getting by then, so unformed their conversation began and ended with "Grampa, haow do yew spell 'Kat'?"

By the time I met Louis in 1965 he'd become a virtuoso of hypochondria, the complaints generally starting with his feet, on which he'd tried every kind of shoe, yes, including Earth Shoe, with no amelioration. Just a few years earlier there'd still been, reportedly, "traces of a Fred Astaire charm and vertigo," something I saw just once, in a motel in Orono, Maine, where we all converged to help a university commemorate Pound.

He would dance, he suddenly announced. He smiled and limbered septuagenarian legs, forgetting that his feet were supposed to be hurting; dipped his shoulders, cocked his head. A straw skimmer would have completed the effect. But he'd talk a bit first; *then* he'd dance. . . . Now—but first some more talk; then shall I dance? It was like Danny Kaye in the "Inspector General," with the difference that Kaye danced to keep from having to talk. In forty-five minutes of scintillating monologue Louis never did dance, but finally promised to another time.

The dance now seems as vivid as if it had happened, an effect familiar to readers of Zukofsky's verse, where brisk goings-on often seemed to caper just to one side of the words. A limber and dapper bachelor indeed of thirty-five it must have been who was courting Celia that long-ago year.

"Married (1939) Celia Thaew": What kind of name, I wondered, for heaven's sake, was Thaew? The kind of linguistic accident that made up the texture of the Zukofskys' life. She should have been a Teyve (or Tevye, "as in 'Fiddler on the Roof'"), but when her father came to Ellis Island the Immigration man had known just enough German to write T as Th, ey as a umlaut, ve as w, hence Thaew: much as Bernard Shaw spelled *fish* from enou*gh*, w*o*men, no*ti*on, hence *ghoti*. Except that the fish are proverbially speechless and the Teyves/Thaews were, as Homer would say, much-speaking.

As was Louis, who was born, he loved to assert, in the great East Side ghetto just about when Henry James was paying it a bemused visit (bemused: Muses). He grew up speaking Yiddish in a culture eager to provide. A man with the pen-name Yehoash even imitated Japanese in Yiddish:

> Der regen blezelt sich in shtillen vasser.
>   Kuk ich vee dee ringen shpreyten sich fanander:
> Shimauneh-San, du Sumurai blasser,
>   Ven vestu kum'n fun dein vaiter vander?
>   Shimauneh-San, mein heller shtern . . .

—serviceable doggerel. Zukofsky's wonderfully cadenced homage is to its intent, not to its meter, and begins like this:

> Rain blows, light, on quiet water
> I watch the rings spread and travel
> Shimaunu-San, Samurai
> When will you come home?—
> Shimaunu-San, my clear star

"Hiawatha," even, was available in Yiddish, and reading it was one of Zukofsky's spurs to learn English.

As he did; who better? Not I. Though my trade is professing "English," when the Zukofskys came to Baltimore I felt (anew) a gross ignorance of the language. They knew, to begin with, the name of simply everything, notably every sprig of vegetation, every flower. (Look this instant toward greenness; can you name the first thing you see?)

Beyond the name (and naturally the Linnaean binomial) they also knew, especially Louis knew, every remote shading the *Oxford English Dictionary* had recorded for 1,500 years' usage: likewise associated legends and private lore. And in "Eighty Flowers," which he'd meant for his eightieth birthday (1984) but luckily finished before his death this year, you'll also have to remember that "flowers" can be a verb. That was one of his pleasures with English, anything could be any part of speech.

His chief books are *All*, the collected short poems which won't be wholly all till "Eighty Flowers" has joined them; *"A"*, the half-century's magnum opus, which the University of California Press will be issuing in one volume late this year; *Prepositions*, his essays, another California agendum; and *Bottom: On Shakespeare*, the most idiosyncratic of homages to the greatest master of English. They will still be elucidating all of them in the twenty-second century, and perceiving what Zukofsky saw in words such as a, the, from, to, about.

He read ' "*A*"-11' for my microphone; on the tape a little dog (not Thomas) is audible two or three times. Louis rather welcomed the little dog's *obbligato*, something more even than he'd put into the poem. ' "*A*"-11' ("for Celia and Paul") causes the poem itself to console his wife and son after his death. He wrote it thirty-eight years ago, forethoughted. "Raise grief to music" is its burden. It reaches back seven centuries for its structure to the Cavalcanti canzone from which Eliot derived the opening of *Ash-Wednesday*, and forward into what was then the fore-time of Paul's becoming a violin virtuoso, "the fingerboard pressed in my honor." Each stanza ends with "honor," and the last two are of dazzling intricacy. I'll let him speak the last lines:

> . . . four notes first too full for talk, leaf
> Lighting stem, stems bound to the branch that binds the
> Tree, and then as from the same root we talk, leaf
> After leaf of your mind's music, page, walk leaf
> Over leaf of his thought, sounding
> His happiness: song sounding
> The grace that comes from knowing
> Things, her love our own showing
> Her love in all her honor.

Thomas: A Record
of His Sayings

Privately circulated among his many friends.

His most memorable saying was "A-*woo*-woo-*woo*-woo-*wooooooo!*," the last phrase spoken with a rising inflection. This may be mistaken for one of the North American Indian languages, but was actually idiomatic in a language much studied by the North American Indians, that of the wolf (*canis lupus*), a powerful totem. Any wolf who said this said, "I am HE," and was a he-wolf. He was also, if he said it with conviction, an Alpha Male, which is pidgin Greek for Top Wolf. Pidgin Greek is a language written by ethologists.

Thomas spoke Wolf like a native, his father having been an Alaskan wolf. His mother, offspring of a union between a German Shepherd and a Malamute, had the fortune to come into season at a place where male wolves abounded. One of these briefly visited. She was subsequently brought south by a man whose destiny was to be a California milkman; at our door, in 1968, he spoke of "puppies." At that time Thomas was a puppy.

He was a sad-eyed puppy, and remained sad-eyed his long life.

Huge though he grew, his eyes were never alight: always the mirrors of his secret mind, which revolved some primitive woe: that there is no going back, that there is mortality. Through the wolves, his mind reached to the Ice Age, and before.

It was Louis Zukofsky who divined this in him. We had feared that the tail of Thomas would knock over Louis, who weighed ninety-five pounds. Louis, astonishingly, achieved instant dominance: mind acknowledging mind. Thomas would beg at the table: Louis would feed him. Louis would sit discoursing, the massive paw of Thomas on his knee. "Thomas," Louis stated, "is a contemplative." He even mentioned Aquinas.

In an earlier, smaller, nervous dog we had perceived the retired Latin master at an all-girls' school. So we thought we saw in Thomas something big and glumly hearty: a German truck driver, perhaps. But Louis was right, and Thomas in his new role commenced to look, at times, not only sad but anxious. Once a master taxonomist has fixed you, you are *responsible*. It had happened to Queen Victoria at eighteen. It happened to him.

Was he contemplating in appropriate depth? Did he have the Pythagorean Theorem exactly right, not to mention Euclid's proof that there is no largest prime? What of Kung, should Hans Kung be admitted into his deliberations? (On the whole he thought not.) What of Derrida? What indeed? What, for that matter, of *us*?

What of his pack, moreover? For he ruled a Pack.

An Alpha Male is defined by his dominance over a Pack. The Pack of Thomas consisted of two females, Teresa, LaBelle; also, in late times, three cats. These latter he disdained: lesser dogs might harry them as necessary. His dealings with his pack were of Senecan brevity. "A-*woooo*" was enough; that and jaws closing around the offender's muzzle. No one dared to eat till he had eaten, or for some minutes after.

The origin of the Pack was this. He bred, eagerly, briefly, with a female from Columbia, Maryland, an AKC German Shepherd with Papers, Gretchen by name, who did not awe him. The litter registered disdain for her papers. There were huge pure white males from the Ice Age, there were shaggy brutes, there were . . . but there was one winsome little female, wraith-like even long later when full-grown, Teresa, "spooky Teresa"; her mother's image, and the one we picked. She became his devoted consort.

She came into season in season, and we caged her. He broke, Kong-like, into the cage. Their moment of incestuous rapture sired seven puppies. The night they were born he kept busy breaking the cauls, washing them, while she panted. Briefly, he was ruler of a pack of eight. We gave six pups away, and kept Belle, the runt.

The runt grew and displayed wolf ancestry in every bone: even commanded (in Baltimore!) a wolf howl. She grew as heavy as he, but shorter, stockier, and shaggy.

His response to her was frequently "Wufff" (in disdain) or "Hrwurrf" (in outrage) or silence. But he knew she was his. His. She owes her survival to that knowledge.

If he had not sired you, he had another way of knowing you were of the Pack. That was the knowledge that admitted humans to safety, and it was transmitted via the paw-shake. At the word "Shake!," one of the few English words he acknowledged, the huge paw would rise toward the stranger, who was required to grasp it. From that moment there was peace between them. He respected what he now knew, that his pack had a courtesy member.

He knew that as he knew that poodles were not his, nor of his kin. In his prime he weighed some ninety pounds, or about six poodles. Poodles were errors of nature, to be exterminated along with creeping things. No poodle did he ever extinguish, but he tried mightily. One morning, prompted by the spirit of Dada, a *poodle* barked at *Thomas* from a passing *Cadillac*! Being otherwise powerless, he moved his bowels.

He was an institution, mentioned annually in the *New York Times Book Review* without knowledge of the editors, who would have swooned. He came regularly to Johns Hopkins University, and guarded an office to the caution of secretaries and the terror of students. The three students he bit were all of them males with eyeglasses. Each of his victims immediately got employment: hence a further legend. He never aggressed a female, nor a child.

He was huge, gentle, eloquent, stoical. The cancer that vanquished him at fifteen (a Methuselan age) subdued but did not alter his unquenchable devotion, his care for his pack and his family and his house. He was wild and a friend and to everyone including the timid an ambassador of dogdom, something that preceded us and has outlived the woolly mammoths, and knows its secret of survival in the discipline of the pack.

Design by David Bullen
Typeset in Mergenthaler Palatino
by Wilsted & Taylor
with Michelangelo Titling display
Printed by Maple-Vail
on acid-free paper